J O H N

Messenger of Salvation

T A Y L O R

JOHN
Messenger of Salvation
TAYLOR

MATTHEW J. HASLAM

Covenant Communications, Inc.

Cover images courtesy of LDS Family and Church History Department Archives
©Intellectual Reserve, Inc.

Cover design copyrighted 2002 by Covenant Communications, Inc.

Published by Covenant Communications, Inc.
American Fork, Utah

Printed in Canada
First Printing: September 2002

08 07 06 05 04 03 02   10 9 8 7 6 5 4 3 2 1

ISBN 1-57734-913-X

TABLE OF CONTENTS

~INTRODUCTION~

After having been an active participant in several Methodist congregations both in his native England and in Canada, John Taylor joined the Church while living in Toronto. Concerning his conversion he subsequently commented, "When I first entered upon Mormonism, I did it with my eyes open. I counted the cost. I looked upon it as a life-long labor, and I considered that I was not only enlisted for time, but for eternity also."[1] While Taylor saw his commitment to the Church as a lifelong endeavor, one can wonder whether he ever anticipated how involved he would become in the new church or what that participation might entail. This book focuses on the remarkable and remarkably varied forms of service that John Taylor performed during his first 25 years in the Church.

As a young man growing up in England, John Taylor received a few years of formal schooling before being apprenticed as a barrel maker. When his master's business failed, he was apprenticed as a carpenter in northern England. During this second apprenticeship he associated himself with a Methodist congregation, becoming an "exhorter" or local preacher. After moving to Canada with his family, John Taylor again joined a Methodist congregation and continued his work as a carpenter. These experiences, however, little prepared him for all he would be called to do as a new member of The Church of Jesus Christ of Latter-day Saints.

Though he had been a Methodist teacher just prior to his conversion in 1836, shortly after his baptism he was ordained as the presiding elder over the newly formed branches in Canada. Less than two years later, John Taylor became Elder Taylor when he was called to be an Apostle. No longer only a local "exhorter," he was "to declare

[Christ's] gospel, both unto Gentile and unto Jew" (D&C 18:26). His calling as an Apostle took him on numerous missions. In 1839 he left Illinois with Wilford Woodruff and traveled to England to preach the gospel. In 1846 he returned to England for a few brief months to take care of Church business and meet with the Saints. Only a couple of years later, in 1849, John Taylor took leave of his family once again, this time to go on a mission to France. Then, during the mid-1850s, Elder Taylor oversaw the Church in the eastern United States.

In addition to preaching the gospel through sermons and lectures, John Taylor became adept at doing so with his pen. Starting with the *Times and Seasons* in Nauvoo, he began a career as a newspaper editor in 1842. During the ensuing 15 years, he printed five different newspapers in four different cities and in three different languages. With the last paper, published in New York City, he demonstrated his skill in refuting misconceptions and falsehoods about the Church. Even after returning to Salt Lake he continued to actively defend the Church in writing, at one point engaging the vice president of the United States in a written exchange concerning the issue of polygamy.

While living in Nauvoo, John Taylor became deeply involved in city affairs. In addition to being editor of two Nauvoo newspapers, he served on the board of regents for the planned university, and he was a member of the Nauvoo city council. As a close confidant of the Prophet, he accompanied Joseph and Hyrum Smith to Carthage. He remained with the two brothers when they were imprisoned, and only Taylor, of the three men shot, survived the ordeal.

As a member of the Twelve, Elder Taylor provided guidance to the Saints as questions abounded about who was to lead the Church. Eventually, he became an expedition leader as he helped Parley P. Pratt lead the second group of pioneers—comprised of nearly 1,500 Saints—across the plains in 1847, arriving in the Salt Lake Valley in October of that year.

Key to understanding John Taylor's service to the Church is the vision of the gospel that he developed. In December 1844 he wrote,

> This church has the seeds of immortality in its midst. It is not of man, nor by man it is the offspring of Deity: it is organized after the pattern of heavenly things, through the

principles of revelation; by the opening of the heavens, by the ministering of angels, and the revelations of Jehovah. It is not affected by the death of one or two, or fifty individuals; it possesses a priesthood after the order of Melchisedec, having the power of an endless life, "without beginning of days, or end of years." It is organized for the purpose of saving this generation, and generations that are past; it exists in time and will exist in eternity. This church fail? No! Times and seasons may change, revolution may succeed revolution, thrones may be cast down, and empires be dissolved, earthquakes may rend the earth from centre to circumference, the mountains may be hurled out of their places, and the mighty ocean be moved from its bed; but amidst the crash of worlds and the crack of matter, truth, eternal truth, must remain unchanged, and those principles which God has revealed to his Saints be unscathed admist the warring elements, and remain as firm as the throne of Jehovah.[2]

John Taylor's lifelong devotion to the Church was grounded in the supreme confidence that their cause was "not of man, nor by man" but was directed by Deity. His vision was an eternal vision, and it was a vision that enabled him to be a guiding presence in the Church.

NOTES TO INTRODUCTION

1. Roberts, *Life of John Taylor,* 48.
2. "The City of Nauvoo" *Times and Seasons* (15 Dec. 1844):744.

Abbreviations

In citing works in the notes, short titles have generally been used. Works frequently cited have been identified by the following abbreviations:

D&C   Doctrine and Covenants

JD   *Journal of Discourses*

HC   *History of the Church*

CHC   *A Comprehensive History of the Church*

MS   *The Latter-day Saints' Millennial Star*

T&S   *Times and Seasons*

~PROLOGUE~

On 23 July 1857, Brigham Young and his counselors, Heber C. Kimball and Daniel Wells, led a procession of Saints traveling by wagon, carriage, or horseback from Salt Lake City to Big Cottonwood Canyon. By evening, 2,587 Saints, along with 1,028 horses and 332 oxen and cows, had made their way up the canyon where the main group camped near Silver Lake. It was here that these Saints gathered with the First Presidency and other Church officials to celebrate the pioneer company's arrival in the Salt Lake Valley ten years previous. In a report published in the *Deseret News* six days later, George Watt wrote:

> At sunset of the 23rd, the notes from a bugle summoned the Saints from an eminence near the center of the camp ground, when President Brigham Young made a few remarks, recounting the mercies of God to his people in delivering them from the power of their enemies, in making the desert places blossom like the rose, and the sterile places yield luscious fruits and golden grain, in loading the leaves of the trees and shrubbery with dew, and in increasing our flocks and herds in a marvelous manner.
>
> After President Young had concluded his remarks, President Heber C. Kimball offered a prayer of thanksgiving unto God for his goodness to his people, prayed for Israel and Israel's enemies, and dedicated and consecrated unto God, the ground, the waters, the timber, the rocks and all the elements pertaining to the stream upon whose head waters we were assembled to celebrate the tenth anniversary of the entrance of the pioneers into these valleys.

Three spacious boweries, with plank floors, had been
provided by the Big Cottonwood Lumber company, and a
large number passed the evening in the joyous dance.[1]

On the morning of 24 July, the group assembled once again. A
choir sang "On the Mountain Tops Appearing," and Elder George A.
Smith's prayer was followed by instructions from President Kimball
concerning how they were to proceed with the day's activities. This was
a day for prayer, remembrance, feasting, and recreation. "Hand in hand
with little children, who had seen nothing of the great world beyond
their native valley, walked silver-haired elders and apostles, who had
passed through all the tribulations of Kirtland and Nauvoo. . . . Some
[spent the day] strolling among the trees, some were fishing in the lake,
some were dancing, some busied with games."[2] Military salutes and
parades added to the festivities.

At noon, four men rode into the camp on horseback. Two of the
men, Abraham O. Smoot, the 43-year-old mayor of Salt Lake City,
and Judson Stoddard, had just completed a 20-day, 1,000-mile
journey from Fort Leavenworth, Kansas, to the Salt Lake Valley.
Upon finding Brigham Young absent from the city, they traveled to
Big Cottonwood Canyon to meet with the prophet. They entered
Brigham Young's tent and informed him and other Church leaders
that 2,500 men from the United States Army had been ordered by
President Buchanan to march toward Utah. Accompanying the army
was the newly appointed governor of the Utah Territory, Alfred
Cumming of Georgia. "Believing that the Mormons would not
accept the new governor unless forced to do so, Buchanan . . .
ordered General William S. Harney of Fort Leavenworth, Kansas, to
take command of a substantial military force that would accompany
Cumming and ensure his installation."[3] After ten years of relative
isolation from their enemies, the Saints now faced a potential armed
conflict with the government whose flag had been attached to the
tallest trees on two peaks overlooking their celebratory camp.

This news, though most unwelcome, did not disrupt the day's
activities. The bands played on, and the Saints continued in their
revelry. It was not until evening that the rest of the party was
apprised of the approaching army. Watt commented, "At sunset the

camp assembled for prayers, when President Wells made a few remarks in relation to the latest tidings from the States, upon the order of leaving the ground in the morning, and concluded with prayer." These "tidings," however, did little to dampen the participants' festive enthusiasm as "dancing and general hilarity continued to a late hour."[4]

According to B. H. Roberts, the Saints were not too concerned with the news of the approaching force:

> Quite contrary to what might have been expected the announcement of the coming of the United States army to Utah created but little excitement in Salt Lake City and other principal settlements. The colonists of Utah were too inured to opposition—even to organize opposition—to be easily excited by its appearance, though it approached in a new form and seemed more formidable than hitherto. There was to be resistance to manifest injustice, of course, yet there would be no hysterical nervousness in that opposition. Confidence in the righteousness of their cause, and confidence in their leaders was too great to admit of undue excitement.[5]

Though Roberts's description does not necessarily account for the varied feelings of individuals, it reflects the Church leaders' outlook on the situation. Two weeks following confirmation that the United States Army was marching toward Utah, Brigham Young told the gathered Saints in Salt Lake how he perceived their political situation:

> With regard to the present contention and strife, and to our position and situation, there are few things to be considered, and there is much labour to be performed. Let the Saints live their religion; let them have faith in God, do all the good they can to the household of faith and to everybody else, and trust in God for the result; for the world will not believe one truth about us. . . . What are we to do, under these circumstances? Live our religion. Are you going to contend against the United States? No. But when they come here to take our lives solely for our religion, be ye also ready.

Do I expect to stand still, sit still, or lie still, and tamely let them take away my life? I have told you a great many times what I have to say about that. I do not profess to be so good a man as Joseph Smith was. I do not walk under their protection nor into their prisons, as he did. And though officers should pledge me their protection, as Governor Ford pledged protection to Joseph, I would not trust them any sooner than I would a wolf with my dinner; neither do I trust in a wicked judge, nor in any evil person. I trust in my God, and in honest men and women who have the power of the Almighty upon them. What will we do? Keep the wicked off as long as we can, preach righteousness to them, and teach them the way of salvation.[6]

In addition to living their religion, the Saints made numerous preparations for the pending conflict. As commander in chief of the Nauvoo Legion, Brigham Young issued calls to the various colonels and majors to recruit men and report for duty. Directed by Daniel H. Wells, the men of the Legion were instructed to be ready to march on short notice to wherever they might be needed in the territory. They were told, "See that the law is strictly enforced in regard to arms and ammunition, and as far as practicable that each Ten be provided with a good wagon and four horses or mules, as well as the necessary clothing, etc., for a winter campaign. . . . Avoid all excitement, but be ready."[7] Armaments of various kinds were made. Volunteers and those employed by the Church worked to make guns, bullets, and cannon-balls. A shop set up on Temple Square was soon producing revolvers, and a chemical laboratory was established for making gunpowder.[8]

Since foodstuffs were to be of particular import during any conflict, the Legion was instructed to "let [their] influence be used for the preservation of the grain."[9] Grain was to be guarded cautiously, and nothing was to be sold to immigrants passing through the territory on their way to destinations beyond the Rocky Mountains. In addition to building fortifications, Brigham Young ordered his Minute Men—a group he had previously formed to leave at a moment's notice to retrieve stolen cattle or horses—to disrupt travel of the army and its supply trains. They were to stampede the army's animals, create disturbances so the troops could not sleep, and steal what guns they could.

Exploration parties were even sent out to look for suitable places where the Saints could relocate if the need arose. To further prepare, members of the Quorum of the Twelve were called to return home, as were Church missionaries throughout the world. Colonists living in the surrounding Mormon settlements, including those in San Bernardino, California; Carson City, Nevada; and northern Idaho were likewise directed to return to Utah.

JOHN TAYLOR'S RETURN TO SALT LAKE

It was amidst these circumstances that John Taylor arrived in the Salt Lake Valley on 7 August 1857, along with his fellow Apostle Erastus Snow. Each Apostle had been in charge of missions in the East with Taylor in New York and Snow in St. Louis, and they were already en route to Utah when the call to return was sent forth. This journey was Taylor's third trip across the plains, having previously made the crossing with the emigration camp in 1847 and again in 1852 when returning from his mission to France and Germany. Taylor had been absent from his Rocky Mountain home for nearly three years with this most recent call.

Two days following his return to the valley, Elder Taylor spoke to the Saints gathered in the Bowery in Salt Lake. He began by stating how difficult it was "to concentrate my thoughts so as to express the feelings that are in my bosom, if in fact I could express them."[10] He then spoke at length about the differences between those with whom he had associated in the East and the fellowship that he felt amongst the Saints. Regarding his just-completed mission, he told those gathered that

> I have been for some length of time past associated with the Gentiles. I have been engaged in battling corruption, iniquity, and the foul spirits that seem to fill the atmosphere of what you may term the lower regions, if you please; and the Lord has been with me, His Spirit has dwelt in my bosom, and I have felt to shout, Hallelujah! and to praise the name of the God of Israel, that he has been pleased to make me a messenger of salvation to the nations of the earth, to communicate the rich blessings flowing

from the throne of God, and put me in possession of truth that no power on this or on the other side of hell can controvert successfully.[11]

The remainder of his speech continued largely as a political diatribe, condemning the dishonest methods of politicians and newspaper editors. He critiqued the religious affairs of those in the East, stating his belief that "those who love the truth are scarce," and that "it is impossible to produce any effect on the feelings of the people" by teaching them the gospel.[12] He concluded by commenting on his limited familiarity with the current political situation. However, he announced that "in relation to any policy that may be pursued here, I feel it is just right. I know that President Young and his brethren associated with him are full of the spirit of revelation, and they know what they are doing. I feel to acquiesce and put my shoulder to the work, whatever it is. If it is for peace, let it be peace; if it is for war, let it be to the hilt. It has got to come some time, and I would just as lief jump into it today as any other time."[13]

On 8 September, a Captain Stewart Van Vliet, quartermaster for the "Utah Expedition," as the advancing army was called, arrived in Salt Lake to make arrangements for the troops' encampment in the territory. His first order of business was to meet with city and Church leaders and deliver a letter from General Harney, the original commander of the expedition. Van Vliet sought to purchase the needed supplies for the army and tried to persuade these leaders of the army's purported peaceful intentions. He accomplished neither. After leaving Salt Lake, he reported that "the governor [Young] informed me that there was an abundance of everything I required for the troops, such as lumber, forage, etc., *but that none would be sold to us.*"[14] The Saints were in no way going to aid those marching toward them. Nor could they be persuaded that the army was anything but a force of aggression. Concerning this situation, B. H. Roberts explained:

[I]n the light of experiences of the Latter-day Saints, and in the absence of any clear understanding of what were the intentions of the administration—beyond the personal assurances of Captain Van Vliet, that could not be very emphatic because of his own but partial knowledge of the purpose of the "Expedition;" and ignorant also as they were of the excellent personnel of the officers in command—all this considered, it was not possible for the Latter-day Saint Church leaders to be so assured of the pacific intentions of the administration. The "Expedition" was an army, and an army meant war, not peace. It meant coercion, and very likely the subordination of the civil to the military authority. The coming of that armed "Expedition," therefore, meant to the Latter-day Saints of Utah the subversion of their constitutional rights, the destruction of their liberties—their religious freedom; their right of community self-government; perhaps, even, their community existence.[15]

Van Vliet spent part of his time in Salt Lake scouting the valley for a suitable military camp. He visited Rush Valley to the west of Salt Lake, investigating the recommendation of a previous army officer, but he found the place inadequate for the expedition's needs. On 12 September he met with Brigham Young for a lengthy interview, in which both discussed candidly their feelings about the political situation. During the course of their conversation, Van Vliet acknowledged that the government officials sent to the Utah Territory had little interest in the people there. The Mormons, he said, had been lied about "[worse than] any people he had ever seen."[16] He further admitted that President Buchanan, in part, had ordered the expedition based on the suspect reports submitted by several such officials, a Judge Drummond in particular. One of the most reviled officials sent to Utah, Drummond made claims that the Mormons and their leaders were not loyal to the United States government, and they followed only the dictates of Brigham Young.

Before leaving, Van Vliet was invited to attend meetings in the Tabernacle. On this Sunday morning, 13 September 1857, he heard speeches by Brigham Young and John Taylor. In his speech, President Young introduced Van Vliet to the congregation:

> The officer in command of the United States' army, on its way to Utah, detailed one of his staff, Captain Van Vliet,

who is now on the stand, to come here and learn whether he could procure the necessary supplies for the army. Many of you are already aware of this, and some of you have been previously acquainted with the Captain. Captain Van Vliet visited us in Winter Quarters (now Florence); . . . From the day of his visit to Winter Quarters, many of this people have become personally acquainted with him. . . . He has invariably treated them kindly . . . for that is his character. He has always been found to be free and frank, and to be a man that wishes to do right; and no doubt he would deal out justice to all, if he had the power.[17]

Following President Young's discourse, John Taylor arose to speak and discussed the Saints' position in relation to the United States government. Partway through the speech, he explained that when he was in the East editing the *Mormon* in New York, he suggested that if the government would "send all to Utah that wanted to come, we would send all back that wanted to go." He then added, "That would be a fair bargain, you know; but I think they would have the heaviest job on hand."

BRIGHAM YOUNG

In response to his observation, some in the audience acknowledged aloud, "We know they would."

Taylor continued by asking, "What was your object in coming here? Was it to rebel against the General Government?"

This time it was President Young who responded: "To get away from Christians." Elder Taylor reported to the audience what he heard: "Brother Young says it was to get away from Christians—from that unbounded charity which you had experienced amongst them. In consequence of their treatment, you had to come away to seek a home in the desert wilds, and to obtain that protection among savages which Christian philanthropy denied you."[18]

After explaining both to the audience and Van Vliet why Church members have confidence in their leaders and their God, Elder Taylor posed the following questions: "What would be your feeling if the United States wanted to have the honour of driving us from our homes and bringing us subject to their depraved standard of moral and religious truth? Would you, if necessary, brethren, put the torch to your buildings, and lay them in ashes, and wander houseless into the mountains?"

Elder Taylor then confidently asserted, "I know what you would say and what you would do." Yet President Young suggested that he do more, telling Taylor to "try the vote." He did so by asking those in attendance, "All you that are willing to set fire to your property and lay it in ashes, rather than submit to their military rule and oppression, manifest it by raising your hands." The congregation was unanimous in their vote. Taylor then continued by repeating that he knew their feelings on the matter, adding, "We have been persecuted and robbed long enough; and, in the name of Israel's God, we will be free!" To his emphatic assertion the congregation responded, "Amen." And President Young added, "I say amen all the time to that."[19] According to one account, Captain Van Vliet was "astounded" at what he heard. He had, to his surprise, found a people not in open rebellion against their government but willing to defend themselves against what they perceived to be the egregious acts of a misguided administration in Washington.[20]

Two days later, the captain left Salt Lake along with Dr. John D. Bernhisel, Utah's nonvoting delegate to Congress. When they passed the slow-traveling troops, Van Vliet advised them not to enter the Salt Lake Valley that winter, as he had been unsuccessful in acquiring the requisite provisions. The two men then continued across the plains on their way to Washington, D.C., where Van Vliet reported to the secretary of war. According to B. H. Roberts, "The captain is to be commended for his accuracy of statement and his evident intention to serve both his country and the people of Utah by representing conditions as he found them." It was Roberts's opinion that "his course doubtless contributed much to bring about the final composition of the difficulties."[21]

CORRESPONDENCE WITH CAPTAIN R. B. MARCY

Approximately a month after addressing the Saints in Captain Van Vliet's presence, Elder Taylor received a letter dated 13 October 1857 from another officer in the Utah Expedition, a Captain R. B. Marcy. In his letter Marcy explained that he carried with him a letter of introduction from a mutual friend in New York. Given the slowness of the army's progress, Marcy decided to forward the letter with a note of his own. In part he wrote, "Suffer me to assure you that within the circle of my observation among the officers of this army, there has not been the slightest disposition to meddle with or in any way interfere with the religious or social customs of your people." On the contrary, he suggested that from the beginning of the expedition there had been amongst the officers "an almost universal manifestation of a desire for a kind and friendly intercourse."[22]

Elder Taylor promptly composed a lengthy reply, which he dated 21 October 1857. In his opening Taylor acknowledged and even commended Marcy's position as an officer in the military, yet he adamantly dismissed the purported friendly stance of the expedition's officers.

> One must naturally suppose that among gentlemen educated for the army alone, who have been occupied by the study of the art of war, whose pulses have throbbed with pleasure at the contemplation of the deeds of our venerated fathers . . . that there is not much time and less inclination to listen to the low party bickerings of political demagogues, the interested twaddle of sectional declaimers, or the throes and contortions of contracted religious bigots. You are supposed to stand on elevated ground. . . . That many of you are thus honorable, I am proud as an American citizen to acknowledge, but you must excuse me, my dear sir, if I cannot concede with you that all your officials are so high-toned, disinterested, humane and gentlemanly, as a knowledge of some of their antecedents would expressly demonstrate.[23]

Taylor went on in the letter to provide a poignant assessment of President Buchanan's administration. Regarding the "rabid tone and false, furious attacks of a venal and corrupt press," he commented that "the [press] are merely the mouthpiece, the tools, the barking dogs of a corrupt administration." He then rhetorically asked, "Why is it that Utah is so *knotty a question? . . .* Why, again I ask, could Drummond and a host of other mean scribblers, palm off their bare-faced lies with such impunity and have their infamous slanders swallowed with such gusto? Was it not that the administration and their satellites having planned our destruction, were eager to catch at anything to render specious their contemplated acts of blood?"[24] According to Taylor's assessment, "Buchanan, with Douglas, Cass, Thompson and others of his advisers, after failing to devise legal means, hit upon the expedient of an armed force against Utah, and thus thought by the sacrifice of the 'Mormons' to untie the knotty question . . . by religiously expatri-ating, destroying or killing a hundred thousand innocent American citizens to satisfy the pious, humane, patriotic feeling of their constituents, take the wind out of the sails of the Republicans, and gain to themselves immortal laurels."[25]

Despite the perceived injustices committed by the federal govern-ment, Elder Taylor reassured Marcy that the Saints sought for peace. "As I before said we wish for peace, but that we are determined on having if we have to fight for it. We will not have officers forced upon us who are so degraded as to submit to be sustained by the bayonet's point. We cannot be dragooned into servile obedience to any man." He emphasized his point with the ironic understatement: "Minie rifles, Colt's revolvers, sabres and cannon may display very good workman-ship and great artistic skill, but we very much object to having their temper and capabilities tried upon us. We may admire the capabilities, gentlemanly deportment, heroism and patriotism of United States offi-cers; but in an official capacity as enemies, we would rather see their backs than their faces. The guillotine may be a very pretty instrument and show great artistic skill, but I don't like to try my neck in it."[26]

KINGDOM OF GOD OR NOTHING

A few days after responding to Captain Marcy, Elder Taylor found himself again addressing the Saints gathered in the Tabernacle. He began this discourse with subtle humor, referring, as he did on occa-sion, to the gospel according to St. Young, St. Brigham, or St. Heber. On this afternoon he informed the audience, "I shall take the liberty, this afternoon, of selecting a text. In the Second Epistle and last verse of the Gospel according to St. Brigham to Colonel Alexander [the new commander of the Utah Expedition], will be found the following words:—'WE SAY IT IS THE KINGDOM OF GOD OR NOTHING.'"[27] It was this statement, though attributed to President Young, that became the motto for Taylor's life. Though not merely a personal maxim nor simply a response to the political situation at hand, this belief in the kingdom of God reflected his vision for what the Saints were attempting to accomplish through their varied efforts. They were, as he told them, "eternal beings, associated with eternity that was and with eternity that is to come—beings that dwelt in eternal light before we came here, we are now seeking for salvation, preparing for celestial inheritances in the eternal worlds. This is what we are after: we are trying to lay a foundation for ourselves, for our progenitors, and for our posterity, that will endure and extend while countless ages roll."[28]

As he was well versed in the Saints' predicament and policies, his discourse focused predominantly on these issues. After reminding those in the audience why they came to Utah and rehearsing the United States government's dealings with their territory, he commented on President Buchanan's decision to send armed troops "to trample upon the rights of 100,000 American freemen." He told them that "it becomes a serious question with us what to do under these circumstances." And then he asked them,

> Shall we lie down and let those scoundrels cut our throats? is the first question. Shall we untie our neckcloths and tell them to come on and cut and carve away as they please, and knock down, drag out, and introduce their abominations among us—their cursed Christian institutions—to prostitute our women and lay low our best men? Shall we suffer it, I say? . . .
>
> If they have a mind to cut each other's throats, we have no objections. We say, Success to both parties. But when they come to cut ours, without ceremony, we say, Hands off, gentlemen. We are not so religious as to sit down meekly and tamely submit to these things. We understand something of the difference between what some call treason, or treasonable acts, and base submission to the will of a

tyrant, who would seek to bring us into servile chains—
into perfect submission to his sway.

We are engaged here in protecting ourselves, our wives, and
families,—in guarding everything that is sacred and
honourable among men from invasion and oppression of
some of the most corrupt wretches that ever disgraced the
footstool of God.

"This is pretty plain talk," say you. *I meant to talk plain: I
do not wish to be misunderstood.*[29]

He also addressed a theme oft repeated in his speeches since his
return to Utah—the cause of the evil that the Saints had to endure.
He again proceeded by asking questions:

What is the cause, then, of the evil planned against us? It is
because we are the Church and kingdom of God. Have we
ever left our houses to interfere with other people anywhere?
Did you ever hear of a crusade by a set of "Mormons" upon
any other people? Did the "Mormons," when in Nauvoo, go
to Carthage, La Harpe, Warsaw, or to any place, and interfere with the rights of anybody? Have we done it here? Have
we gone to Mexico, California, Kansas, Nebraska, Oregon,
Minnesota, or to any of the surrounding districts, to interfere with their business or rights? . . .

If we do not interfere with anybody else, what right has
anybody else to interfere with us? I speak now as an
American citizen. I speak, if you please, as a politician. On
this ground I ask what right any people or number of
people have to come and interfere with us? There is no
such right in the catalogue, gentlemen.

They, however, do interfere with us; and what is the cause
of it? It is because of the kingdom of God—because of the
truth of God—because of the Spirit of God and certain
principles that exist among this people.[30]

Concluding his remarks, he returned to discuss President Young's decree—the kingdom of God or nothing. He spoke passionately as he continued with his questions:

> And now, having been forced from the United States, after having been driven time and time again from our homes by our murderous enemies—having fulfilled all the requirements that God or man could require of us, and kept every law necessary for us to observe,—after all this, and more, I say, shall we suffer those poor, miserable, damned, infernal scoundrels to come here and infringe upon our sacred rights?[31]

In response, the audience shouted a resounding "NO!" that made the Tabernacle walls tremble. He reiterated their answer and went on to provide further observation: "NO! It shall be 'The Kingdom of God or nothing' with us. That is my text, I believe; and we will stick to it—we will maintain it; and, in the name of Israel's God, the kingdom of God shall roll on, and all the powers of earth and hell cannot stop its progress. It is onward, ONWARD, ONWARD, from this time henceforth, to all eternity." Some in the audience voiced their approval with cries of "Amen." He then added, "'Are you not afraid of being killed?' you may ask me. No. Great conscience! who cares about being killed? They cannot kill you. They may shoot a ball into you, and your body may fall; but you will live. Who cares about dying? We are associated with eternal principles: they are within us as a well springing up to eternal life. We have begun to live for ever."[32]

After this address to the Saints, Elder Taylor went with the militia to keep under surveillance the movement of the United States troops, who were then approaching Fort Bridger, 115 miles from Salt Lake City. Eventually the army established a winter encampment in the area surrounding the burned-out fort. The Mormon Militia, having burned army provisions, harassed the members of the army, and stolen hundreds of cattle, finally retreated to Salt Lake once the December snows effectively blocked passage to the valley. Elder Taylor made his way back to the valley in order to serve in the territory legislature, having been elected by the constituents of Salt Lake County.

A peaceful resolution to the Utah War had its genesis in the arrival of Colonel Kane to Salt Lake in February 1858. After meeting with President Buchanan, Kane traveled at his own expense and without an official office to Utah, sailing from New York to Panama. After traversing the isthmus, he boarded a ship that sailed up the California coast. His arrival at the Mormon community in San Bernardino was followed by a wagon trip to Salt Lake. As a friend of the Saints (he had visited the Saints in Winter Quarters twelve years previous), Kane had been an advocate for their cause and was well known by many Church leaders. In discussions with Brigham Young, he was able to negotiate an agreement whereby Alfred Cumming, the presidential appointee, would be acknowledged as governor of the Utah Territory, provided he came without the accompanying army. Cumming agreed to the arrangement, and in March he was escorted by the Mormon Militia to Salt Lake, where he took over for Brigham Young as governor. Kane then returned to Washington and reported to President Buchanan. Seeking to eradicate himself from what some had come to call "Buchanan's blunder," the president issued a declaration pardoning Church leaders and others for their purportedly seditious acts. The war finally ended after the army's peaceful journey through a deserted Salt Lake City on their way to their permanent encampment in Cedar Valley, 40 miles southwest of the city.

A SERVANT OF GOD REVEALED

These two speeches to the Saints, along with his letter to Captain Marcy, do much to reveal the personality of the man who would become the third prophet and President of the Church in this dispensation. They illustrate the characteristics exemplified in John Taylor's service in the kingdom of God, and clearly demonstrate his expansive vision of the gospel. As he told the Saints on 1 November 1857, "We believe in adapting our lives and actions to the positions that we now occupy as servants of the true and living God—as God's representatives on the earth—as those who are destined to lay the foundation of that kingdom which shall stand for ever."[33] More than seeking personal salvation through righteous living, he believed the Saints were engaged in a cause that would outlast any worldly institution. They were, as he explained, "lay[ing] a foundation for ourselves, for our progenitors, and for our posterity, that will endure and extend while countless ages roll." And their efforts, unlike any others in the preceding 1,800 years, were founded on correct principles and directed by the "holy Priesthood—by the revelations of God."[34] In making these comments, Taylor reiterated the sentiments he expressed in Nauvoo at the last conference before Joseph Smith's death, when he told the Saints, "We are laying the foundation of a kingdom that shall last forever;—that shall bloom in time and blossom in eternity. We are engaged in a greater work than ever occupied the attention of mortals; we live in a day that prophets and kings desired to see, but died without sight."[35]

Taylor's vision of the gospel had been nurtured through the twenty years of service since his baptism into Christ's Church. He had been an Apostle for nearly nineteen years and had served three missions that took him to the British Isles, France, and Germany. He later served a fourth mission to the eastern United States. Elder Taylor, along with others of the Twelve, also spent the years of 1841 to 1844 under the personal tutelage of the Prophet Joseph Smith in Nauvoo.

These public addresses also exhibited his confidence in the Church's leadership. He assured the Saints that though he was not fully aware of the preparations for the coming army, he knew their leaders were doing right. In the speech attended by Captain Van Vliet, he demonstrated his willingness to sacrifice his material possessions in fighting for the Saints' rights. Not merely inflammatory rhetoric, his readiness to set his property aflame reflected what Taylor, along with numerous other Saints, had done on several previous occasions: abandoned their homes to join or gather anew with the body of Saints. Upon learning of his forthcoming call to join the Quorum of the Twelve, Taylor acquitted his furniture business in Toronto in 1838 and traveled to Missouri, where he arrived at the climax of hostilities against Church members. His stay in Far West was short-lived, and he soon joined Brigham Young in leading the Saints to Quincy, Illinois. When the Saints were driven from Nauvoo six years later, Taylor left behind property worth $10,000, including his furnished brick home, a brick store, and another brick building that housed the printing office.

In describing his willingness to die for the gospel, he was not merely making an empty pledge or displaying false bravado. Rather, he was again speaking from experience. As he did often in speeches, he referred to the fateful day in June 1844 when he was shot along with Joseph Smith and the Prophet's brother Hyrum. He told the Saints on 13 September 1857, "I do not care anything about shooting: I have been shot. Neither do I care anything about dying; for I could have died many a time if I had desired to; but I had not got ready."[36] In both discourse and in practice, he demonstrated a willingness to sacrifice all for the kingdom of God.

In his speeches, writings, and publishing efforts, Elder Taylor was forthright, bold, and at times, confrontational. He spoke plainly so as to not be misunderstood. Upon returning from his mission in the East, he told the Saints that "people back East used to blame me for speaking and writing plain."[37] He was frank in evaluating the character of the politicians, newspaper editors, and other public figures whom he met, and he was candid in assessing the religious and moral life of Saints and Gentiles alike. In his 9 August 1857 speech, he provided a harsh critique of the political and social practices that left men and women in ideological and economic bondage. "Every man," he told the Saints, "bows down his neck to his fellow, and they have their parties of every kind in the United States; and every man must be true to his party, no matter what it is. Politicians are bound by their parties, editors by their employers, ministers by their congregations, merchants by their creditors and Governors and President by political cliques. Divisions, strife, contention, and evil are everywhere increasing, and there is little room for truth in the hearts of the people." He went on to add, "I believe, notwithstanding, there are thousands of honest people in the United States; but so much evil prevails, and so much corruption, that it is next to impossible for them to discover the difference between truth and error."[38]

Taylor's ardor for defending the Saints was reflected in his disdain for the hypocrisy exhibited by politicians and his intolerance of the injustices repeatedly inflicted upon the Saints. His 1857 speeches echo statements he previously made to a Major Warren, who had been assigned by Governor Ford to ensure, with military force, the peace in Hancock County, Illinois. When Major Warren confronted President Young and Elder Taylor about their purported resistance to the law, the latter responded:

> Sir, I stand before you as a victim of law. I feel warm on
> this subject—who would not? I have seen my best friends

shot down while under legal protection. What is our governor? These scenes have been enacted under his supervision. What are our generals and judges? They have aided in these matters. . . . What are all these legal men but a pack of scoundrels? And you will talk to us of law and order, and threaten us with punishment for disobeying your commands and protecting our rights! What are we? Are we beasts? I tell you for one, sir, I shall protect myself, law or no law, judge or no judge, governor or no governor. I will not stand such infernal rascality, and if I have to fight it out, I will sell my life as dearly as I can.[39]

Concerning the injustice he experienced since coming to the United States, he told Warren:

I have endured as much as I feel willing to endure under this government. I feel myself oppressed and wronged. I have never violated any law in the United States, and to be vexed and annoyed continually with vexatious law suits and illegal prosecutions, I do not feel disposed tamely to submit to. If it is not enough for me to be deprived of my rights and my liberty; if it is not enough for me to sacrifice my property and to become an exile; if I can not have the short space of six months to dispose of my effects and to leave the state—if the governor will only tell me, I will leave now; but I cannot and will not endure a continuation of these wrongs. I do not mean to be taken by any unjust requisition and thrust into prison; if I am, I must go there dead; for they shall not take me there alive. I have no personal feelings against you, Major Warren, but I will not put up with these accumulated wrongs.[40]

Though he did not seek the many confrontations forced upon the Church, he was adamant that he would not submit meekly to the injustices the Saints faced. Much like Brigham Young, he did not "profess to be so good a man as Joseph Smith was," as he would not "walk under their protection nor into their prisons," and he "would not trust them any sooner than [one] would a wolf with [his] dinner."

His rather simple statement that he would speak "as a politician" was, in many ways, prophetic of what was to come in the remaining years of his Church service. It foreshadowed a way of speaking that would be commonplace for him, a way of speaking necessitated by the political impact on religious matters. In his last conference addresses to the Church—which had to be read to the congregation because President Taylor was on the run from the law and could not attend the meetings—the political was inseparable from the religious; he discussed at length the legal circumstances that Mormons in Utah, Idaho, and Arizona found themselves in as they attempted to live the law of celestial marriage while the federal government outlawed the practice of polygamy. In 1857 he asked, "How can we live under the dominion and laws of the United States and be subjects of another kingdom?"[41] With this question, he raised a recurring issue that the Church had to address for years to come. The need to be both a practitioner of religion and a student of politics was emphasized in 1862 when he told the "elders of Israel" that they needed to "begin to understand that they have something to do with the world politically as well as religiously, that it is as much their duty to study correct political principles as well as religious, and to seek to know and comprehend the social and political interests of man, and to learn and be able to teach that which would be best calculated to promote the interests of the world."[42] It had become clear that the Saints could not deal with the gentile world solely on a religious basis.

As a servant of the Lord, John Taylor was passionate in his commitment to the gospel. The loyalty he demonstrated to Joseph and Hyrum in Carthage typified his allegiance to the Church. For the last 40 years of his life he carried with him the scars of Carthage as a reminder of all that was required of the Lord's anointed. Resolute in defending gospel truths and in advocating the Saints' cause, his personal welfare and comfort was often secondary to that which the Lord required. In so many ways, he lived a life that exemplified his motto: "the Kingdom of God or Nothing."

NOTES TO PROLOGUE
1. Nibley, *Brigham Young: The Man and His Work,* 285–286.
2. Bancroft, *History of Utah, 1540–1886,* 504.
3. Arrington, *Brigham Young: American Moses,* 252.

4. Nibley, *Brigham Young: The Man and His Work,* 287–88.

5. *CHC* 4:239.

6. *JD* 5:123.

7. "The Echo Canyon War," *Contributor* (March 1882): 177.

8. Arrington, *Brigham Young: American Moses,* 261.

9. "The Echo Canyon War." *Contributor* (March 1882): 177.

10. *JD* 5:112.

11. Ibid., 5:113.

12. Ibid., 5:121.

13. Ibid., 5:122.

14. *CHC* 4:263–64, emphasis in original.

15. Ibid., 4:262.

16. Ibid., 4:265.

17. *JD* 5:227.

18. Ibid., 5:244.

19. Ibid., 5:247.

20. Bancroft, *History of Utah,* 508–509.

21. *CHC* 4:271.

22. Ibid., 4:336.

23. Ibid., 4:336

24. Ibid., 4:337, emphasis in original.

25. Ibid., 4:338.

26. Ibid., 4:440.

27. *JD* 6:18.

28. Ibid., 6:26.

29. Ibid., 6:21, emphasis added.

30. Ibid., 6:22, emphasis added.

31. Ibid., 6:26.

32. Ibid., 6:26–27.

33. Ibid., 6:19.

34. Ibid., 6:26.

35. "Conference Minutes," *T&S* (15 July 1844): 578.

36. *JD* 5:248.

37. Ibid., 5:117.

38. Ibid., 5:120–21.

39. *CHC* 2:529.

40. Ibid., 2:530.

41. *JD* 6:24.

42 . *JD* 9:340.

~ ONE ~

THE CALLING *of an* APOSTLE

In a revelation given to Joseph Smith, Oliver Cowdery, and David Whitmer in Fayette, New York, in June 1829, the Lord informed them, "Behold, there are others who are called to declare my gospel, both unto Gentile and unto Jew. Yea, even twelve; and the Twelve shall be my disciples . . . and the Twelve are they who shall desire to take upon them my name with full purpose of heart" (D&C 18:26–27). It would be nearly six years before this divine injunction was fulfilled. On Sunday, 8 February 1835, Joseph Smith called Brigham Young and Brigham's brother Joseph to visit with him at his home near the temple in Kirtland. During their stay, the Youngs engaged the Prophet in discussion and song. Joseph Smith explained that he wanted to call a meeting of all who had participated in Zion's Camp, as he desired to give them a blessing. The Prophet, according to Joseph Young, told the two brothers:

> "Brethren, I have seen those men who died of the cholera in our camp; and the Lord knows, if I get a mansion as bright as theirs, I ask no more." At this relation he wept, and for some time could not speak. When he had relieved himself of his feelings, in describing the vision, he resumed the conversation, and addressed himself to Brother Brigham Young. He said to him, "I wish you to notify all the brethren living in the branches, within a reasonable distance from this place, to meet at a general conference on Saturday next. I shall then and there appoint twelve Special Witnesses, to open the door of the Gospel to foreign nations, and you [speaking to Brigham] . . . will be one of them."[1]

Brigham did as requested, and the meeting was convened the following Saturday, 14 February 1835. Those invited met in the new school located under the printing office, which was housed in a building behind the yet-to-be-completed temple.

Joseph Smith began the meeting by reading from John 15, and telling those gathered that he had been commanded of God to call the assembly. After making remarks concerning the calling of the Twelve, he informed those in attendance that the Three Witnesses to the Book of Mormon would make the callings. Following a united prayer and a blessing from the First Presidency, Oliver Cowdery, David Whitmer, and Martin Harris made their selections: Lyman E. Johnson, Brigham Young, Heber C. Kimball, Orson Hyde, David W. Patten, Luke S. Johnson, William E. McLellin, John F. Boynton, Orson Pratt, William Smith, Thomas B. Marsh, and Parley P. Pratt. Of these men, only Lyman Johnson, William E. McLellin, and Thomas B. Marsh had not participated in the march to Missouri. Shortly thereafter, the Quorum was restructured so that seniority in the Quorum was based on age. As such, Thomas B. Marsh became head of the Quorum, and Lyman Johnson, the youngest at age 23, occupied the twelfth position. By revelation, the Twelve were appointed to be "traveling councilors" who were to be "special witnesses of the name of Christ in all the world." They were to "form a quorum, equal in authority and power to the three presidents" (D&C 107: 23–24).

Despite their lofty calling, it wasn't long before these men ceased functioning as a quorum.[2] Initially, the Twelve were given less prominence than other Church councils, which provoked the ire of some Apostles who thought they were not being honored in their calling. Brigham Young's view on the situation was slightly different from some of his fellow Apostles; he reported that Joseph "snobed us [the Twelve] and when we proved ourselves willing to be everybody's servant for Christ's sake, then we are worthy of power."[3] By 1837 most in the Quorum gave little consideration to their duties as special witnesses of Christ. According to Eliza R. Snow, "A spirit of speculation had crept into the heart of some of the Twelve, and nearly, if not every quorum was more or less infected."[4] Lyman Johnson and John Boynton joined a group of 30 others who sought to overthrow Joseph

Smith and install David Whitmer as the presiding Church leader. Luke Johnson and William McLellin likewise joined apostate groups, and Orson Hyde, Orson Pratt, and his brother Parley P. Pratt began to seriously question the Prophet's calling.

So open and bold were some in their rebellion that a skirmish took place in the temple, which had been in the previous year the site of miraculous visions and heavenly visitations. Warren Parrish, who had marched with the Prophet in Zion's Camp and had been a successful preacher, brought his apostate group to the temple one Sunday morning. Concerning Parrish's actions Eliza R. Snow wrote:

> One Sabbath morning, he, with several of his party, came into the Temple armed with pistols and bowie-knives, and seated themselves together in the Aaronic pulpits, on the east end of the Temple, while Father Smith and others, as usual, occupied those of the Melchisedec Priesthood on the west. Soon after the usual opening services, one of the brethren on the west stand arose, and just after he commenced to speak, one on the east interrupted him. Father Smith, presiding, called to order—he told the apostate brother that he should have all the time he wanted, but he must wait his turn—as the brother on the west took the floor and commenced first to speak, he must not be interrupted. A fearful scene ensued—the apostate speaker becoming so clamorous, that Father Smith called for the police to take that man out of the house, when Parrish, John Boynton, and others, drew their pistols and bowie-knives, and rushed down from the stand into the congregation; J. Boynton saying he would blow out the brains of the first man who dared to lay hands on him. Many in the congregation, especially women and children, were terribly frightened—some tried to escape from the confusion by jumping out of the windows. Amid screams and shrieks, the policemen, in ejecting the belligerents, knocked down a stovepipe, which fell helter-skelter among the people; but, although bowie-knives and pistols were wrested from their owners, and thrown hither and thither to prevent disastrous results, no one was hurt, and after a short, but terrible scene to be enacted in a Temple of God, order was restored, and the services of the day proceeded as usual.[5]

When John Taylor arrived in Ohio in March 1837, 10 months after his baptism, Kirtland was besieged by dissension, bickering, and violence. He came to meet the Prophet and learn more of the gospel from the man who ushered in the new dispensation. Taylor visited Joseph Smith in his home and was entertained by the Smith family. During his visit Taylor encountered Parley P. Pratt, the man who had baptized him only a few months before. By his own admission, Pratt had been caught up in the "jarrings and discords in the Church at Kirtland," and as such he "also was overcome by the same spirit in a great measure, and it seemed as if the very powers of darkness which war against the Saints were let loose upon me."[6] He tried to persuade his

THE KIRTLAND TEMPLE

recent convert that Joseph Smith was in error. Taylor, however, was not convinced. "How am I to believe you?" he asked. "I was told by you one year ago that if I were to obey the Gospel I should know of the doctrines whether they were of God. I have obeyed and I know for myself, and am no longer dependent upon your testimony, and you cannot make me now unknow it. No matter what your ideas and notions are, now I know for myself."[7] He told Pratt, "It is not the man that I am following, but the Lord. The principles you taught me led me to Him, and I now have the same testimony that you then rejoiced in. If the work was true six months ago, it is true today; if Joseph Smith was then a prophet, he is now a prophet."[8]

This was not the only public defense of Joseph Smith that Taylor made during his visit to Kirtland. On one Sunday he attended a meeting in the temple where the Prophet was absent. During the meeting Warren Parrish made a verbal attack on the Prophet, which was supported by many in attendance. Though unknown to those gathered, Taylor requested that he might address the audience. After referring to the ancient Israelites who had murmured against God and His servant Moses, Taylor asked, "From whence do we get our intelligence, and knowledge of the laws, ordinances and doctrines of the kingdom of God? Who understood even the first principles of the doctrines of Christ? Who in the Christian world taught them? If we, with our learning and intelligence, could not find out the first principles, which was the case with myself and millions of others, how can we find out the mysteries of the kingdom?" He went on to explain, "It was Joseph Smith, under the Almighty, who developed the first principles, and to him we must look for further instructions. If the spirit which he manifests does not bring blessings, I am very much afraid that the one manifested by those who have spoken, will not be very likely to secure them."[9] Though his speech did little to influence the gathered apostates, it clearly reflected his views about Joseph Smith's divine calling. Not only was Taylor convinced of the gospel's truthfulness, he was willing to boldly proclaim this knowledge.

Upon leaving Kirtland, John Taylor had mixed feelings about his experiences. Though thrilled to have met the Prophet and received his counsel, he was dismayed about encountering Parley P. Pratt, who was "passing under a dark cloud."[10] He explained, "I was pained on the one hand to witness the hard feelings and severe expressions of apostates; while on the other, I rejoiced to see the firmness, faith, integrity and joy of the faithful."[11] On the return trip to Toronto, Taylor's party found themselves near Niagara Falls on a Sunday. Before searching for a place in Queenstown where they might preach, his group retreated to an isolated place below the falls where they joined in prayer. During the meeting Taylor spoke in tongues. Though not a stranger to outward manifestations of the Spirit—he had witnessed miraculous healings and received heavenly manifestations—he found comfort in this experience. He said there was "an invisible manifestation of the Spirit of the living God, bearing witness with mine that this was the work of God that He had established in the last days."[12] In the days following his return from Kirtland, Taylor also received spiritual confirmation that he would eventually be called as an Apostle.[13]

Though John Taylor had only been a Church member for a short time, much had taken place in the preceding years that prepared him to accept the gospel when preached to him, and to become a special witness of Jesus Christ and His gospel.

COMING OF AGE IN ENGLAND

The second son of James and Agnes Taylor, John Taylor was born 1 November 1808 in Milnthorpe, England. The Taylor family lived in Milnthorpe until 1814, when they moved to Liverpool where James Taylor worked for the English government. They stayed in this port city on the eastern coast of England until 1819, when the family returned north to the village of Hale. James Taylor had inherited a small estate that he and his sons began to farm. It was while the Taylors were living in Hale that John received his last three years of formal education. At age 14 it was time for John to learn a vocation, so he was apprenticed to a cooper, or barrel maker, in Liverpool. His master's business failed within the year, so John returned to the family farm in Hale. His stay, however, was relatively short, as he was subsequently apprenticed to a carpenter in the city of Penrith, near the Scottish border. John spent the next five years learning his craft, eventually completing his apprenticeship in 1828 at the age of 20.

It was in northern England that John Taylor cultivated a religious disposition at an early age. At John's birth, James and Agnes Taylor belonged to the Church of England. His parents had him baptized as a child, and they attended church where, he reported, they "confessed every Sunday that we had 'done the things that we ought not to have done, and left undone the things which we ought to have done,'" acknowledging they were "miserable sinners."[14] Eventually, however, John came to distance himself from the religion of his birth. As a 16-year-old in Penrith, the impressionable John Taylor became interested in Methodism. About this experience he wrote, "I heard the Methodist doctrine preached and as it seemed to me more a matter of fact, personal thing than the Church of England, which I was nominally united, I became a Methodist. I was strictly sincere in my religious faith and was very zealous to learn what I then considered the truth."[15] He began to spend his free time studying the Bible and reading works on theology. He also sought out his Heavenly Father in prayer. He would go "into the fields and concealing myself behind some bush, would bow before the Lord and call him to guide and direct me."[16] He even attempted to persuade other boys his age to join him in his secluded prayers, yet he had little success in sharing his religious fervor.

When he was 17, Taylor became a Methodist "exhorter," a type of local preacher. In this capacity he visited towns surrounding the city of Penrith. On his first assignment, he and a fellow congregation member traveled to a country town seven miles away. While en route, he stopped in the road and told his partner, "I have a strong impression on my mind, that I have to go to America to preach the gospel!"[17] Though he knew little about America and was unsure what he would preach, this impression would become a guiding force in his life. This experience was not, however, his only spiritual manifestation. He indicated that "often when alone and sometimes in company, I heard sweet, soft, melodious music, as if performed by angels or supernatural beings."[18] As a boy he also saw a vision in which he beheld an angel flying in the heavens, blowing a trumpet.

With his apprenticeship complete, John returned to Hale in 1828 to begin work as a carpenter. A short time later in 1830, the Taylor family decided to immigrate to Canada. John was left behind to sell the family property, which he was able to do the following year. He then set sail for the United States, arriving in New York, and from there he traveled to Toronto to reunite with his family. His journey to America was not without peril. Soon after leaving its British port, his ship encountered a weeklong storm in which officers expected the ship would sink. John Taylor, however, did not share their sentiments; he was assured that he would make it to America, as it was there he had a calling to preach the gospel. "So confident was I of my destiny," he wrote, "that I went on deck at midnight, and amidst the raging elements felt as calm as though I was sitting in a parlor at home. I believed I should reach America and perform my work."[19]

A METHODIST PREACHER IN TORONTO

John Taylor continued his association with Methodism by joining a congregation in Toronto and becoming a preacher. It was in performing his religious duties that he met Leonora Cannon, the woman who eventually became his wife. Originally from the British Isles, Leonora came to Canada with a close friend whose husband, a colonel in the British army, had been appointed secretary to the governor of Canada. As a devout Methodist, she quickly joined with a congregation in Toronto. John Taylor came to know Leonora as he served as her class leader at church. Eventually he proposed to her and was promptly rejected. She was 12 years his senior, and she had intended from the beginning of her journey to return to her family and home on the Isle of Man. A dream, though, led her to reconsider his offer. She envisioned herself with John and became convinced that she ought to marry him.[20] Thus, another proposal was accepted, and they were married on 28 January 1833 in Toronto. Their first child, George John, was born a year later on 31 January 1834. While they were still living in Toronto, their first daughter, Mary Ann, was born on 23 January 1836.

In Toronto John Taylor applied his trade as a carpenter to support his growing family. On Sundays he had appointments to preach at various places. Often Leonora would accompany him as he went about his duties, and on occasion she made reference to her husband's impression as a youth that he would preach the gospel in America. He told her, however, "This is not the work; it is something of more importance."[21] Not completely satisfied with his current religion, Taylor joined a group of preachers from his congregation, along with other well-educated men, who met to study the Bible. Of this coterie he explained:

> [A] number of us met together for the purpose of searching the Scriptures; and we found that certain doctrines were taught by Jesus and the Apostles, which neither the Methodists, Baptists, Presbyterians, Episcopalians, nor any of the religious sects taught; and we concluded that if the Bible was true, the doctrines of modern Christendom were not true; or if they were true, the Bible was false. Our investigations were impartially made, and our search for truth was extended. We examined every religious principle that came under our notice, and probed the various systems as taught by the sects, to ascertain if there were any that were in accordance with the word of God. But we failed to find any.[22]

Much of the group's time was spent quarreling with one another about the differing doctrines. Of those gathered he commented,

"One was a brother Methodist, and another was a brother Presbyterian; and we used to fall out about which was right—whether the doctrine of freewill or of fate was right; for we did not know which was right. . . . There was also much wrangling as to whether infants that died went to hell or not."[23] In addition to their disputations and research, the group gathered to pray and fast. "[T]he substance of our prayers was, that if [God] had a people upon the earth anywhere, and ministers who were authorized to preach the Gospel, that He would send us one."[24] Their prayers were answered with the arrival of Elder Parley P. Pratt from Kirtland, Ohio.

PARLEY P. PRATT'S PROPHETIC CALLING TO PREACH IN CANADA

In the spring of 1836, Elder Pratt found himself in a quandary. Several of the elders were preparing to depart on missions to various destinations, and he was inclined to go with them. However, he was also substantially in debt for expenses incurred over the winter and because he had purchased land in Kirtland and had built a home for himself and his wife. These circumstances left him in doubt concerning his appropriate course of action. By April he had yet to make up his mind. One evening while Pratt was at home, there was a knock at the door. Elder Pratt reported that when he opened the door,

PARLEY P. PRATT

> Elder Heber C. Kimball and others entered my house, and being filled with the spirit of prophecy, they blessed me and my wife, and prophesied as follows:
>
> "Brother Parley, thy wife shall be healed from this hour, and shall bear a son, and his name shall be Parley; and he shall be a chosen instrument in the hands of the Lord to inherit the priesthood and to walk in the steps of his father. He shall do a great work in the earth in ministering the Word and teaching the children of men. Arise, therefore, and go forth in the ministry, nothing doubting. Take no thoughts

for your debts, nor the necessaries of life, for the Lord will supply you with abundant means for all things.

"Thou shalt go to Upper Canada, even to the city of Toronto, the capital, and there thou shalt find a people prepared for the fulness of the gospel, and they shall receive thee, and thou shalt organize the Church among them, and it shall spread thence into the regions round about, and many shall be brought to the knowledge of the truth and shall be filled with joy; and from the things growing out of this mission, shall the fulness of the gospel spread into England, and cause a great work to be done in that land.

"You shall not only have means to deliver you from your present embarrassments, but you shall yet have riches, silver and gold, till you will loath the counting thereof."[25]

Along with the promise of finding a people prepared to hear Christ's gospel in Toronto, the blessing was remarkable in what was promised Parley and his wife, Thankful Halsey Pratt. For six years Thankful had suffered from consumption, and doctors had considered her condition incurable. In addition to this ailment, the Pratts had been unable, for the ten years of their marriage, to have children. Now they were promised that Thankful would be cured and they would be able to conceive if Parley were to proceed with this mission. Parley complied with Elder Kimball's directive, and he was soon ready to leave. By coach he traveled with a Brother Nickerson, who paid their expenses to Niagara Falls and then on to the town of Hamilton, located on the shores of Lake Ontario.

When he arrived in Hamilton, Pratt was left to travel alone, as Nickerson returned to his home. To continue on to Toronto, Pratt could either catch a steamer that crossed the lake in two hours, or he could travel for several days by foot around the lake. Though he would have chosen the quicker alternative, he lacked the two dollars necessary for the boat passage. "Under these circumstances I pondered what I should do. I had many times received answers to prayer in such matters; but now it seemed hard to exercise faith, because I was among strangers and entirely unknown. The Spirit seemed to whisper to me to try the Lord, and see if anything was too hard for him, that I might know and trust Him under all circumstances."[26] Choosing a secluded forest outside of town, Pratt knelt down in supplication, asking the Lord for the necessary means to continue his journey. He returned to town, where he struck up a conversation with several residents. It was but a few minutes before a stranger approached Pratt, asked his name, and inquired where he was going. The stranger offered him ten dollars and gave him a letter of introduction to one John Taylor, a resident of Toronto. Pratt subsequently crossed the lake and soon found himself at his destination.

In Toronto, Pratt immediately found the Taylors' home and showed them the letter given to him by the generous stranger in Hamilton. Initially, Leonora cordially received this unknown preacher from the United States. After she called her husband from his carpenter's shop, she and John shared tea with Pratt. He explained that he had come to Toronto to preach the gospel of Christ. Despite their hospitality, neither John nor Leonora did much to suggest any interest in his message. In fact, John felt put upon by the friend who had written the letter of introduction, and he told Pratt, "I do not know what to think about you 'Mormons.' I do not believe any kind of fanaticism: I profess to be acquainted with the Bible; and . . . in any conversation we may have I wish you to confine yourself to the Bible; for I tell you I shall not listen to anything in opposition to that word."[27] As the letter of introduction did not facilitate finding a place of preaching, the following day Pratt visited the clergy in the city to see if he might lecture before their congregations. These visits yielded no invitations. He then sought use of the courthouse and a public room in the marketplace and was likewise rebuffed. With no place to preach, he pondered the prophecy about a people prepared for the gospel in Toronto, and he prayed that somehow the promises of success in the city might be brought to pass. He soon exhausted his options in finding a place to preach, and as he prepared to leave the city, he called upon the Taylors one last time.

After visiting with the Taylors, Pratt was delayed by inquiries from John. During their conversation, an acquaintance of the Taylors knocked on the door and entered. She began speaking with Leonora in an adjoining room. Pratt reported what Leonora told her friend: "Mrs. Walton, I am glad to see you; there is a gentleman here from the

United States who says the Lord sent him to this city to preach the gospel. He has applied in vain to the clergy and to the various authorities for opportunity to fulfil his mission, and is now about to leave the place. He may be a man of God; I am sorry to have him depart." Mrs. Walton then responded:

> "Well, I now understand the feelings and spirit which brought me to your house at this time. I have been busy over the wash tub and too weary to take a walk; but I felt impressed to walk out. I then thought I would make a call on my sister, the other side of town; but passing your door, the Spirit bade me go in; but I said to myself, I will go in when I return; but the Spirit said: go in now. I accordingly came in, and I am thankful that I did so. Tell the stranger he is welcome to my house. I am a widow; but I have a spare room and bed, and food in plenty. He shall have a home at my house, and two large rooms to preach in just when he pleases. Tell him I will send my son John over to pilot him to my house, while I go and gather my relatives and friends to come in this very evening and hear him talk; for I feel by the Spirit that he is a man sent by the Lord with a message which will do us good."[28]

A PEOPLE PREPARED

By that evening, Mrs. Walton had gathered some of her acquaintances to listen to Pratt preach. Her guests all sat around a large table in her parlor while he told them of Joseph Smith, his calling as a prophet, and the restoration of Christ's established Church. When he concluded, several acknowledged this was the message they had awaited and they desired to be baptized. He bade them wait until others could be taught and accept these teachings. Initially, few attended the meetings at Mrs. Walton's, but soon the two rooms were filled, and would-be listeners spilled out into the yard. On the following Sunday, Pratt chose not to hold meetings, "not wishing to show opposition" to other denominations.[29] Instead, he accompanied a friend to hear a certain preacher. Following the meeting he was introduced to the preacher, who invited Pratt and his friend to dinner. During the course of their mealtime conversation, they were invited to attend another meeting, this time in the home of a Mr. Patrick, a wealthy gentleman employed by the government. Regarding this meeting Pratt reported:

> In a large apartment, well furnished, was soon convened a solemn, well dressed, and, apparently, serious and humble people, nearly filling the room. Each held a bible, while Mr. Patrick presided in their midst, with a bible in his hand and several more lying on the table before him. With one of these I was soon furnished, as was any other person present who might lack this, apparently, necessary article. In this manner these people had assembled twice each week for about two years, for the professed purpose of seeking truth, independent of any sectarian organization to which any of them might nominally belong.

> Here had assembled John Taylor, his wife, Mrs. Walton and some others who now knew me, although to the president and most of the congregation I was entirely unknown, and, from my appearance, was supposed to be some farmer from the country, who had dropped in by invitation.

The meeting began with singing and prayer, and then each in attendance was free to introduce an appropriate discussion topic.

On this evening, John Taylor arose and spoke first. He read from the New Testament account of Philip going to Samaria to preach the gospel. Elder Pratt recorded:

> Closing the book, [Taylor] remarked that the Samaritans received the Word with joy; and were then baptized, both men and women; after which the two Apostles, Peter and John, came from Jerusalem, and laid their hands on them in the name of Jesus, and prayed that they might receive the Holy Ghost; and they received it, and spake with tongues, and prophesied. "Now . . . where is our Philip? Where is our receiving the Word with joy, and being baptized when we believed? Where is our Peter and John? Our apostles? Where is our Holy Ghost by the laying on of hands? Where are our gifts of the Holy Ghost? Echo answers, where?"[30]

Taylor continued asking his questions: "Is this the pattern of the Christian Church, the model for the organization in all after times? If so, we, as a people, have not the ministry, the ordinances, the gifts which constitute the Church of Jesus Christ."[31] He continued speaking of those elements in Christ's Church that were notably missing in their churches, including apostles and spiritual gifts. He concluded by asking, "If we are not members of the Church of Christ, wherein do we differ from the heathen?"[32] His comments prompted extensive discussion by those in attendance. During the debate, the preacher who had invited Elder Pratt indicated that there was a stranger amongst them who might have something to say on the matter. Pratt introduced himself, and it was determined that he would meet the group the following evening. Elder Pratt's initial invitation to speak was followed by a request that he address the group on two successive evenings.

Upon hearing the gospel for the first time, John Taylor explained:

> I was struck at once with [what was taught]. I was well acquainted with the Bible, yet I had never heard such teaching before; had never seen such principles developed; had never listened to such words as came from his mouth, illustrating, making manifest and explaining the Scriptures, the Book of Mormon and the revelations of God, and opening the heavens as it were to my view. It was to me one of the greatest things I had ever heard. He said to me, "If you will be baptized in the name of Jesus Christ for the remission of sins you shall receive the gift of the Holy Ghost, inasmuch as you go in faith, and humility and obedience to the law of God and forsake your sins," &c. This was precisely the same thing that Peter told the people in his day.[33]

Pratt's message, however, was belittled by the ministers he knew. "The first thing that I heard from a priest, after hearing the Gospel preached by Parley P. Pratt . . . was the cry of 'Delusion!' I was immediately informed that 'Joe Smith was a money-digger,' that he tried to deceive people by walking on planks laid under the water, and that he was a wicked and corrupt man, a deceiver, and one of the biggest fools in creation, and so forth." The criticism did not impede John Taylor's careful investigation of the doctrines put forth by this preacher from America. As part of his analysis, he wrote down six of the sermons given by Pratt so that he might compare them with passages in the Bible. Taylor sought to find any discrepancies that might exist, yet as he explained, "I could easily controvert any other doctrine, but I could not overturn one principle of 'Mormonism.'"[34] Pratt's preaching eventually led Taylor to examine the Book of Mormon and read the Doctrine and Covenants. Shortly thereafter John Taylor was baptized along with his wife and others in their study group.

Hearing the new doctrine heightened Taylor's ministerial zeal. Even before he was baptized, he accompanied Elder Pratt on his preaching appointments. On one occasion they visited the home of John Taylor's friend Joseph Fielding. Fielding, however, was quite reluctant to receive them and told his visitors that he wished they had not come. He opposed the meeting they planned to hold in the neighborhood, and he opposed a new religion that went against the Bible. When Pratt convinced him that he would preach nothing but "the old Bible gospel," Fielding agreed to attend. Eventually Fielding and those in his family, including Mary Fielding (who would become Hyrum Smith's wife and mother to Joseph F. Smith) were convinced of the truth and agreed to be baptized. Following his baptism, Fielding asked Taylor to write a letter to Joseph Fielding's brother, who was a minister in Preston, England, introducing him to the gospel. Subsequently, in 1837 Joseph Fielding accompanied Heber C. Kimball and Orson Hyde on the first mission overseas, and the first place they preached was in Joseph Fielding's brother's chapel.

Elder Kimball's prophecy was fulfilled as Elder Pratt found in Toronto a people prepared for the gospel. The gospel then spread to surrounding areas, and Elder Pratt's efforts led to the eventual introduction of the gospel to England. Before Pratt returned to Kirtland (where he found his wife healed), he appointed John Taylor to be the presiding elder in Canada, with responsibility to nurture the new branches of the Church.

NOTES TO CHAPTER ONE
1. *HC* 2:181.
2. Esplin, "Joseph, Brigham, and the Twelve: A Succession of Continuity,"

BYU Studies (Summer 1981): 301–41. Esplin suggests that they worked together for only approximately 15 months.

3. Arrington, *Brigham Young: American Moses,* 52.
4. Smith, *Biography and Family Record of Lorenzo Snow,* 20.
5. Ibid., 20–21.
6. Pratt, *Autobiography of Parley P. Pratt,* 168; hereafter cited as *Autobiography of Parley P. Pratt.*
7. *JD* 10:131.
8. Roberts, *Life of John Taylor,* 40; hereafter cited as *Life of John Taylor.*
9. Ibid., 40–41.
10. Ibid., 40.
11. Ibid., 41.
12. *JD* 10:130.
13. Taylor, *Succession in the Priesthood,* 15. About this confirmation, John Taylor wrote, "I knew about this calling and appointment before it came, it having been revealed to me. But not knowing but that the devil had a finger in the matter, I did not say anything about it to anybody."
14. *JD,* 21:218.
15. "History of John Taylor by Himself," quoted in Paul Thomas Smith, "Young John Taylor," *Ensign* (June 1993): 8.
16. *JD* 22:314–15.
17. *Life of John Taylor,* 28.
18. Ibid., 27–28.
19. Ibid., 29.
20. Ibid., 30.
21. Ibid., 30.
22. *JD* 23:30.
23. Ibid., 5:240.
24. Ibid., 23:30.
25. *Autobiography of Parley P. Pratt,* 130–31.
26. Ibid., 134.
27. *JD* 5:239.
28. *Autobiography of Parley P. Pratt,* 135–36.
29. Ibid., 139.
30. Ibid., 140.
31. Ibid., 140.
32. Ibid., 141.
33. *JD* 10:129–30.
34. Ibid., 5:239.

∽ TWO ∽

MINISTERING *for a* NEW FAITH

In August 1837, the Prophet Joseph Smith, Sidney Rigdon, and Thomas Marsh, President of the Twelve Apostles, visited the churches in the Toronto region. The Prophet sought out John Taylor, the presiding elder, before conducting Church business in the area. The Prophet was dismayed to find that Taylor had relinquished his duty to a Dr. Sampson Arvard, who had come earlier in the year claiming that he had been sent from Kirtland to preside over the Canadian branches. Taylor at this time was a novice in Church affairs and gave up this responsibility when he viewed Arvard's credentials from his high priest's quorum. This subterfuge had been initiated by a group of apostates in Kirtland, and when Joseph Smith arrived in Canada, he informed Taylor that he had not authorized the change in leadership. During the Prophet's visit, when Smith, Rigdon, and Marsh traveled about holding conferences in various towns, it was John Taylor who procured a wagon for them and accompanied these leaders. Concerning his experience with the Prophet, John Taylor commented, "This was as great a treat to me as I ever enjoyed. . . . I had daily opportunity of conversing with them, of listening to their instructions, and in participating in the rich stores of intelligence that flowed continually from the Prophet Joseph."[1] At a conference in Scaboro, Dr. Arvard was in attendance, and Joseph Smith chastised him for usurping the position given to John Taylor by the rightful authority. He was even critical of Taylor for succumbing to the deception. Having visited the churches, the Prophet prepared to return to Kirtland. Before leaving though, the Prophet ordained John Taylor a high priest on 21 August 1837, and reappointed him to preside over the churches in that area.

In the fall of 1837, John Taylor received an unexpected letter notifying him of a call to become a member of the Quorum of the Twelve Apostles. The directive from Joseph Smith indicated that he was to journey to Far West as soon as he could make the necessary arrangements. (John Taylor knew of this calling in advance of the letter, as he had been apprised of it in a personal revelation. The call was formally recognized in a revelation Joseph Smith received in July 1838.)[2] Previously the Taylors had planned to leave Toronto and join the Saints in Kirtland, not Missouri; they had even gone so far as to purchase property in Ohio in anticipation of their move. They would now have to forgo these arrangements to adhere to the issued call. Much like Parley P. Pratt a year and a half earlier, the Taylors found themselves without the means to make the requisite trip. Their purchases in Kirtland had depleted their resources, and John had spent increasingly less time working as a wood turner since his new ministry consumed a good deal of his time, though it afforded no remuneration. Despite their situation, John went ahead with plans to take his family to Missouri. He visited the branches he was responsible for one last time to make sure all was in order, notifying the Saints at each stop of his intended departure. As the designated day gradually approached and their circumstances remained unchanged, Taylor remained confident that the Lord would provide for them as needed.

A few days before they planned to leave, John Mills, who had intended to travel with the Taylors when they left for Kirtland, visited the family. When Taylor explained that they would now be going to Far West, Brother Mills responded, "Well, I'll go to Far West too. Won't you go with me, Brother Taylor, I have plenty of teams?" Taylor informed him that he could not pay him for taking them, but Mills replied that it mattered not. When Taylor countered that he did not wish to get into debt without any prospects of being able to pay, Brother Mills explained there would be no need to pay him back. In response Taylor said, "Well, if you'll clear me of all responsibility in the matter, and take the Lord for your paymaster, I'll go with you."[3] Other Church members in the area provided abundant food and warm clothing for the Taylors to make their journey. Thus, John, a pregnant Leonora, George John (age three), and Mary Ann (age one) set out with John Mills that winter, headed for Far West.

Their travels first took them south to Kirtland, where they stopped at what had been their original destination. Kirtland, however, was no longer the desirable destination for the Saints that it once had been. In early 1838 the town had become, according to one Church member, "a hell to all Saints." Fires were "laid by the dozens in the basements, windows of Saints." In addition, "the apostates and mobocrats had control of the law in Kirtland, and many of our good Saints were accused of crimes and thefts that they never committed, were tried and convicted and had to pay a big sum of money or get out of town."[4] In the months that followed, the Saints left Kirtland in droves. Regarding what he witnessed, John Taylor observed, "Distress, ruin and poverty . . . seemed to prevail. Apostates and corrupt men were prowling about as so many wolves seeking whom they might devour. They were oppressive, cruel, heartless; devising every pretext that the most satanic malignity could invent to harrass the Saints. Fraud, false accusation and false swearing, vexatious law suits, personal violence, and bare-faced robbery abounded. They were truly afflicted, persecuted and tormented."[5] The Taylors and Mills's stay in Kirtland was short, and they soon journeyed on.

When they arrived at Indianapolis, Mills stopped to find employment. As he had done on several occasions along their journey, John Taylor found work as a carpenter. The Taylors lodged with a Brother Miller, and it was in Indiana that Leonora gave birth to their third child, Joseph James—named after the Prophet and John's father—on 8 June 1838. The family stayed in the city for two months while John Taylor worked and preached, establishing a branch of the Church there. Anxious to get to Far West, the Taylors chose not to wait for Mills, and the family left Indianapolis, traveling on their own. Their journey was interrupted when John fell from their carriage as it was descending a hill. He was injured severely when a wheel ran over his arm. Fortunately, they were near De Witt, Missouri, where numerous Saints had settled, and they were cared for by fellow Church members.

Shortly thereafter, De Witt was attacked by a mob led by two ministers, Sashiel Woods and Abbot Hancock. John Taylor gave an account of the situation.

> I had no arms . . . and heretofore considered that I needed
> none in a Christian civilized land; but I found I had been

> laboring under a mistake. The civilization here was of a very low order, and the Christianity of a very questionable character. I therefore threw off the sling and bandages from my lame arm, suppressed my repugnance to fighting, borrowed a gun, bought a brace of pistols, and prepared myself at least for defensive measures.[6]

Though the Saints in DeWitt were considerably outnumbered by the mob, an armed conflict was avoided at the time. After this incident, the Taylor family completed the last leg of their journey, arriving in Far West at the end of summer.

A REVELATION FROM THE LORD

While the Taylors were making their way toward Far West, the Prophet Joseph Smith received a revelation from the Lord on 8 July 1838, in which he was directed to organize the Twelve and have "men be appointed to supply the place of those who are fallen" (D&C 118:1). At the conclusion of the revelation, the Lord named the new members of the Twelve: John Taylor, John E. Page, Wilford Woodruff, and Willard Richards.[7] These replacements were necessitated by the excommunications of four original members of the Twelve. Though John F. Boynton and Luke S. Johnson had both joined apostate groups and were in open rebellion against the Church and its leaders by the end of 1837, they were not officially cut off from the Church until 12 April 1838. On the following day, the high council at Far West rendered the same judgment against David Whitmer, one of the Three Witnesses, and Lyman E. Johnson, the man the Three Witnesses first chose as an Apostle. Then, at a bishop's court on 11 May 1838, William McLellin lost his membership. At the quarterly conference held in Far West in October, John Taylor's calling to the Twelve was voted upon by Church members. At the conference Elder Taylor shared his feelings about his call, telling those gathered "that he was willing to do anything that God would require of him."[8] His ordination, however, was delayed an additional two months until 19 December 1838, when Brigham Young and Heber C. Kimball laid their hands on his head, making him a "special witness" of Christ.[9]

With the Prophet Joseph, his brother Hyrum, and Sidney Rigdon in jail, the responsibility of leading the Saints out of Missouri primarily fell upon the Twelve. In some ways this miniexodus served as preparation for the much larger exodus from Nauvoo seven years later. Along with many others, the Taylors gave up their newly settled home in Far West, Missouri, and left for Quincy, Illinois, where the Saints found a temporary refuge before moving up the Mississippi River to Commerce. It was in Quincy on 17 April 1839 that a conference of the Church was held in which George A. Smith, the Prophet's 21-year-old cousin, was sustained as the newest member of the Twelve. Also discussed at the conference was the Lord's directive in Doctrine and Covenants 118:4–5 that the Twelve "go over the great water, and there promulgate my gospel," leaving from the "building-spot" of the temple in Far West on 26 April 1839. When the revelation had been given in July the year previous, the Saints still resided in Missouri and anticipated building up Zion there. Ten months later much had changed. Governor Boggs had issued his extermination order, Joseph Smith and others were in Missouri jails, nearly all Church members had fled to Illinois, and many of the Twelve were marked men in Missouri. Because enemies of the Church knew of the revelation and the day and place from which the Twelve were to depart, they vowed to prevent its fulfillment, thereby demonstrating that "Joe Smith" was no prophet. Thus, the Twelve's assignment to leave from Far West had become considerably more complicated.

During the conference the Twelve and other Church members debated what should be done. About their discussions Wilford Woodruff reported:

> As the time drew nigh for the accomplishment of this work, the question arose, "What is to be done?" . . . The Missourians had sworn by all the gods of eternity that if every other revelation given through Joseph Smith were fulfilled, that should not be, for the day and date being given they declared that it should fail. The general feeling in the Church . . . was that, under the circumstances, it was impossible to accomplish the work; and the Lord would accept the will for the deed. This was the feeling of

Father Smith, the father of the Prophet. Joseph was not
with us. . . . .When President Young asked the question of
the Twelve, "Brethren, what will you do about this?" the
reply was, "The Lord has spoken and it is for us to obey."
We felt that the Lord God had given the commandment
and we had faith to go forward and accomplish it, feeling
that it was His business whether we lived or died in its
accomplishment.[10]

The following day, on 18 April, Brigham Young and Orson Pratt
left in Wilford Woodruff's wagon, while John Taylor and George A.
Smith rode with Alpheus Cutler, who had previously been designated
the master builder of the temple, and who would aid the Twelve in
laying the cornerstone of the temple in Far West. Along the way, this
group came across John E. Page headed for Quincy with his family.
When they helped him right his overturned wagon, Page left his
family to join his fellow Apostles on their journey to Far West.

On the evening of 25 April, the Apostles and their group stayed
in the home of a Church member who was still imprisoned by the
mob. Sometime after midnight on 26 April they rode into the town
square. According to Taylor, "It was early in the morning when we
rode into the square, but beautifully clear and moonlight; all seemed
still as death, except the noise that was made by the trampling of our
horses and the rumbling of our wagons."[11] There they met with
Heber C. Kimball, who had secreted himself in Far West awaiting
their arrival. With Heber joining them, a majority of the Quorum
was now in attendance. Of the other Apostles, Parley P. Pratt was still
in jail, Willard Richards, who had been named in the 8 July 1838
revelation, was in England and had yet to be ordained, and the other
two, William Smith and Orson Hyde, had engaged in recent conduct
for which they would temporarily lose their Apostolic calling.

Their conference began in the home of Brother Samuel Clark,
and twelve people were cut off from the Church. The seven Apostles,
accompanied by 18 others, made their way to the temple grounds to
fulfill the revelation. They sang a hymn, and Brother Cutler rolled the
cornerstone into place. While seated on the cornerstone, Wilford
Woodruff and George A. Smith were ordained members of the

Twelve by their fellow Apostles, and Darwin Chase and Norman Shear were ordained members of the Seventy. Each of the seven Apostles was called upon to pray aloud, and a concluding hymn was sung. After the meeting the Apostles wandered about Far West, surveying what had been, until recently, their homes. Despite the predictions by the Missouri mobs, the Apostles were unmolested as they laid the cornerstone. Taylor observed of the mob that "it seemed as though a deep sleep had fallen upon them, for although we rode into the place right among the houses, with a number of horses and two four-wheeled carriages, we were not observed." As they left, he explained, we "took our leave of the Saints, and started . . . without being observed or it being known that we were there, except by a few women whose husbands were not in the Church, and one individual, an apostate from this Church, whom elder Turley called up to let him know that the word of the Lord had been fulfilled in relation to the above-named revelation."[12] Before sunrise, the Apostles and several others left Far West, having fulfilled the requirements spelled out by the Lord.

LEAVING FOR ENGLAND WITHOUT PURSE OR SCRIP
> It was a trying time, and nature would have recoiled and shrunk from the task, and sickened at the idea of leaving our families thus situated, and go a distance of 5,000 miles without purse or scrip; but they acquiesced, and said, "we will trust in the Lord;" and we said, "It is the word of the Lord, let him do what seemed him good."[13]
> —John Taylor on leaving for his mission to England

After leaving Far West, the Twelve did not immediately make their journey east. Rather they headed back to Quincy, where they arrived within the week. While the Twelve had been away, Joseph Smith and his brother had "escaped" from prison and finally made their way to Illinois. On 3 May the Apostles met with the Prophet, and the following day, Church leaders convened a general conference near Quincy. Before the Apostles could leave for England, there was much to be accomplished. Since Quincy was only a temporary refuge, the brethren made arrangements for the Saints to settle just to the north in

Commerce, Illinois. As there were few homes in Commerce and much of the land was yet uninhabitable, some sought accommodations across the river in Montrose, Iowa. Many of the Twelve, including Brigham Young, Wilford Woodruff, Orson Pratt, and John Taylor, found housing for their families in one-room sections of an old army barracks.

With Joseph Smith now back in their midst, there was much to learn as they prepared to go forth. The Prophet counseled and instructed them on important gospel doctrines. On 2 July 1839, a conference was held specifically for those leaving on missions. The Presidency of the Church blessed those men ordained in Far West and gave blessings to the missionaries' wives. The Prophet instructed the elders that they needed to be humble and not "exalt themselves, until they exalt themselves so high that they will soon tumble over and have a great fall." They were "not sent out to be taught, but to teach," and they were to "be honest, open, and frank in all [their] intercourses with mankind."[14] They were also given one of the keys of the mysteries of the kingdom. Joseph Smith informed them of "an eternal principle, that has existed with God from all eternity: That man who rises up to condemn others, finding fault with the Church, saying that they were out of the way, while he himself is righteous, then know assuredly that that man is in the high road to apostasy; and if he does not repent, will apostatize, as God lives."[15] In his instructions the Prophet did not tell them how to preach the gospel, where they should go, or how long they should stay. Nor did he instruct them in terms of administration or organization. They were to go and be led by the Spirit in all things.[16]

As they prepared to leave, only John Taylor escaped the ravaging sickness that laid low all those who intended to leave. According to the newly ordained Wilford Woodruff, it was as if the devil were trying to kill them before they could depart.[17] It was Woodruff who accompanied John Taylor when they left Nauvoo on 8 August 1839. Regarding their departure Elder Woodruff related:

> Early upon the morning of the 8th of August, I arose from my bed of sickness, laid my hands upon the head of my sick wife, Phoebe, and blessed her. I then departed from the embrace of my companion, and left her almost without food or the necessaries of life. . . .

Although feeble, I walked to the banks of the Mississippi River. There President Young took me in a canoe (having no other conveyance), and paddled me across the river. When we landed, I lay down on a side of sole leather, by the post office, to rest. Brother Joseph, the Prophet of God, came along and looked at me. "Well, Brother Woodruff," said he, "you have started upon your mission." "Yes," said I, "but I feel and look more like a subject for the dissecting room than a missionary." Joseph replied: "What did you say that for? Get up, and go along; all will be right with you."

Several years later, Taylor reflected back on this experience.

I left Montrose, Lee County, Iowa, . . . having previously dedicated my wife and family to the care of the Lord and blessed them in His name. The thoughts of the hardships they had just endured, the uncertainty of their continuing even in the house they were in, the prevalence of disease— more than one half of the saints being afflicted with bilious fever, there not being a sufficient number well to wait upon the sick—the poverty of the brethren, their insecurity from mobs, together with the uncertainty of what might happen during my absence, produced feelings of no ordinary kind, not to mention those of paternal and conjugal affection, enhanced by a knowledge of the time and distance that was about to separate us; but the thought of going forth at the command of the God of Israel to revisit my native land, unfold the principles of eternal truth, and make known the things that God had developed for the salvation of the world, overcame every other consideration.[19]

They left Commerce after being offered a ride and came across Parley P. Pratt and Heber C. Kimball, both cutting logs for cabins. When Kimball saw them on their way, he informed them he had no money to give them but could contribute an empty purse. Seeing what Heber had done, Pratt provided them a dollar—sending them on their way with both purse and scrip.

As they traveled in the wagon of Brother Zebedee Coltrin, Elder Woodruff suffered from chills and fever every other day. When they stopped in Springfield, Illinois, for a few days, Elder Taylor took the opportunity to publish 1,500 copies of a pamphlet he wrote describing the persecution Church members had experienced in Missouri. Taylor had, until this point, avoided the prevalent sickness, yet on 28 August he "was attacked with a violent fever," which, he explained, "took such hold upon my frame that when I got out of the carriage in which I was riding I dropped down senseless in the highway, and was some time before I recovered, Being determined, if possible, to proceed, I got into the vehicle, and travelled on, but the next and following day I dropped down in the road as before, and the last time it was with difficulty that I was restored to anima-tion."[20] By now the party had arrived at Germantown, Indiana, where they found a tavern in which to stay. On Sunday, Taylor held a meeting in which both Apostles spoke, though Taylor was notably fatigued by his efforts. The following morning it was determined that it would be best if Taylor stayed behind. Brother Coltrin was anxious to continue on, and Elder Woodruff was in no condition to provide assistance to his fellow Apostle.

During his stay in Germantown, John Taylor wrote Leonora a letter in which he told her that after being ill for three weeks, "I have got clear of my fever and am fast recovering—i[t] brought me however to the gates of death several times. It laid hold of me like a strong man armed and I was led to quail beneath the power of the adversary for I believe his hand was in it." He then added:

> You may ask me how I am going to prosecute my journey, with my trunk a distance of 300 miles or upwards by land, without means. I do not know, but one thing I do know, that there is a being who clothes the lillies of the valley and feeds the ravens and he has given me to understand that all these things shall be added and that is all I want to know. . . . He stopped me on my road and I am content. When my way is open to proceed I shall go on my way rejoicing.[21]

WILFORD WOODRUFF

His way was opened for departure a couple of weeks later. While convalescing, Elder Taylor had preached at a chapel near the inn. As he readied to leave, a man approached and said, "Mr. Taylor, you do not act as most preachers do, you have said nothing about your circumstances or money: yet you have been here some time sick and have frequently preached to us, in which we were very much interested. Your doctors', hotel and other bills must be heavy, and I and some friends have been speaking about this matter, and would like to assist you, but we have been afraid of giving any offense."[22] Elder Taylor accepted his offer, which paid the expenses incurred and provided means to continue the trip. The following day he traveled 40 miles to Dayton, Ohio, where he fell ill again and had to remain another three weeks. While in Dayton, though, he met George A. Smith and others he knew, and when he felt better they traveled with him to Kirtland, Ohio. This trip again left him too sick to continue, and Taylor stayed in Kirtland for three weeks. It was not until 13 December 1839 that John Taylor finally arrived in New York City.

Back in Montrose, John Taylor's family was not faring much better than he. In a letter dated 9 September 1839, Leonora wrote, "This has been a distressed place since you left, with Sickness. Allmost evry individual in evry Family sick."[23] In one passage she explained:

> My dear John when I wrote last I in this, all was well. Now I am Sitting watching by the Bed side of our dear George and Joseph late at Night. On Monday last I washed, on Tuesday I went out on the Prairy some Miles after the Cow as she stays away two days together if not fetched up. The Grass wet and cold morning. At Night it pourd of rain when I Milked and got wet through. On Wednesday Morning I had a sever Chile and Feaver in consequence of Cold I had taken. The next day Mary A[nne] had Chils and Feaver, thought she was going into Fits. I had to wean my sweet Child lest he should get the Chils from me. The first Night he cryd all night, afterwards he lay about the flore as if his heart was broken. On Friday he had a Chill and has evry day since and no comfort at all for it. All this time George was my only help. He went to the Well and did all he could. On Sunday he fell back to the flore in a Fit and had Chile and Feaver. I watchd him all

Night. To day he came to him self so as to talk to me. About noon he fell into the most dreadful fit, and out of that into another and got his Toung between his teeth his Fingers all turnd back. I thought I must die. My dear John I hope the Lord will not lay more upon [undecipherable] Pils. I sufer in My head a great deal; what I have past through since you left has hurt my Head a great deal.[24]

In addition to all the illness, a dispute with Brigham Young led Leonora Taylor and her family to move out of their room with the Youngs and into Sarah Pratt's room. Shortly after her husband's departure, there came the prospect of the Taylors being provided a home in Commerce. At one point in the letter she told John that her fate would be decided in the Church conference the following Saturday. However, following the conference she wrote, "I have no more prospect of a house that I had. The[y] say I shall have one but when I dont know. I live in Sister Woodrufs with Mrs. Prat. Pray for me dear."[25] Her circumstances would change little while her husband was away. When he returned in 1841, John Taylor found his family still living in the barracks and his wife so sick that he called on 20 elders to administer to her and restore her health.

PREPARING TO LEAVE FOR ENGLAND

When John Taylor finally arrived in New York City, he first traveled to Parley P. Pratt's house. Despite the fact the latter had left Illinois after Taylor, he had arrived some time before his fellow Apostle and was now presiding over the mission in the East. At Pratt's home, several of the Church brethren inquired about Taylor's financial situation. Not wishing to divulge his true state of affairs, he told them he had plenty of money, which was reported to Pratt. At the time Pratt was in the process of publishing his tract *Voice of Warning* and another publication and was in need of financial assistance. He subsequently sought out John Taylor.

"Brother Taylor, I hear you have plenty of money?"

"That is true."

"Well I am very much in need of money now, and if you could furnish me two or three hundred dollars I should be much obliged."

When Taylor told his fellow Apostle he was welcome to anything that he had, Pratt responded, "I never saw a time when it would be of more use to me." Writing later of the incident Taylor explained, "I pulled out my [only] cent and offered it to him, whereupon we had a hearty laugh." When Pratt questioned him about having plenty of money, he responded, "Yes, and so I have, I am well clothed, you furnish me plenty to eat and drink and good lodging. With all these things and a cent over, as I owe nothing, is not that plenty?"[26]

At a council meeting held that evening, Elder Pratt proposed to those in attendance that they provide Elder Taylor the means to accompany Elder Woodruff to England. Taylor refused such help, suggesting that any money go to Pratt to cover his expenses. Following the meeting Wilford Woodruff expressed his dismay at Taylor's response to the overtures for financial help. Woodruff, who had been waiting for his companion to arrive in New York, had already booked passage on a ship leaving in a week and wished that Taylor travel with him.

"Well, Brother Woodruff, if you think it best for me to go, I will accompany you."

"But where will you get the means?"

Having received an impression that he could readily acquire the money, he replied, "Oh, there will be no difficulty about that, go and take me a passage on your vessel, and I will furnish the means."

When Brother Theodore Turley heard Taylor's pronouncement, he expressed his desire to accompany the men, offering to cook for them. Taylor then added, "Then Brother Woodruff take another passage for Elder Turley and I will furnish you the means for him and me."[27]

During the following week, Elder Taylor preached to the Saints in New York and met each individually. As he did so, he informed them that he would soon leave for England, and they readily supplied him with the money necessary to pay for the two passages, as he had promised Elder Woodruff. The Church members also provided the three missionaries with bedding and sufficient food for their 22-day journey to England.

RETURNING HOME TO PREACH THE GOSPEL

Their ship, the *Oxford*, landed in Liverpool on 11 January 1840, a little over five months after Taylor and Woodruff left their homes in

Montrose, Iowa. It had been nearly nine years since John Taylor had left this same port on his journey to America. Upon arriving in England, Elder Woodruff commented:

> As England was the native place of Elders Taylor, and Turley, of course it appeared natural unto them; but it being the first time that I had set my feet upon the soil of England, it appeared unto me like an old world sure enough, for all the fires, from the parlor to the largest public works of every name and nature, being fed alone from stone coal, that it causes the whole horizon, air, elements, earth, buildings, and everything visible to be covered with gas, soot and smoke, that it makes the towns and cities appear at the first sight something similar to a coal pit, or smoke house. The buildings in England are mostly composed of stone or brick, the plain walls of which show that the majority of them were built more for durability and profit, than outward show; while others indicate great architecture, splendor, and magnificience. We past through Liverpool New Market, had a view of the Custom house, and Lord Nelson's monument, which is quite noted in England, all of which were quite splendid.[28]

JOSEPH FIELDING

The three missionaries proceeded to the Liverpool home of George Cannon, Leonora Taylor's brother. Though George was not home, John Taylor spoke with his sister-in-law for the first time and indicated they would return the next day, Sunday. The following day when George was home, they ate dinner with the Cannons. During their visit Elder Taylor began to teach them the gospel, giving them copies of the *Voice of Warning* and the Book of Mormon, which George read twice in the next month.

The following day George Cannon accompanied the elders and Brother Turley to the rail station. The three missionaries boarded a train for Preston, where they were to meet with the mission presidency—Joseph Fielding,

Willard Richards, and William Clayton—to discuss what was to be done until the remainder of the Twelve arrived. On 16 January 1840, Taylor encountered his old friend Joseph Fielding. "[I] was rejoiced to see him as he was also to see me. I thank God that he has preserved him & given him wisdom for the arduous duties devolving upon him. We felt something like Jonathan & David after an absence of 3 Years."[29] During their meeting on 18 January, the brethren decided that the two friends from Canada would return to Liverpool to preach and Elder Woodruff and Brother Turley would travel to the Potteries.

After Taylor and Fielding made their way back to Liverpool, they went to the Cannons' home and had tea with George. They began their proselyting efforts immediately, calling upon various preachers. While visiting with a Mr. Kent, a man named Steward, a Church of England minister, entered. The two missionaries proceeded to share their testimony with him and, following the Prophet's directive to be honest and frank with those they met, they "warned him in the name of The Lord & told him that if he opposed these things that portion of the spirit which he had received should leave him that he would be brought into darkness & the concerns in which he was engaged would not prosper." They also warned him "against baptizing any more as he was without authourity."[30] The minister, "a learned & highly polished man," was adamant in his rejection of their message, telling them their work "was from hell."[31] Following this rebuff, Taylor reported that, in accordance with revelation given to the Prophet Joseph Smith, "we washed our feet & bore testimony before the Lord—Saying Oh Lord our Heavenly Father we thy servants have bore testimony of the truth of those things that thou hast revealed to Mr. Steward & he has rejected our testimonys. . . . If thou canst forgive him & lead him to the truth do, we pray the[e] Oh Father. We do this that we may fulfill thy word & bear this testimony before thee according to thy command & now O Father we leave him in Thy hand praying thee to guide us into all truth & fulfill all Righteousness."[32]

The following Sunday they went to an Aitkenite church where Joseph Fielding's brother-in-law, a Mr. Matthews, was a minister. Though Matthews was absent on this particular Sunday, the two missionaries stayed and listened to the preacher. About the meeting Taylor explained, "I had peculiar feelings when I heard him & saw the situation of the people & felt Oh that I could have an opportunity of unfolding to them the glorious things of the Gospel."[33] At the sermon's conclusion, Taylor sought the chance to say a few words. He was directed by some of the preachers to go to the vestry, where he might address them. There Taylor explained his interest in what he had heard and then told them, "Bretheren & friends we are the humble followers of Jesus Christ & are from America. I have lately arrived in this place, have come a distance of 2000 miles without purse or scrip & testify to you bretheren that the Lord has revealed himself from Heaven & put us in possession of those things that you are so anxiously looking for & praying that you may receive." He went on to tell them, "I feel an anxious desire to deliver this testimony. I feel the word of the Lord like fire in my bones & am desirous to have an opportunity of proclaiming to you these blessings that you are looking for, that you may rejoice with us in those great & glorious things which God has revealed for the salvation of the world in these last days."[34] His message received a mixed response: some wept at what he said, while others were angry. One informed them of the "unfavorable opinion" that Mr. Matthews and Mr. Aitkens had of the Mormons, indicating that these ministers had told them Mormonism was of the devil.

During the afternoon, Taylor and Fielding visited other congregations in Liverpool. Concerning these visits Elder Taylor wrote, "We called upon many of the leading ministers of different denominations, and delivered our testimony to them, some received us kindly, some otherwise but none would let us have their Chapels to hold forth in, they were so good in general, and so pure, that they had no room for the gospel, they were too holy to be righteous, too good to be pure, and had too much religion to enter into the kingdom of heaven."[35] That evening they returned to the Aitkenite chapel, where they again attended services. After the meeting one of the preachers, William Mitchell, and his wife invited them to preach at their home. When Taylor and Fielding arrived on Tuesday evening, the elders of the Aitkenite church had done much to persuade Mr. Mitchell not to listen to the preachers from America. Despite this pressure, Mr.

Mitchell kept the appointment, and when Taylor and Fielding arrived, the house was nearly full of eager listeners. They met at the Mitchell's home several times that week, sharing their testimonies with those gathered.

By the following Sunday evening, Taylor and Fielding had found a place of their own in which to preach. They had rented a room that held approximately 300 persons, and in spite of little publicity on their part the room was nearly full of people "who joined in singing & gave good attention." Elder Taylor began his sermon by speaking of the many reformers—among them Luther, Calvin, Wesley, and Whitfield—who had sought to restore the ancient Church yet had been unable to do so entirely. Taylor explained, "I then shewed what the gospel was as presented by Peter Paul Phillip &c. Began at the day of Pentecost &c. Spoke of the Order Spirit Doctrines Ordinances Gifts, Blessings &c. of the gospel & shewed that if it was true then it was true now, that if it was the privilege to enjoy these thing it was ours now to possess as great blessings through the same gospel."[36] Taylor told them their prayers had been answered, as he had traveled 2,000 miles to testify to them that this ancient Church had been restored. Brother Fielding made a few remarks and then bore his testimony of the gospel. When the meeting was over, Elder Taylor explained:

> Many wept others rejoiced & praised the Lord. The spirit of the Lord indeed was with us & bore testimony to what we said & I plainly saw that it was the power of God & not the wisdom of man—that I could do nothing unless the spirit of God bore testimony to that word. After the meeting a young man came to me & told me that the Lord had showed these things to him in a vision. He rejoiced & said that he would be baptized. A young woman come to me & wept & said that she knew it was the truth, the power of God & the word of God. Several said that they beleive we were the Servants of God & wanted to obey the Gospel. It caused our hearts to rejoice. Mr. Mitchell spoke to many of his class who were present & told them that these things were of God & that he could not resist, them that he would obey the gospel & hoped that they would consider seriously about it.[37]

Following this outpouring, the two missionaries made an appointment to baptize those willing at three o'clock on Tuesday. At the determined hour, ten were baptized. Shortly thereafter, Leonora's brother George and his wife joined the new converts and were baptized, becoming "brother & sister in Jesus Christ." When Leonora received word of their baptism, she wrote her husband:

> Dear Husband, I went over the river yesterday, and I got a letter from you, dated 15th Feb.; I never received a letter that gave me so much real comfort as it has done. I do rejoice, and praise God for what he has done in bringing my dear brother George, and sister Ann, into the church, (the only church with which the Lord is pleased.) I do hope that the rest of our dear scattered ones may yet be gathered into the fold, and yet live and reign with our blessed Lord and Savior.[38]

TAKING THE GOSPEL TO IRELAND

On 27 July 1840, John Taylor left Liverpool for Ireland, joined by James McGuffie and William Black, both natives of that country. Brother McGuffie, who had joined the Church in Liverpool, persuaded Taylor to join him on a trip to his former home, and Brother Black had been designated in the previous Church conference to go to Lisbourne, Ireland, to preach. That evening they boarded a ship that would take them to their destination. They disembarked only a few miles from Newry, where many of McGuffie's former acquaintances and friends lived. Before Elder Taylor could make arrangements to preach, McGuffie celebrated his renewed friendships with a few rounds of whiskey, leaving him quite intoxicated. His drunken revelry was not limited to this single occasion, yet it was in this particular state of intoxication that he announced to the townspeople that he was a member of The Church of Jesus Christ of Latter-day Saints. "He not only told them what he was . . . he did not fail to tell them that he was accompanied by one of the Twelve Apostles, and he boasted about him, how eloquent he was and what a knowledge of the scriptures he had."[39] This, however, was not the type of introduction Elder Taylor sought as he was about to preach the first sermon in this country. They made arrangements to hold a meeting in the Sessions House, or courthouse, which was attended by hundreds. Yet so raucous was the audience that Taylor dismissed them, indicating that he did not wish to speak but that he was willing to answer questions that individuals might have. A subsequent meeting held in a country barn went much better, with numerous young men from the nearby college making inquiries concerning the precepts taught.

As Elder Taylor and Brothers Black and McGuffie subsequently headed to Lisbourne, they traveled past the farm of a Mr. Thomas Tait, whom Taylor had met previously at McGuffie's home in Liverpool. When Tait had left McGuffie's house that evening, Taylor prophesied that Tait would be the first convert in Ireland; at the time, however, there was no one preaching in the country. Now the men stopped at Tait's farm and conversed with him. As they gathered to resume their journey, Mr. Tait joined them. At a small lake near the road on which they traveled, he asked to be baptized. Elder Taylor replied, "If thou believest with all thine heart, thou mayest." Tait responded, "I believe that Jesus Christ is the Son of God, and I believe also the principles which you teach."[40] With that, Elder Taylor baptized him, confirmed him, and ordained him a priest, making Brother Tait one of two converts that Taylor baptized in his quick excursion to Ireland. Leaving McGuffie and Black in Ireland to preach, Taylor went on to Scotland, preaching to branches in Glasgow and Paisely before returning to Liverpool.

PREACHING IN LEONORA'S HOMETOWN

On 17 September 1840, John Taylor left Liverpool once again to preach the gospel elsewhere. This time he boarded a ship with Hyrum Clark, a missionary from America, and William Mitchell, a new convert from Liverpool. The three were leaving for the Isle of Man, an island located between Ireland and England. They disembarked in the capital city of Douglas. Here the three missionaries stayed for a few days before Brothers Clark and Mitchell went on to the city of Ramsey to preach. It was in Douglas that John Taylor's wife, Leonora, had grown up, and it was where she was living when she agreed to accompany her friend to Canada. Elder Taylor began his work by contacting former acquaintances of his wife. He also rented out the

Wellington Room, a large hall that could seat 1000 people, and he began giving lectures before "attentive and respectable congregations."[41] Concerning the response to his lectures, Taylor reported that "great excitement prevailed and a persecuting spirit soon manifested itself."[42] During his lecture on the third evening, a group of Methodist and Wesleyan preachers sought to disrupt the proceedings. "[H]ad it not been for some gentlemen present who interfered, who possessed more prudence than religious bigotry, it would have been difficult to prevent an indignant public from putting them out of doors."[43] Despite their failure to prevent Taylor from speaking, this group of ministers was not ready to abandon their challenge of Mormonism.

The following day they sent Elder Taylor a letter claiming he had misquoted the Bible and was guilty of blasphemy, thus deceiving the citizens of Douglas. In the letter, a Mr. Hamilton challenged Taylor to a debate in Wellington Hall, which was agreed upon. Each would have an hour to speak, followed by a half an hour each in which they could reply to the other. Mr. Hamilton was to speak first. A newspaper on the island, the *Manx Liberal*, gave a report of the evening.

> All preliminaries being over and chairman chosen, Mr. H. was called to defend his charges. He instantly rose and commenced his harangue by shewing what a clever fellow he had been, what he had done, and by inference, what he was still able to do. He said that he once took part in a similar discussion, and so effectual were the weapons of his oratory that his antagonist died within three days, and that on a subsequent occasion he was equally successful. This, as might be expected, raised some excitement in the meeting, and created some alarm for the safety of his opponent, who seemed domed to fall beneath the fatal influence of his death-striking logic.—But as he proceeded it soon became apparent that he was a mere braggadocia, possessing no qualifications save ignorance and presumption. His countenance void of every trace of intelligence—his common-place expressions abounding with tautology—the stiffness of his attitude—the inaccuracy of his language and the monotony of his tone—all indicated

his utter inability to effect his purpose, so that the missionary had nothing to fear from the inoffensive weapons of the harmless Hamilton.[44]

Hamilton's speech did nothing to address the charges levied against Taylor, who in turn explained that all divisions in religion originated with the opinions of man rather than by divine decree. And, he argued, as the gospel was unchangeable, Christ's Church ought to be the same as it was anciently. When Hamilton arose, he failed to address Taylor's claims. Instead he spoke of his knowledge of Greek, although the report indicated that he was "a perfect stranger to the syntax of his mother tongue."[45] He claimed that in the Greek Testament he could find the word *bapto*, which meant to sprinkle with the hand. He went on to claim that this was how baptism was correctly performed, adding that in countries where there was no water, they baptized with oil. At the end, "Mr. Taylor again rose, not to defend his principles, for they had not been attacked, but, as soon appeared, to inflict deserved chastisement on the arrogant simpleton, who had given the challenge without being able to utter a single sentence against his opponent; and this he did right well, for while poor Mr. Hamilton writhed beneath his heavy flagellation, it was truly heart-rending to witness his (Mr. H.'s) agony."[46]

Commencing with Hamilton's challenge, the attacks against the gospel on the Isle of Man had just begun. A Wesleyan minister, Reverend Robert Hayes, attacked the character of Joseph Smith and the credibility of the Book of Mormon in his writings and sermons. Elder Taylor responded by publishing two tracts, *Calumny Reputed and the Truth Defended*, and *Truth Defended, and Methodism Weighed in the Balances and Found Wanting*. A letter to the editor of the *Manx Liberal*, a newspaper on the Isle of Man, gives some indication of the success enjoyed by Elder Taylor. After first declaring his surprise at the stride made by "that modern delusion, viz. 'Mormonism,'" the letter's author wrote, "Above all, I imagined the two pamphlets issued by that holy, religious, and devout man of God, Mr. Hays, Wesleyan minister, (to which connection I have the honour to belong,) would have been quite sufficient to prove the fallacy of such a system, and prevent its further spread—but, sir, alas! alas! the case is quite the reverse;

numbers continually flock to the Wellington rooms and listen with eagerness to the principles there advocated." He then went on to say:

> Oh, Mr. Editor! I quake for the consequences—such a wholesale conversion to Mormonism was never before witnessed in any town or country. What will become of our society? what will become of our class meetings? what will become of our brethren in the faith? and above all, what will become of poor Mr. Hays, that nice and humble man, who so nobly stod forward to expose the errors of the Mormon system—God bless him, and preserve him from want. But, Mr. Editor, what makes the case worse, is, that a rumour is prevalent that all these pious men are to be baptised! that is, duly immersed in the salt water of Douglas Bay, by that abominable creature, Taylor. Surely there must be something enchanting about the vile man— immersion!! (my hand shakes while I write) and in winter too. Oh, sir! the thought chills my very soul—surely this American dipper intends to drown them.[47]

Though there were no reports of any drownings, the "American dipper" reported that at the end of his mission there were 100 Church members on the island.

As he readied to leave the Saints in England, Elder Taylor wrote to the *Millennial Star* a letter which he concluded by saying:

> I feel to rejoice before God that he has blessed my humble endeavours to promote his cause and kingdom and for all the blessings that I have received from this island; for although I have travelled 5,000 miles without purse or scrip, besides travelling so far in this country on railroads, coaches, steam-boats, wagons, on horseback, and almost every way, and been amongst strangers and in strange lands, I have never for once been at a loss for either money, clothes, friends, or a home, from that day until now; neither have I ever asked a person for a farthing. Thus I have proved the Lord, and I know that he is according to his word. And now as I am going away, I bear testimony that this work is of God.[48]

NOTES TO CHAPTER TWO

1. *Life of John Taylor*, 43.
2. Concerning his call, John Taylor reported: "I was living in Canada at the time, some three hundred miles distant from Kirtland. I was presiding over a number of churches in that region, in fact, over all the churches in Upper Canada. I knew about this calling and appointment before it came, it having been revealed to me. But not knowing but that the devil had a finger in the matter, I did not say anything about it to anybody. . . . A messenger came to me with a letter from the First Presidency, informing me of my appointment, and requesting me to repair forthwith to Kirtland, and from there to go to Far West. I went according to the command" (Taylor, *Succession in the Priesthood*, 14–15).
3. *Life of John Taylor*, 49–50.
4. Quoted in Anderson, *Joseph Smith's Kirtland*, 237.
5. *Life of John Taylor*, 52.
6. Ibid., 56–57.
7. Regarding the timing between John Taylor's call to be an Apostle and the revelation given in Doctrine and Covenants 118, B. H. Roberts wrote: "There is a revelation in the Doctrine & Covenants, Sec. 118, that was given at Far West on the 8th of July, 1838, in which John Taylor, John E. Page, Wilford Woodruff and Willard Richards, are called to the Apostleship; and direction is given that they should be officially notified of their appointment. But it is quite evident that Elder Taylor was notified of his appointment previous to 8th July, 1838, as he wound up his affairs and prepared to leave Canada, because of his being informed of this call to the Apostleship in the fall of 1837" (*Life of John Taylor*, 47).
8. *HC* 3:154.
9. Ibid., 3:240–41.
10. *JD* 13:159.
11. "Communications," *MS* (May 1841):13.
12. Ibid., 13.
13. Ibid., 13.
14. *HC* 3:384.
15. Ibid., 3:385.
16. Arrington, *Brigham Young: American Moses*, 73.
17. *JD* 13:159.
18. Cowley, comp., *Wilford Woodruff: History of His Life and Labors*, 109.
19. Taylor, "Reminiscences," *Juvenile Instructor* (30 October 1875): 256.

20. "Communications," *MS* (May 1841): 13–14.

21. Esplin, "Sickness and Faith, Nauvoo Letters," *BYU Studies* (Summer 1975): 433.

22. Taylor, "Reminiscences," *Juvenile Instructor* (13 November 1875): 267.

23. Esplin, "Sickness and Faith, Nauvoo Letters," *BYU Studies* (Summer 1975): 427.

24. Ibid., 430, emphasis in original.

25. Ibid., 431.

26. Taylor, "Reminiscences," *Juvenile Instructor* (13 November 1875): 268.

27. Ibid., 268.

28. "Theological," *T&S* (15 February 1841): 313.

29. "John Taylor to Leonora Taylor, January 30, 1840," in Allen, *Men With a Mission, 1837–1847*, 364; hereafter cited as *Men with a Mission*.

30. Ibid., 364.

31. Ibid., 364–65.

32. Ibid., 365.

33. Ibid., 365.

34. Ibid., 365–66.

35. *T&S* (1 May 1841):401.

36. *Men With a Mission,* 368.

37. Ibid., 369.

38. "Good News from America," *MS* (July 1840):64.

39. "Missionary Sketches," *Juvenile Instructor* (15 October 1870): 167.

40. Ibid., 167.

41. "Communication—To the Editor of the Star," *MS* (March 1841): 276.

42. *T&S* (1 May 1841):401.

43. "Communication—To the Editor of the Star," *MS* (March 1841): 276–77.

44. "Public Discussion on the Isle of Man," *MS* (November 1840): 179.

45. Ibid., 179.

46. Ibid., 180.

47. "Methodism in Trouble," *MS* (May 1841): 6–7, emphasis in original.

48. "Communications," *MS* (May 1841): 15–16.

∼THREE∼

JOHN TAYLOR *in* NAUVOO

At the beginning of April 1841, nine members of the Quorum of the Twelve gathered in Manchester, England, where council meetings were held for several days before the Apostles attended the conference of English Saints on 6 April 1841. The day following the conference, the Apostles gave Orson Hyde, who had recently joined the other Twelve in England, a blessing as he prepared to travel to Palestine to complete his mission there. A week later, on 15 April, the remaining Twelve traveled by train from Manchester to Liverpool, where they met a large group of converts readying themselves to emigrate and join with the Saints in Illinois. On 20 April, Brigham Young, Heber C. Kimball, Willard Richards, Wilford Woodruff, George A. Smith, Orson Pratt, and John Taylor boarded the ship *Rochester*. The following day the ship exited the harbor and sailed west. Their departure brought to an end John Taylor's 15-month mission to his homeland. It would not, however, be Taylor's only departure from his native land, as he would return to England in 1846 and again in 1849.

After arriving in New York on 20 May, the seven Apostles dispersed. Orson Pratt stayed in New York to print a book he originally published in Scotland. George A. Smith went to Philadelphia until he had the means to travel to Illinois. Brigham Young, Heber C. Kimball, and John Taylor left New York together on 4 June 1841 to return to Nauvoo. On the first leg of the journey, they went from Philadelphia to Pittsburgh, traveling 400 miles by train and canal. In Pittsburgh, they boarded the steamboat *Cicero* in order to travel by river to Nauvoo. Due to the low water levels, their boat ran aground several times, on one occasion leaving them stranded for three days.

Concerning the three Apostles' arrival in Nauvoo three weeks later, Heber C. Kimball wrote:

> We landed in Nauvoo on the 1st of July and when we struck the dock I think there were about 300 Saints there to meet us, and a greater manifestation of love and gladness I never saw before. President Smith was the first one that caught us by the hand. I never saw him feel better in my life than he does at this time; this is the case with the Saints in general. When we got in sight of Nauvoo, we were surprised to see what improvements had been made since we left home. You know there were not more than thirty buildings in the city when we left about two years ago, but at this time there are twelve hundred, and hundreds of others in progress, which will be finished soon.[1]

Two days later, on Saturday, 3 July, the nearly 8,000 citizens of Nauvoo gathered for an Independence Day celebration in which the Nauvoo Legion marched and Sidney Rigdon addressed the gathering. On Sunday, 4 July, 5,000 Saints gathered in a grove of trees near the temple to hear the newly returned missionaries report the details of their mission to England. It was in Nauvoo that John Taylor spent the next five years with his family, assuming a prominent role in both city and Church leadership.

"LET ALL MY SAINTS COME FROM AFAR"

When John Taylor left Montrose, Iowa, in August 1839, the Saints were just making the transition from Quincy, Illinois, upriver to Commerce. Sparsely populated, there were few permanent structures in Commerce, and there was little there at the time that would suggest the dramatic change that would take place in the two intervening years. Before returning to America from England, the Twelve issued an epistle to those immigrating to Nauvoo that reminded the English Saints they were "not going to enter upon cities already built up, but are going to '*build* cities and inhabit them.'"[2] When John Taylor and his fellow Apostles arrived in Nauvoo (the city's name now officially changed), they found a city that had been largely built up. Hundreds of buildings and homes had been constructed. Elder Kimball explained that "when we built our houses in the woods, there was not a house within a half mile of us. Now the place, as wild as it was at that time, is converted into a thickly populated village."[3]

By 1841 Nauvoo had become another gathering place for the Saints, with thousands of Church members living in and around the newly formed city. Some members openly questioned the wisdom of gathering the Saints into a single place, as the previous attempts to gather together in Ohio and Missouri had ended in perceived failure. However, in a revelation given to Joseph Smith on 19 January 1841, the Lord affirmed that it was His desire that the Saints once again assemble themselves together. He told the Prophet, "And again, verily I say unto you, let my saints come from afar" (D&C 124:25). In an epistle "To the brethren scattered abroad on the Continent of America," the Twelve confirmed the divine injunction to come to Nauvoo. In their letter they praised the citizens of Illinois, who are "inspired with a love a liberty" such that "the saints have found a resting place, where, freed from tyranny and mobs, they are beginning to realize the fulfilment of the ancient prophets, 'they shall build houses and inhabit them, plant vineyards and eat the fruit thereof, having none to molest or make afraid.'"[4] Lots were for sale, which were "for the inheritance of the saints, a resting place for the church a habitation for the God of Jacob." The gathering was also to aid the temporal affairs of the Church, helping it pay off the land purchased by Joseph Smith in 1839.

Having explained the need for the gathering, the Twelve reminded their audience that "the journeyings and gatherings, and buildings of the saints are nothing new." In the last dispensation, which "comprehends all the great works of all former dispensations," the Saints "must gather as did the fathers, must build a house, where they may be endued, and be found together worshipping and doing as their fathers did, . . . and if these things are not in this generation then we have not arrived at the dispensation of the fullness of times as we anticipate and our faith and prayers are vain."[5] In another "epistle," the Twelve further explained the doctrine of gathering, telling the Saints, "Our situation is such in these last days; our salvation spiritually, is so connected with our salvation temporally, that if one fail, the other necessarily must be seriously affected if not wholly destroyed."[6] The Saints were told that "if the church will arise unitedly" and "unite all their means, faith, and energy, in one grand mass, all that they desire can speedily be accomplished." And with them united, "no power on the earth, or under the earth can prevail against them; but while each one acts for himself, many, very many, are in danger of being overthrown."[7]

The January 1841 revelation directed the gathering Saints to bring with them their gold, silver, precious stones, and antiquities along with "all the precious trees of the earth" for the purpose of building "a house to my name, for the Most High to dwell therein" (D&C 124:26–27). Having failed to build a house to the Lord in Missouri, the Saints were commanded that they should now build one in Nauvoo. On the eleventh anniversary of the Church's organization, 6 April 1841, Church members gathered to lay the cornerstones for another temple. At noon a procession of the Nauvoo Legion arrived at the temple grounds, and once the leading officers were seated in a stand near the main cornerstone, the religious meeting commenced. The Saints sang a hymn, and following a prayer "the architects then, by the direction of the First Presidency, lowered the first (the south-east corner) stone to its place, and President Joseph Smith pronounced the benediction as follows: This principal corner stone in representation of the First Presidency, is now duly laid in honor of the Great God; and may it there remain until the whole fabric is completed; and may the same be accomplished speedily; that the Saints may have a place to worship God, and the Son of Man have where to lay His head."[8] The meeting adjourned for an hour, and the other three cornerstones were subsequently put in place.

POLITICAL AND DOCTRINAL DEVELOPMENTS IN NAUVOO

In the months prior to John Taylor's return to Nauvoo, there were several political and ecclesiastical events that significantly impacted what his life would be like in Nauvoo. In December 1840 the state legislature approved the Nauvoo city charter. In a proclamation to

Church members issued shortly thereafter, Joseph Smith, Sidney Rigdon, and Hyrum Smith commended the "legislators of this state, who, without respect to parties, without reluctance, freely, openly, boldly, and nobly, have come forth to our assistance, owned us as citizens and friends, and took us by the hand, and extended to us all the blessings of civil, political, and religious liberty, by granting us, under date of December 16, 1840, one of the most liberal charters, with the most plenary powers ever conferred by a legislative assembly on free citizens."[9] The charter provided for the structure of the city government and allowed the city council to pass laws so long as they were in accordance with state laws. It also provided for a municipal court to be established, with officials chosen from the city's citizens. On the date the charter went into effect, 1 February 1841, the first municipal elections were held, with John C. Bennett elected mayor of the city.

The legislative action also provided charters for the University of the City of Nauvoo and the Nauvoo Legion. The former, the Church presidents wrote in their proclamation, "will enable us to teach our children wisdom, to instruct them in all the knowledge and learning, in the arts, sciences, and learned professions. We hope to make this institution one of the great lights of the world, and by and through it to diffuse that kind of knowledge which will be of practicable utility, and for the public good, and also for private and individual happiness." The university was to be governed by a board of regents, which would supervise all education affairs in the city. The Nauvoo Legion was to be the city's unit in the Illinois State Militia. In light of the Saints' experiences in Missouri, where the state militia had been used in their expulsion from their homes, the charter for the Legion was an important addition, as it legally established a military force that could protect the Saints. As the proclamation explained, the Nauvoo Legion "will enable us to perform our military duty by ourselves, and thus afford us the power and privilege of avoiding one of the most fruitful sources of strife, oppression, and collision with the world."[10] On the day the Legion was formally created in February 1841, Joseph Smith was named lieutenant general, and by September of that year, the Legion was made up of 16 companies, totaling 1,490 officers and men.[11]

In addition to these important political developments, Joseph Smith introduced the practice of celestial marriage. Though the

Prophet first received a revelation concerning plural marriage as early as 1831, it was while the Twelve were still in England that Joseph undertook the steps to introduce this principle to a select group of Saints and to enter into plural marriages. And though the revelation would not be recorded for several years, on 5 April 1841, the day before the temple cornerstones were laid, the Prophet was sealed to Louisa Beaman.[12] It was during the summer of 1841, when the Twelve began to return from their mission, that the Prophet instructed them concerning this principle and advocated their practice of it.

THE MANY HATS OF JOHN TAYLOR IN NAUVOO

When he returned to Nauvoo, John Taylor soon became involved in directing Church affairs. On 16 August 1841 a special conference was held during which the Prophet outlined the duties of the Twelve. He informed them that "the time had come when the Twelve should be called upon to stand in their place next to the First Presidency, and attend to the settling of immigrants and the business of the Church at the stakes, and assist to bear off the kingdom victoriously to the nations."[13] In assuming responsibility for Church business in Nauvoo, the Twelve would relieve a great burden from the Prophet, enabling him, as he explained, to "attend to the business of translating." The several "epistles" from the Twelve about gathering in Nauvoo reflect their recently gained responsibilities. During the August conference, assignments were also made regarding which Apostles would attend conferences held in nearby cities. As part of his responsibility, John Taylor accompanied Brigham Young and Willard Richards the following month to a conference in Lima, Adams County, Illinois, where all three Apostles addressed those in attendance.

At the October 1841 conference of the Church, John Taylor was given an additional task. During the Sunday evening meeting, Brigham Young called upon the conference to select a committee to petition Congress for redress of the injustices experienced in Missouri. Elias Higbee, John Taylor, and Elias Smith were appointed to the committee, and John Taylor was designated to present the petition in Washington, D.C. The men drafted a memorial similar to one that had already been sent to Congress. Their petition began as follows:

> Your Memorialists Elias Higbee, John Taylor, and Elias Smith would most respectfully represent, that they have been delegated by their brethen and fellow Citizens the Latter Day Saints, (commonly called Mormons) to prepare, and present to your honorable Bodies a statement of their wrongs, and a prayer for their relief, which they now have the honour to submit to the consideration of the Congress of the United States.
>
> This memorial Showeth: That in the Summer of the year 1831 a portion of the people above named commenced a settlement in the County of Jackson, in the State of Missouri. The individuals making that Settlement had emigrated from almost every State in the Union to that lovely spot in the "Far West" in the hope of improving their condition; of building homes for themselves, and posterity and of erecting Temples, where they and theirs might worship their Creator, according to the dictates of their own consciences.[14]

The petition went on to describe in detail the wrongs the Saints had suffered while in Missouri. Accompanied by numerous individual petitions, Taylor, Higbee, and Smith's petition was presented before Congress by Illinois representatives John T. Stuart and John D. Reynolds, and Illinois senator Richard M. Young. Their efforts to support the Mormon cause failed, and the petition was sent to the judiciary committee, which did nothing but send it on to the National Archives.[15]

As a member of the Twelve, John Taylor often sat in council with the Prophet. Shortly after the Twelve returned to Nauvoo, the Prophet explained, "I spent the day [10 August] in council with Brigham Young, Heber C. Kimball, John Taylor, Orson Pratt, and George A. Smith, and appointed a special conference for the 16th instant. I directed them to send missionaries to New Orleans; Charleston, South Carolina; Salem, Massachusetts; Baltimore, Maryland; and Washington, District of Columbia. I also requested the Twelve to take the burthen of the business of the Church in Nauvoo, and especially as pertaining to the selling of Church lands."[16] On 27 December 1841, the Prophet wrote, "I was in council with Brothers Brigham Young,

TIMES AND SEASONS.

"Truth will prevail."

Vol. IV. No. 1.]   CITY OF NAUVOO, ILL. NOV. 15, 1842.   [Whole No. 61

From the Millennial Star.

ELECTION AND REPROBATION.

"Do you believe in Election and Reprobation?"
To prevent the necessity of repeating a thousand times what may be said at once, we purpose to answer this oft asked question in writing; so that the saints may learn doctrine, and all who will, may understand that such election and reprobation as is taught in the old and new Testaments, and other revelations from God, we fully believe, in connexion with every other principle of righteousness; and we ask this favor of all, into whose hands our answer may come, that they will not condemn till they have read it through, in the spirit of meekness and prayer.

The Lord (Jehovah) hath spoken through Isa. (42, 1) saying, behold my servant, whom I uphold, mine elect in whom my soul delighteth; evidently referring to the Lord Jesus Christ, the Son of God chosen or elected by the Father, (1 Peter, i: 20, who verily was fore-ordained before the foundation of the world, but was manifest in these last times for you, who by him do believe in God,) to serve him in the redemption of the world, to be a covenant of the people, (Isa. xlii: 6,) for a light of the Gentiles, and the glory of his people Israel; having ordained him to be the judge of the quick and dead, (Acts, x: 42) that through him forgiveness of sins might be preached (Acts xiii: 38) unto all who would be obedient unto his gospel

Every high priest must be ordained (Heb. v: 1,) and if Christ had not received ordination, he would not have had power to ordain others, as he did when he ordained the twelve (Mark iii: 14) to take a part in the ministry which he had received of his father: also, (John xv: 16) ye have not chosen me, but I have chosen you, and ordained you that ye should go and bring forth fruit, (Heb. v: 4) for no man taketh this honor unto himself but he that is called of God as was Aaron, (v: 5.) So also Christ *glorified not himself* to be *made* an *high priest*, but he that said unto him thou art my Son, this day have I begotten thee.

No being can give that which he does not possess; consequently no man can confer the priesthood on another, if he has not himself first received it; and the priesthood is of such a nature that it is impossible to investigate the principles of election, reprobation, &c. without touching upon the priesthood also; and, although some may say that Christ as God needed

no ordination, having possessed it eternally, for Christ says (Matt. xxviii: 18) all *power* is *given* unto me in heaven and on earth; which could not have been if he was in eternal possession: and in the previously quoted verse we discover that he that said unto him, i. e. his father glorified him *to be made* an high priest, or ordained him to the work of creating the world and all things upon it; (Col. i: 16) for by him were all things created that are in heaven and that are in the earth, and of redeeming the same from the fall; and to the judging of the quick and dead; for the right of judging rests in the priesthood; and it is through this medium that the father hath *committed* all judgment unto the Son (John v: 22) referring to his administration on the earth.

If it was necessary that Christ should receive the priesthood to qualify him to minister before his father unto the children of men so as to redeem and save them, does it seem reasonable that any man should take it upon him to do a part of the same work, or to assist in the same priesthood, who has not been called by the spirit of prophecy or revelation as was Aaron, and ordained accordingly? And can it be expected that a man will be called by revelation who does not believe in revelation? Or will any man submit to ordination, for the fulfilment of a revelation or call in which he has no faith?— We think not.

That we may learn still further that God calls or elects particular men to perform particular works, or on whom to confer special blessings, we read (Isa. xlv: 4) for Jacob my servant. sake, and Israel mine elect, I have called thee (Cyrus) by thy name: to be a deliverer to my people Israel, and to help to plant them on my holy mountain, (Isa. lxv: 9, see connexion) for mine elect shall inherit it, and my servants shall dwell there; even on the mountains of Palestine, the land of Canaan, which God had before promised to Abraham and his seed; (Gen. xvii; 8) and the particular reason why Abraham was chosen or elected to be the father of this blessed nation, is clearly told by the Lord, (Gen. xviii: 19) for I know him, that he will command his children and his household after him; and they shall keep the way of the Lord, to do justice and judgment; that the Lord may bring upon Abraham that which he hath spoken of him; and this includes the general principle of election, i. e. that God chose, elected, or ordained, Jesus Christ, his son, to be the Creator,

Heber C. Kimball, Willard Richards and John Taylor, at my office, instructing them in the principles of the kingdom, and what the Twelve should do in relation to the mission of John Snyder, and the European conferences, so as to forward the gathering of means for building the Temple and Nauvoo House."[17] The Twelve also met regularly among themselves to discuss matters related to their newly assigned duties. At a meeting in John Taylor's home on 7 October 1841, they met to determine which elders should be sent on missions and where they ought to go. Then on 20 November 1841, seven of the Twelve met at the home of Brigham Young to discuss an issue that would soon have particular relevance for Elder Taylor: the Twelve were not pleased with the editorial direction of the Nauvoo newspaper *Times and Seasons*, and they debated what action should be taken.[18] (Not quite a year later on 15 November 1842, John Taylor became the paper's editor after serving as associate editor during Joseph Smith's nine-month tenure as editor.) With numerous meetings of the Twelve to attend, Church conferences to speak at, and special assignments to fulfill, there was much to keep Elder Taylor occupied.

Early in 1842, Taylor accompanied Joseph Smith when the Prophet convened a meeting of 20 women in the upper room of his Red Brick Store. Among the women in attendance were the Prophet's wife Emma, as well as Leonora Taylor, Sarah M. Kimball, Nancy Rigdon, and Eliza R. Snow. The meeting was held on 17 March for the purposes of formally organizing "The Female Relief Society of Nauvoo." About what transpired as they met, Joseph Smith recorded, "I gave much instruction, read in the New Testament, and Book of Doctrine and Covenants, concerning the Elect Lady, and showed that the elect meant to be elected to a certain work, &c., and that the revelation was then fulfilled by Sister Emma's election to the Presidency of the Society, she having previously been ordained to expound the Scriptures."[19] Emma Smith was unanimously chosen president and Sisters Elizabeth Ann Whitney and Sarah M. Cleveland were selected as her counselors. Following the selection of this presidency, it was John Taylor who "ordained" these women to their callings as leaders of the women in Nauvoo.

As a close associate and confidant of the Prophet, Elder Taylor had the privilege of participating in the sacred ordinances associated with the temple. Six weeks following the October 1841 conference in which the Prophet spoke of salvation for the dead, the basement rooms of the temple were completed such that a temporary roof was set up and baptisms could be performed. In the late afternoon on Sunday, 21 November 1841, the Twelve met in council at Brigham Young's home, after which they proceeded to the baptismal font in the temple's basement. There, "Elders Brigham Young, Heber C. Kimball and John Taylor baptized about forty persons for the dead. Elder Willard Richards, Wilford Woodruff and George A. Smith confirming. These were the first baptisms for the dead in the font."[20] By May 1842, Joseph Smith began meeting with Church leaders in his Red Brick Store to instruct them concerning the endowment ceremony. Among the Twelve, early recipients of the endowment included Brigham Young, Heber C. Kimball, and Willard Richards. By the following year, John Taylor had received these priesthood ordinances, and eventually, the nine Apostles who served in England "received the fullness of the priesthood ordinances in Nauvoo under the prophet's direction."[21]

In addition to his many religious responsibilities, John Taylor assumed several positions within the city government. The death of Robert Thompson and the Prophet's brother Don Carlos Smith left two vacancies on the university's board of regents. In September 1841, John Taylor and Heber C. Kimball were elected to take their places. By the following January, John Taylor joined the city council, initially serving on the police committee. He would remain on the city council throughout his tenure in Nauvoo, and he was involved in the council's critical decision to rid the city of the *Nauvoo Expositor*.

FAMILY LIFE IN NAUVOO

In her letter dated 9 September 1839, Leonora Taylor told her husband, "We are separated for a short time but I hope we shall yet to part no more for ever."[22] While her wish that they might not be separated "for ever" would be delayed considerably, the period in Nauvoo from 1841 to 1846 would prove to be the most continuous time they would spend together between 1839 and 1857. Despite this time together, their relationship was challenged by events that occurred in Nauvoo.

Upon his return from England, John Taylor found his wife and three children still living in the run-down barracks across the river in

Iowa. He quickly set about obtaining a lot in Nauvoo proper, and he constructed a frame house at the corner of Parley and Granger Streets, on property adjacent to Brigham Young's. Before the year was out, his family moved into their new home. About this time, Leonora became pregnant with their fourth child, a little girl who was born 1 June 1842. Leonora Agnes Taylor only lived to be 15 months old, passing away in September 1843.

In April 1843, the Taylor family welcomed additional arrivals. Leonora's brother George Cannon and his family left Liverpool in September 1842 so they could join the Saints in Nauvoo. George's wife, Ann, however, never arrived in Nauvoo, as she had died during the voyage and was buried at sea. After wintering in St. Louis, George and his children boarded the *Maid of Iowa*, which finally brought them to Nauvoo. At the dock Leonora greeted her brother and his six children, ranging in ages from two to sixteen. George Cannon's family stayed a short time with the Taylors until George purchased a home. Even after George moved out, two of his children, George Q., who was 16, and 12-year-old Ann, remained with their aunt and uncle, and George Q. soon found himself employed in his uncle's office at the *Times and Seasons*.

Dealing with his youngest daughter's death was not the only struggle John Taylor faced during this time. In the summer and fall of 1841, Joseph Smith, who had recently entered into plural marriages, taught the Twelve they needed to do likewise. However, the Twelve were most reluctant. Of these circumstances John Taylor explained, "We [the Twelve] seemed to put off, as far as we could, what might be termed the evil day."[23] Taylor was not the only one who expressed his desire to avoid the Prophet's directive. Brigham Young explained, "If any man had asked me what was my choice when Joseph Smith revealed that doctrine [plurality of wives], provided that it would not have diminish my glory I would have said, 'Let me have but one wife.' . . . I was not desirous of shrinking from any duty, nor of failing in the least to do as I was commanded, but it was the first time in my life that I desired the grave."[24] John Taylor explained, at length, his feelings about the matter.

> I had always entertained strict ideas of virtue, and I felt as a
> married man that this was to me, outside of this principle,

an appalling thing to do. The idea of going and asking a young lady to be married to me when I had already a wife! It was a thing calculated to stir up feelings from the inner-most depths of the human soul. I had always entertained the strictest regard of chastity. I had never in my life seen the time when I have known of a man deceiving a woman—and it is often done in the world, where, notwithstanding the crime, the man is received into society and the poor woman is looked upon as a pariah and an outcast—I have always looked upon such a thing as infa-mous, and upon such a man as a villain.[25]

In response to the Twelve's reluctance to enter into plural marriages, the Prophet explained that it was not his wish but the Lord's will. According to Taylor:

Joseph Smith told the Twelve that if this law was not prac-ticed, if they would not enter into this covenant, then the Kingdom of God could not go one step further. Now, we did not feel like preventing the Kingdom of God from going forward. We professed to be the Apostles of the Lord, and did not feel like putting ourselves in a position to retard the progress of the Kingdom of God. The revela-tion says that "All those who have this law revealed unto them must obey the same." Now, that is not my word. I did not make it. It was the Prophet of God who revealed that to us in Nauvoo, and I bear witness of this solemn fact before God, that he did reveal this sacred principle to me and others of the Twelve, and in this revelation it is stated that it is the will and law of God that "all those who have this law revealed unto them must obey the same."[26]

It was only this knowledge—this directive was from God and not man—that persuaded Taylor to practice this principle. He indicated that "with the feelings I had entertained, nothing but a knowledge of God, and the revelations of God, and the truth of them, could have induced me to embrace such a principle as this."[27]

Despite this knowledge, John Taylor was still reluctant to approach his wife about the matter and seek out another woman to marry. Eventually, the Prophet became insistent concerning obedience to the principle.

> Some time after these things were made known unto us, I was riding out of Nauvoo on horseback, and met Joseph Smith coming in, he, too, being on horseback. . . . I bowed to Joseph, and having done the same to me, he said: "Stop;" and he looked at me very intently. "Look here," said he, "those things that have been spoken of must be fulfilled, and if they are not entered into right away the keys will be turned."
>
> Well, what did I do? Did I feel to stand in the way of this great, eternal principle, and treat lightly the things of God? No. I replied: "Brother Joseph, I will try and carry these things out."[28]

Eventually, John Taylor proposed to marry his wife's cousin, Elizabeth Kaighin. Also from the Isle of Man, Elizabeth had moved to Canada, where she had been baptized by Parley P. Pratt. The proposal was accepted, and the two were married on 12 December 1843. Fifteen months later, Elizabeth gave birth to a daughter, Josephine, the last of John Taylor's children to be born in Nauvoo. Before leaving Illinois, John married two more times. On 25 February 1844, John Taylor was sealed to 30-year-old Jane Ballantyne, and a year later he was sealed to 19-year-old Mary Ann Oakley.

JOHN TAYLOR AS EDITOR

Using a press that had been buried when mobs attacked the Saints in Far West, Don Carlos Smith, the Prophet's brother, first published the *Times and Seasons* in November 1839. When Don Carlos died in August 1841, his assistant, Ebenezer Robinson, took over. It was at this time that the

> **The Times and Seasons,**
> IS EDITED BY
> **JOHN TAYLOR.**
> Printed and published about the first and fifteenth of every month, on the corner of Water and Bain Streets, Nauvoo, Hancock County, Illinois, by
> **JOHN TAYLOR & WILFORD WOODRUFF**
> TERMS.—Two DOLLARS per annum, payable in all cases in advance. Any person procuring five new subscribers, and forwarding us Ten Dollars current money, shall receive one volume gratis. All letters must be addressed to John Taylor, editor, POST PAID. or they will not receive attention.

Twelve became increasingly dissatisfied with the way the *Times and Seasons* was run. In a council meeting at Brigham Young's on 30 November, they voted to purchase the newspaper. If Robinson rejected the offer, they planned to purchase a press and start a Church-owned paper in competition. Though Robinson initially resisted their inquiries to buy the paper, on 28 January 1842 the Prophet received a revelation concerning the matter.

> Verily thus saith the Lord unto you, my servant Joseph, go and say unto the Twelve, that it is my will to have them take in hand the editorial department of the *Times and Seasons,* according to that manifestation which shall be given unto them by the power of my Holy Spirit in the midst of their counsel, saith the Lord. Amen.[29]

Within the week a deal was struck, and the printing office, located on the corner of Bain and Water streets, was sold to the Prophet. In the next issue of the paper, Robinson announced his resignation, explaining the Prophet would fill the "editorial chair" and would be assisted by John Taylor. In concluding his announcement, Robinson explained, "I feel confident that the agents and friends of the Times and Seasons will exert themselves to support the press; knowing that while it is under the supervision of him whom God has chosen to lead his people in the last days, all things will go right."[30] He then cordially bid farewell to his readers.

Joseph Smith's tenure in the editorial chair was much abbreviated. Only nine months after his predecessor had done so, he issued a "valedictory" stating that it was impossible for him to fulfill the demands of the position. In his place he appointed John Taylor, whom the Prophet described as "less encumbered and fully competent to assume the responsibilities of that office [editor], and I doubt not but that he will give satisfaction to the patrons of the paper." In the same issue, Taylor, as the new editor, made sure to align himself with his predecessor, telling readers that the Prophet "promised to us the priviledge of referring to his writings, books, &c., together with his valuable counsel, when needed, and also to contribute to its columns with his pen when at leisure, we are in hopes that with his assistence, and other resources that we have at our command, that the Times and Seasons will continue to be a valuable periodical, and interesting to its numerous readers."[31] Thus began an editorial career for John Taylor that continued throughout the time the Saints lived in Nauvoo and eventually took him to New York City, where he published a newspaper for two and a half years.

When Taylor became the editor of the *Times and Seasons*, it was not the only paper in the city. In April 1842 William Smith, Joseph Smith's brother and an Apostle, published the first issue of the *Wasp*, a "public journal" that covered topics concerning agriculture, science, and commerce, as well as local, national, and even international news. The name of the paper indicated that it "would not hesitate to 'sting' those who opposed the editor's views, particularly those distorting Mormonism and advocating hate and persecution against the rising city of the Saints."[32] After he was elected to the state legislature in the fall of 1842, William Smith had to give up editorial control of the paper. On 10 December he published his valedictory, ceding the position of editor to John Taylor, who was "to take a more conservative approach with the [paper], no doubt hoping to lessen the ill feelings mounting against the Mormons in Illinois."[33] In assuming control of this paper, Taylor was now responsible for putting out the *Wasp* weekly and the bi-monthly *Times and Seasons*, both of which he printed at the offices purchased from Robinson.

As part of altering the image of William Smith's newspaper, Taylor issued a front-page announcement in the 15 March 1843 issue of the *Times and Seasons*.

PROSPECTUS

OF A

WEEKLY NEWSPAPER,

CALLED

THE NAUVOO NEIGHBOR.

The prospectus explained, "The little Wasp has held on the even tenor of his way the untiring, unflinching supporter of integrity, righteousness and truth; neither courting the smiles, nor fearing the frowns of political demagogues, angry partizans, nor fawning syco- phants." It went on to add that "as the young gentleman is now nearly a year old, we propose on his birth day to put him on a new dress, and to make him double the size, that he may begin to look up in the world, and not be ashamed of associating with his older brethren; and as he has acted the part of a good samaritan, we propose giving him a new name.—Therefore his name shall no longer be called THE WASP, but the NEIGHBOR." The paper was still to be published by John Taylor, and it would continue to "be devoted to the dissemination of useful knowledge of every description;—The Arts, Science, Religion, Literature, Agriculture, Manufactures, Trade, Commerce and the general news of the day."[34]

In his editorial column, Taylor outlined his views about the paper's purpose.

> By using our efforts in spreading our paper, we shall be instrumental in advancing the cause of truth, spreading the principles of intelligence and removing a large amount of prejudice, arising from misrepresentation, and ignorance, of our principles. . . . Ignorance of our doctrines, principles and policy, is the great evil that we have to cope with, and the more generally we can spread our information, the more will the community appreciate our principles, and be attracted by our doctrines. And as we are commanded, "where we cannot go, to send," if we can make use of the press as a medium, through which to disseminate our prin- ciples and doctrines, we shall be forwarding the work of God, and putting the people in possession of the principles of intelligence.[35]

The press was to be a means to abate the prejudices the Saints faced and to "advance the cause of truth."[36] At the completion of Taylor's first year editing the *Times and Seasons*, he wrote to his readership that in publishing the paper "we have hitherto been governed by the plain principles of truth; it has been our endeavour to lay before our readers those principles which we thought would best conduce to their interest and to the good of the church in general." While the publishers were honored by the praise they received and the help given them, Taylor added, "It affords us pleasure to know that we are engaged in disseminating principles, and publishing a work which in their estimation is of so much importance to the church, and to the world."[37]

In addition to using the newspaper to spread the gospel, Taylor could be outspoken in his criticism. On one occasion he wrote the following editorial:

> Some people are so very religious that their religion sticks out so far that their neighbors tread upon it, and then there is a fuss among the brethren, and surmises, and murmuring, and sometimes a little uneasiness, that somebody has fallen from grace. To prevent such unnecessary trouble, and save many from thinking wrong, and, in fact, from doing wrong, we have thought advisable to caution all against the practice of judging others, until they have been weighed in the balance, and are not found wanting themselves.
>
> The "Times and Seasons" contains religious and political articles, says one: to which we reply, certainly, and so does the Bible. Go ahead saints, and reform the world in religion and politics, in ways and means, in power and glory, in truth and virtue. Instead of judging others, and talking continually about their faults, correct your own. Thou fool! first cast the beam out of thine own eye, and then thou canst see clearly the moat in thy brother's eye. The highest folly that disgraces the United States, is; the truth and holiness, which combined and practiced, compose religion, should not be mixed with power and policy, which is the essence of government:—because some tyro from Gottengin, or some other college, has joined in the yell of demagogues, that that would be uniting "Church and State!" "God save the king!" who ever heard of such weakness? Union, virtue, truth, holiness, policy and power:— look out lest you should combine and give peace to the world, and save treasure and blood: Beware!—beware! lest a "thus saith the Lord" should be a better rule to govern the people, than an "I take the responsibility." Do beware![38]

And though the "sting" had been removed from the *Wasp*, Taylor could still be biting in his commentary.

John Taylor's work as editor of the *Times and Seasons* reflected a change in his responsibilities as an Apostle. Whereas, in 1838, the Lord had directed the Twelve to "depart to go over the great waters, and there promulgate my gospel" (D&C 118:4), the Twelve were now asked by Joseph Smith to oversee the welfare of the Church. For John Taylor this calling involved both secular and religious responsibilities. He officiated in sacred ordinances and ordinations, and he became Church spokesman in print. Having returned to Nauvoo, he was asked, as it were, to wear a good many hats.

NOTES TO CHAPTER THREE

1. "Communications," *MS* (September 1841):77.
2. "An Epistle of the Twelve," *MS* (April 1841):311.
3. 'Communications," *MS* (September 1841):78.
4. "An Epistle of the Twelve," *T&S* (15 October 1841):567.
5. Ibid., 568–69.
6. "An Epistle of the Twelve," *MS* (June 1842):17.
7. Ibid., 18.
8. *HC* 4:329.
9. Ibid., 4:267–68.
10. Ibid., 4:269.
11. Miller and Miller, *Nauvoo: The City of Joseph,* 98.
12. *CHC* 2:100–102.
13. *HC* 4:403.
14. Johnson, *The Mormon Redress Petitions,* 395.
15. Johnson, "Government Responses to Mormon Appeals, 1840–1846," *Regional Studies in Latter-day Saint History: Illinois,* 192.
16. *HC* 4:400.
17. Ibid., 4:486.
18. Ibid., 4:454.
19. Ibid., 4:552–553.
20. Ibid., 454.
21. Esplin, "Joseph, Brigham and the Twelve: A Succession of Continuity," *BYU Studies* (Summer 1981): 313.
22. Esplin, "Sickness and Faith, Nauvoo Letters," *BYU Studies* (Summer 1975): 428.

23. *CHC* 2:102.
24. Ibid., 2:102–103.
25. Roberts, *The Rise and Fall of Nauvoo,* 117.
26. Ibid., 116–17.
27. Ibid., 117.
28. Ibid., 117.
29. *HC* 4:503.
30. "Valedictory," *T&S* (15 February 1842):695–96.
31. "Valedictory," *T&S* (15 November 1842):8.
32. Jolley, "The Sting of the Wasp: Early Nauvoo Newspapers, April 1842 to April 1843," *BYU Studies* (Fall 1982):488.
33. Ibid., 494.
34. "Prospectus of a Weekly Newspaper Called the Nauvoo Neighbor," *T&S* (15 March 1843):129.
35. "Prospectus," *T&S* (15 March 1843):135.
36. Ibid., 135.
37. "To Our Patrons," *T&S* (15 October 1843):359.
38. "A Word to the Wise," *T&S* (1 June 1844):552; emphasis in original.

~FOUR~

A FRIEND to the PROPHET

After he escaped from Missouri in 1839, Joseph Smith continued to be hounded by officers of the law and government officials from that state. Prompted by ex-governor Lilburn W. Boggs, Governor Thomas Reynolds sought an extradition order to bring Joseph Smith back to Missouri to face charges of murder, theft, and arson. When the Prophet was eventually arrested in 1841, he obtained a writ of habeas corpus at Quincy, Illinois, and was tried before Stephen A. Douglas, who dismissed the case and released him. The Prophet's problems escalated when a would-be assassin shot Boggs while he was seated in a chair at home. Despite the severity of his injuries, Boggs survived and sought to have charges brought against Joseph Smith, claiming in an affidavit that Smith was an accessory before the fact. Boggs was again able to persuade Governor Reynolds to seek an extradition order. In hopes of bringing Joseph Smith back to Missouri, Reynolds gained the support of Thomas Carlin, governor of Illinois. The Prophet and his bodyguard, Porter Rockwell, were arrested on 8 August 1842. They immediately sought a writ of habeas corpus from the municipal court in Nauvoo, which prevented, for the moment, their departure. When Governor Carlin ordered the arresting officer to ignore the Nauvoo court's decision, Joseph Smith spent the next several months in hiding.

Heeding the advice of Justin Butterfield, United States attorney for the district of Illinois, Joseph Smith sent a petition to the newly elected governor, Thomas Ford, who forwarded it and the accompanying documents to the Illinois Supreme Court. The court unanimously decided the Missouri writ was illegal. However, the court determined that the matter would best be resolved by judicial proceedings rather than by executive decree. Ford wrote the Prophet that he ought to go to Springfield to have the case tried, telling him that "I would feel it my duty in your case, as in the case of any other person, to protect you with any necessary amount of force, from mob violence whilst asserting your rights before the courts, going to and returning."[1] Following these directions, Joseph Smith subsequently submitted to arrest on Carlin's old order and immediately applied for a writ of habeas corpus in Carthage, Illinois. On 30 December 1842, the Prophet, accompanied by his brother Hyrum, John Taylor, and others, left for Springfield to be tried there.

GOV. LILBURN W. BOGGS

On Sunday, 1 January 1843, the hall used by the state's House of Representatives was made available to the Prophet for preaching. In a morning meeting, it was Elder Orson Hyde who preached, and at two-thirty that afternoon, Elder Taylor preached "from Revelation 14th chapter, 6th and 7th verses, on the first principles of the gospel." According to the Prophet, "There was a respectable congregation, who listened with good attention, notwithstanding the great anxiety to 'see the prophet.'"[2] In the week that followed, the case was tried before Judge Nathaniel Pope, who denied the extradition order and freed Smith. In the *Times and Seasons* issue following the 5 January 1843 verdict, Taylor summarized the case and printed in its entirety Judge Pope's written opinion, which, in part, explained that "the mis-recitals and over-statements in the requisition and warrant are not supported by oath and cannot be received as evidence to deprive a citizen of his liberty, and transport him to a foreign state for trial. For these reasons Smith must be discharged."[3]

Within months, John Taylor once again became intimately involved with the Prophet's legal affairs. In June 1843, the Prophet was indicted in Missouri on the old charge of "murder, treason, burglary, and theft." Again, Governor Reynolds of Missouri sought to extradite the Prophet, and he appealed to Governor Ford, who, this time, supported the Missourians' actions. Joseph Smith was arrested by J. H. Reynolds, sheriff of Jackson County, Missouri, and Mr. Harmon Wilson from

Carthage, Illinois. Pretending to be Mormon preachers, they confronted the Prophet while he was visiting his wife's sister in Dixon, Lee County, Illinois. Before Joseph could be secreted away, several local citizens learned of the situation and informed Reynolds that "if that was their mode of doing business in Missouri, they had another way of doing it in Dixon."[4] A writ of habeas corpus was obtained, and circumstances eventually led the Prophet to be tried before the municipal court in Nauvoo.

In the *Times and Seasons*, Taylor dedicated two full issues and part of a third to the Prophet's trial. Introducing the court proceedings in the 1 July 1843 issue, Taylor began by telling readers:

> It has fallen to our lot of late years to keep an account of any remarkable circumstance that might transpire, in, and about this, and the adjoining states; as well as of distant provinces and nations. Among the many robberies, earthquakes, volcanic eruptions, tornadoes, fires, mobs, wars, &c. &c., which we have had to record, there is one circumstance of annual occurrence, which it has always fallen to our lot to chronicle. We allude not to the yearly inundations of the Nile, nor the frequent eruptions of Vesuvius or Etna, but to the boiling over of Tophet, alias the annual overflow of the excrescence of Missouri. Not, indeed, like the Nile, overflowing its parched banks, invigorating the alluvial soil and causing vegetation to teem forth in its richest attire; but like the sulphurious flame that burns unnoticed in the bowels of a volcano. . . . So Missouri has her annual ebulitions, and unable to keep her fire within her own bosom, must belch forth her sulphuric lava, and seek to overwhelm others with what is burning in her own bowels and destroying her very vitals; and as it happens that we are so unfortunate as to live near the borders of this monster, we must ever and anon, be smooted with the soot that flies off from her burning crater.

Recounting the legal challenges the Prophet faced, the article explained:

> Joseph Smith must therefore be sacrificed at the shrine of the hellish despotism of Missouri, and that of political

aspirants of this State. What was the pledge that Gov. Duncan gave the people, if they would elect him? that he would have the Mormon charters repealed, and deprive them of all their other privileges. Thus the Mormons and Joseph Smith must be at the disposal of such inhuman reckless, blood thirsty, (we had like to have said,) republicans as these. Oh shame where is thy blush! and the attempted murder of Governor Boggs, to them is a good pretext. As if it were impossible that there should be found among the inhabitants of a State who had butchered scores in cold blood, who had robbed an innocent people of hundreds of thousands of dollars worth of property; and who had driven thirteen thousand people from their homes, who had never violated law, a man who was base enough to seek to murder another without having the thing so far fetched as to try to heap it upon the head of a man who had not been in the State for years.[5]

Following an account of Joseph Smith's arrest near Dixon and his subsequent legal wrangling, the article concluded:

Why Governor Ford should lend his assistance in a vexatious prosecution of this kind we are at a loss to determine. He possesses a discretionary power in such cases, and has a right to use his judgment, as the chief magistrate of this State, and knowing, as he does, that the whole proceedings, connected with this affair are illegal, we think that in justice he ought to have leaned to the side of the oppressed and innocent, particularly when the persecuted and prosecuted were citizens of his own State. . . .Why then should our Executive feel so tenacious in fulfiling all the nice punctillios of law, when the very State that is making those demands has robbed, murdered and exterminated by wholesale without law and are merely making use of it at present as a cats-paw to destroy the innocent and murder those that they have already persecuted nearly to the death. It is impossible that the State of Missouri should do justice with her coffers groaning with the spoils of the oppressed and her hands yet reeking with the blood of the innocent.

Shall she yet gorge her bloody maw with other victims?
Shall Joseph Smith be given into her hands illegally? *Never!*
NO NEVER!! NO NEVER!!!⁶

Defended by Cyrus Walker, a well-known lawyer who was
campaigning for United States Congress, the case was tried on its
merits, rather than being dismissed on legal technicalities. The result
was the same for Joseph Smith, and he was discharged once again.

A PRESIDENTIAL CAMPAIGN

In October 1843, an editorial appeared in the *Times and Seasons*
that asked the question: "WHO SHALL BE OUR NEXT PRESI-
DENT?" The opening paragraph explained, "This question we
frequently hear asked, and it is a question of no small importance to
the Latter Day Saints." After reviewing the injustices the Saints
endured in Missouri, John Taylor wrote, "But our wrong cannot
slumber. Such tyranny and oppression must not be passed over in
silence; our injuries, though past, are not forgotten by us." As
American citizens, the article explained, "we claim the privilege of
being heard in the councils of our nation." The short piece then
concluded, "We make these remarks for the purpose of drawing the
attention of our brethren to this subject, both at home and abroad;
that we may fix upon the man who will be the most likely to render
us assistance in obtaining redress for our grievances—and not only
give our own votes, but use our influence to obtain others. . . . We
shall fix upon the man of our choice, and notify our friends duly."⁷
Rather than advocating a certain candidate, the editorial, which the
Prophet copied into his history, affixed the criteria by which the
Saints were to select the next United States president.

That fall, John Taylor and Willard Richards assisted Joseph Smith
as he wrote the leading presidential candidates—John C. Calhoun,
Lewis Cass, Richard M. Johnson, Henry Clay, and Martin Van
Buren—asking, "'What will be your rule of action as it relates to us as a
people, should fortune favor your ascension to the chief magistracy?'"⁸

Only three candidates replied: Calhoun, Cass, and Clay. None of
them indicated a willingness to support the Mormons.⁹ In light of these
rebuffs, the Twelve gathered with Joseph Smith, his brother Hyrum,

and John P. Greene at the mayor's office in Nauvoo on 29 January 1844 to decide "the proper course to pursue in relation to the coming Presidential election."[10] The field had now been narrowed to Henry Clay and Martin Van Buren, and the latter had already made clear to the Prophet his stance concerning the Mormons. At Willard Richards's motion, it was unanimously decided that they would support an independent ticket with Joseph Smith as the candidate. In response the Prophet told them, "If you attempt to accomplish this, you must send every man in the city who is able to speak in public throughout the land to electioneer and make stump speches, advocate the 'Mormon' religion." According to the Prophet's instructions, the April Church conference would be followed by conferences held throughout the nation, where the missionaries would campaign and preach the gospel. The Prophet went on to add, "Tell the people we have had Whig and Democratic Presidents long enough: we want a President of the United States. If I ever get into the presidential chair, I will protect the people in their rights and liberties. I will not electioneer for myself. Hyrum, Brigham, Parley and Taylor must go. . . . There is oratory enough in the Church to carry me into the presidential chair the first slide."[11]

From this meeting sprang the Prophet's presidential campaign. Barely a week later, Joseph Smith spoke at a political meeting held in the assembly hall in which he related his views on the powers of the government. After speeches by Orson Hyde and John Taylor, those in attendance voted to support the Prophet's political views. In the following *Times and Seasons*, Taylor, in an editorial, again asked the question: Who shall be our next president? Emphasizing that this "is a matter of paramount importance," one which necessitated the Saints' "most serious, calm, dispassionate reflection," he acknowledged the importance of the presidential office. Reviewing their failed efforts at seeking redress for the wrongs committed in Missouri, he indicated that appeals to both federal and state governments yielded nothing. Following this introduction, Taylor then asked:

> What shall we do under this state of things? In the event of
> either of the prominent candidates, Van Buren or Clay,
> obtaining the Presidential chair, we should not be placed in
> any better situation. In speaking of Mr. Clay, his politics are
> diametrically opposed to ours; he inclines strongly to the old
> school of federalists, and as a matter of course, would not
> favor our cause, neither could we conscientiously vote for
> him. And we have yet stronger objections to Mr. Van Buren,
> on other grounds. He has sung the old song of congress—
> "congress has no power to redress your grievances."

Disparaging Van Buren further, Taylor told readers that Van Buren
had entered into an agreement with Mr. Benton of Missouri, whereby
if Benton helped Van Buren carry the state, he would use his executive power to further persecute the Mormons. While Taylor wrote,
"We could scarcely credit the statement, and we hope yet for the sake
of humanity, that the suggestion is false," he added "We have too
good reason to believe that we are correctly informed."[12]

It seemed that the Saints had only two poor choices from which
to select their next president. The editorial, however, went on to
suggest another alternative.

> Under these circumstances the question again arises, who
> shall we support? General Joseph Smith. A man of sterling
> worth and integrity and of enlarged views; a man who has
> raised himself from the humblest walks in life to stand at
> the head of a large, intelligent, respectable, and increasing
> society, that has spread not only in this land, but in distant
> nations; a man whose talents and genius, are of an exalted
> nature, and whose experience has rendered him every way
> adequate to the onerous duty. Honorable, fearless, and
> energetic; he would administer justice with an impartial
> hand, and magnify, and dignify the office of chief magis-
> trate of this land; and we feel assured that there is not a
> man in the United States more competent for the task.

In concluding, Taylor told readers, "Under existing circumstances
we have no other alternative, and if we can accomplish our object

well, if not we shall have the satisfaction of knowing that we have acted conscientiously and have used our best judgment; and if we have to throw away our votes, we had better do so upon a worthy, rather than upon an unworthy individual, who might make use of the weapon we put in his hand to destroy us with."[13] Thus, the Prophet's candidacy was announced to the citizens of Nauvoo and to Church members who read the paper in distant cities.

An editorial in the next *Times and Seasons* admonished the Saints as to what course of action they ought to follow: "Having now raised the name of our General and Prophet to the head of our columns, it becomes us, as Latter Day Saints, to be wise, prudent, and enerjetic, in the cause that we pursue; and not to let any secondary influences control our minds, or govern our proceedings. The step that we have taken is a bold one, and requires our united efforts, perseverance, and diligence; but important as it may be, it is no greater than others have taken, and they have conceived that they had a right, without molestation to pursue that course, and to vote for that man whose election, they in their wisdom, thought would be most conducive to the public weal." In part, the article argued that Church members must actively seek to publicize the Prophet's virtues, countering the many misrepresentations and falsehoods that abounded. "It is for us," Taylor wrote, "to take away this false coloring, and by lecturing, by publishing, and circulating his works; his political views; his honor, integrity, and virtue; stop the foul mouth of slander, and present him before the public in his own colors, that he may be known, respected, and supported."[14] This latter suggestion anticipated the help needed from Church members to spread the Prophet's message, making a veiled reference to the subsequent calling for volunteers to electioneer for the Prophet.

In the 15 March 1844 issue of the *Times and Seasons*, Taylor addressed the important issue of mixing religion with politics, admitting that "there are peculiar notions extant in relation to the propriety or impropriety of mixing religion with politics, many of which we consider to be wild and visionary." While recognizing the problems with policies in European nations, he claimed that in America the division of religion and politics had gone too far, suggesting that "in our jealousy lest a union of this kind should take place, we have thrust out God from all of our political movements, and seem to regard the affairs of the nation as that over which the great Jehovah's providence has no control, about which his direction or interposition, never should be sought, and as a thing conducted and directed by human wisdom alone." Rather than evicting God from politics, the Bible, he argued, demonstrates that "God in ancient days had as much to do with governments, kings and kingdoms, as he ever had to do with religion."[15] Accordingly, "if any person ought to interfere in political matters it should be those whose minds and judgments are influenced by correct principles—religious as well as political; otherwise those persons professing religion would have to be governed by those who make no professions; be subject to their rule; have the law and word of God trampled under foot." For this reason, "the cause of humanity, the cause of justice, the cause of freedom, the cause of patriotism, and the cause of God requires us to use our endeavors to put in righteous rulers." Given these criteria, Taylor wrote that General Joseph Smith, as he referred to the Prophet in the editorials, was the perfect candidate. His integrity, "exalted genius," perseverance, and virtue would "prove him to be a patriot and statesman."[16]

At the general conference in April, speeches mingled religious and political messages. Volunteers were sought to go to "all the different States to get up meetings and protracted meetings, and electioneer for Joseph to be the next President."[17] When the call was made for volunteers, 244 came forward. Nearly 100 more were chosen in the following days as the dates and places for the conferences were selected. The first conference in Quincy, Illinois, was to take place on 4 and 5 May, and subsequent conferences were set for Saturdays and Sundays through August. Then in September, conferences on nine consecutive days were to be held in Washington, D.C. With the exception of John Taylor and Willard Richards, the Apostles joined the missionaries in these electioneering efforts. A year previous, when Joseph Smith sent the Twelve out on missions, Taylor was directed to stay behind, the Prophet telling him, "John Taylor, I believe you can do more good in the editorial department than preaching. You can write for thousands to read; while you can preach to but a few at a time. We have no one else we can trust the paper with, and hardly with you, for you suffer the paper to come out with so many mistakes."[18] Elder Taylor stayed behind, and he and Willard Richards were the only Apostles in Nauvoo for the next few months.

WILLARD RICHARDS FAMILY

JOHN TAYLOR'S ROLE IN THE EXPOSITOR AFFAIR

Approximately a month after the April Church conference, on 10 May 1844, a prospectus was issued for a third newspaper to be printed in Nauvoo: the *Nauvoo Expositor*. The weekly paper, the prospectus declared, would advocate the unconditional repeal of the Nauvoo city character and disobedience to political revelations and would oppose the union of church and state. The first issue was to be published Friday, 7 June 1844, by a group of men who had recently been cut off from the Church, including William Law, once a member of the First Presidency. As promised, the paper was printed and distributed on the first Friday in June. Those involved in the paper sought to explain the grounds for their dissension, along with exposing the evil practices of Joseph Smith and the Church. About the paper Taylor wrote;

> Emboldened by the acts of those outside, the apostate "Mormons," associated with others, commenced the publication of a libelous paper in Nauvoo, called the *Nauvoo Expositor*. This paper not only reprinted from the others, but put in circulation the most libelous, false, and infamous reports concerning the citizens of Nauvoo, and especially the ladies. It was, however, no sooner put in circulation than the indignation of the whole community was aroused; so much so, that they threatened its annihilation; and I do not believe that in any other city in the United States, if the same charges had been made against the citizens, it would have been permitted to remain one day. As it was among us, under these circumstances, it was thought best to convene the City Council to take into consideration the adoption of some measures for its removal, as it was deemed better that this should be done legally than illegally. Joseph Smith, therefore,

who was mayor, convened the City Council for that purpose; the paper was introduced and read, and the subject examined. All, or nearly all present, expressed their indignation at the course taken by the *Expositor,* which was owned by some of the aforesaid apostates, associated with one or two others. . . . The calculation was, by false statements, to unsettle the minds of many in the city, and to form combinations there similar to the "anti-Mormon" associations outside of the city.[19]

NAUVOO EXPOSITOR

On Saturday morning, 8 June 1844, the city council debated what might be their best course of action, yet nothing was agreed upon. On Monday, the council members deliberated for another eight and a half hours. Taylor "well remember[ed] the feeling of responsibility that seemed to rest upon all present."[20] Eventually Joseph Smith persuaded the council (with the exception of Councilman Warrington, who sought to impose a $3,000 fine for every libelous statement) to declare the paper a public nuisance. Joseph Smith then ordered the marshal and acting major-general of the Nauvoo Legion to destroy the press, scatter the type, and burn any remaining copies. The order was carried out. When Taylor later discussed the council's actions with Governor Ford, the governor told him, "I cannot blame you for destroying [the press], but I wish it had been done by the mob." In explaining why they pursued the course they did, Taylor explained, "I told him that we preferred a legal course, and that Blackstone described a libelous press as a nuisance and liable to be removed; that our city charter gave us the power to remove nuisances; and that if it was supposed we had contravened the law, we were amenable for our acts and refused not an investigation."[21]

Two days later on Wednesday, 12 June, Joseph Smith was arrested by David Bettisworth, a constable from Hancock County. The

GOV. THOMAS FORD

Prophet petitioned for a writ of habeas corpus, which was granted, and he was tried before the municipal court in Nauvoo and acquitted on charges of inciting a riot. In response to the non-Mormon outcry regarding the events, Smith wrote Governor Ford on Friday, stating, "the City Council decided that it was necessary for the 'peace, benefit, good order and regulations' of [Nauvoo], 'and for the protection of property,' and for 'the happiness and prosperity of the citizens'" to destroy the press.[22] On Monday, 17 June, Joseph Smith was again arrested, along with the city council, for inciting a riot. The men all appeared before Judge Daniel H. Wells and were tried that afternoon, with the judge rendering the same verdict as the previous court.

On Wednesday, 19 June, John Taylor published an extra edition of the *Nauvoo Neighbor* containing the following editorial:

> As a soft breeze on a hot day mellows the air, so does the simple truth calm the feelings of the irritated; and so we proceed to give the proceedings of the City Council relating to the removal of the Nauvoo Expositor as a nuisance. We have been robbed, mobbed and plundered with impunity some two or three times; and as every heart is more apt to know its own sorrows, the people of Nauvoo had ample reason, when such characters as the proprietors and abettors of the Nauvoo Expositor proved to be before the City Council, to be alarmed for their safety.
>
> The men who got up the press were constantly engaged in resisting the authority or threatening something. If they were fined, an appeal was taken, but the slander went on; and when the paper came, the course and the plan to destroy the city was marked out. The destruction of the city charter and the ruin of the Saints was the all-commanding topic.

Our lives, our city, our charter and our characters are just as sacred, just as dear, and just as good as other people's; and while no friendly arm has been extended from the demolition of our press in Jackson county, Missouri, without law, to this present day, the City Council with all the law of nuisance, from Blackstone down to the Springfield charter, knowing that if they exceeded the law of the land a higher court could regulate the proceedings, abated the *Nauvoo Expositor.*

The proceedings of the Council show, as sketched out, that there was cause for alarm. The people, when they reflect, will at once say that the feelings and rights of men ought to be respected. All persons otherwise, who, without recourse to justice, mercy or humanity, come out with inflammatory publications, destructive resolutions, or more especially extermination, show a want of feeling, a want of respect and a want of religious toleration that honorable men will deprecate among Americans as they would the pestilence, famine, or horrors of war. It cannot be that the people are so lost to virtue as to coolly go to murdering men, women and children. No; candor and common sense forbid it![23]

As the "feelings of the irritated" were not to be calmed, Joseph Smith declared martial law in Nauvoo because of the pending threats to the city.

Due to the increasing hostilities, Governor Ford soon headed for Carthage, where he arrived on Friday, 21 June 1844. Following his arrival he sent two men to see Joseph Smith, requesting that a committee be sent to the governor to represent the city council's side in the matter. The city council met that afternoon at four o'clock and reviewed affidavits by those who had participated in the *Expositor*'s destruction. It was decided that Dr. J. M. Bernhisel, who would later represent the territory of Utah in Congress, John Taylor, and Willard Richards would heed the governor's petition. At five o'clock, Bernhisel and Taylor left for Carthage, while Richards remained in Nauvoo preparing more documents. When they arrived in Carthage around eleven o'clock that evening, the two emissaries found a room

at the same hotel as the governor. Though the governor had purportedly gone to bed, they found "the town was filled with a perfect set of
rabble and rowdies, who, under the influence of Bacchus, seemed to
be holding a grand saturnalia, whooping, yelling and vociferating as if
Bedlam had broken loose."[24] That evening men from Carthage tried
to separate Taylor and Bernhisel from one another. At one point, they
knocked on the door and informed Taylor that a Mormon man had
been arrested and he sought Taylor to bail him out. Finding it an odd
hour for such proceedings, Taylor and Bernhisel determined that help
(if any was needed at all) could be rendered in the morning. That
night Taylor slept with his pistols under his pillow.

Nothing further happened that evening, and on the morning of
22 June, they sought an audience with the governor. About the
meeting Taylor wrote, "After waiting the governor's pleasure for some
time we had an audience; but such an audience!"

> He was surrounded by some of the vilest and most unprin-
> cipled men in creation; some of them had an appearance of
> respectability, and many of them lacked even that. . . . I can
> well remember the feelings of disgust that I had in seeing
> the governor surrounded by such an infamous group, and
> on being introduced to men of so questionable a character;
> and had I been on private business, I should have turned to
> depart, and told the governor that if he thought proper to
> associate with such questionable characters, I should beg
> leave to be excused; but coming as we did on public busi-
> ness, we could not, of course, consult our private feelings.

> We then stated to the governor that, in accordance with his
> request, General Smith had, in response to his call, sent us
> to him as a committee of conference. . . .We then, in brief,
> related an outline of the difficulties, and the course we had
> pursued from the commencement of the troubles up to the
> present, and handing him the documents, respectfully
> submitted the whole. . . .

> He opened and read a number of the documents himself,
> and as he proceeded he was frequently interrupted by

"that's a lie!" "that's a God damned lie!" "that's an infernal falsehood!" "that's a blasted lie!" etc.[25]

Despite reading the documents provided, Governor Ford still requested that Joseph Smith and all those involved in destroying the press come to Carthage. Taylor pointed out, however, they had already been tried and acquitted on the matter twice and had "fulfilled the law in every particular."[26] But since people outside Nauvoo felt that justice had not been served, the governor insisted that the involved parties come to Carthage. He directed them to not bring any weapons, and he promised, as governor of the state, that all would be protected and he would guarantee their "perfect safety."

Taylor and Bernhisel returned to Nauvoo late that night and immediately went to see Joseph Smith, who was obviously displeased by the governor's request. None of the men wanted to put themselves in the hands of the mobs by going to Carthage. The Prophet, along with his brother Hyrum, Taylor, Bernhisel, Willard Richards, and others, sat in council for some time discussing their options. When two men seeking an interview with the Prophet disrupted their meeting, Taylor left for home at two in the morning to get some sleep. Awakened only a few hours later, Taylor was much surprised to hear that Joseph, Hyrum, and Willard Richards had fled Nauvoo and crossed the river to Iowa. Recognizing that if men from Carthage attacked Nauvoo, one of the likely targets would be the printing office, Taylor gathered some trusted men and went to the office to remove all the valuable equipment. He then arranged with Cyrus Wheelock and Alfred Bell to likewise take him across to Iowa. By the time Taylor crossed the Mississippi River, he had decided to go to upper Canada if he could not find the Prophet. Needing a traveling companion, he said to Brother Wheelock, "Can you go with me ten or fifteen hundred miles?" Wheelock answered, "Yes." "Can you start in half an hour?" "Yes." Taylor told him to first see his family and then make the necessary arrangements for such a trip; if they were yet unable to find the Prophet, they would leave by nightfall.[27] Shortly before they were to depart for Canada, after the horses had been acquired and the funds arranged for the trip, Brother Elias Smith came to Taylor, who had been waiting in a secluded house, and informed him he had found the Prophet and his companions. They had concluded to go to Carthage after all and wished that Taylor return to Nauvoo so that he could accompany them. About this report Taylor explained, "I must confess that I felt a good deal disappointed at this news, but I immediately made preparations to go."[28] The following Monday, 24 June, Taylor accompanied the Prophet, Hyrum Smith, and others on the city council as they left Nauvoo on horseback, headed for Carthage.

TO CARTHAGE AND BACK

On the morning of 25 June, those who had gone to Carthage from Nauvoo surrendered themselves to the constable, David Bettisworth. Bettisworth subsequently arrested Joseph and Hyrum on charges of treason. That afternoon, all on the city council appeared in court, where they posted bail and were ordered to appear at the county court during its next session. No mention was made concerning the charges of treason against Joseph and Hyrum. As the governor had promised a meeting with the Smith brothers, they waited that evening until they saw him at his hotel room. Shortly after this conversation, Bettisworth reappeared and insisted Joseph and Hyrum go to jail for their arrest on the treason charges. Given the illegality of Bettisworth's order, Taylor sought out the governor to put right the situation.

> I represented to him the characters of the parties who had made oath, the outrageous nature of the charge, the indignity offered to men in the position which they occupied, and declared to him that he knew very well it was a vexatious proceeding, and that the accused were not guilty of any such crime. The governor replied, he was very sorry that the thing had occurred; that he did not believe the charges, but that he thought the best thing to be done was to let the law take its course. I then reminded him that we had come out there at his instance, not to satisfy the law. . . . The governor replied that it was an unpleasant affair, and looked hard; but that it

was a matter over which he had no control, as it belonged to the judiciary; that he, as the executive, could not interfere with their proceedings, and that he had no doubt but that they would immediately be dismissed. I told him that we had looked to him for protection from such insults, and that I thought we had a right to do so from the solemn promises which he had made . . . in relation to our coming without guard or arms; that we had relied upon his faith, and had a right to expect him to fulfill his engagements after we had placed ourselves implicitly under his care, and complied with all his requests, although extra-judicial.[29]

When the governor refused to intervene, the prisoners were carted off to jail. The following morning Joseph Smith had a lengthy interview with the governor, in which he explained the Mormon side of the issues. Governor Ford again promised him protection and told him that if he went to Nauvoo on the morrow, he would assuredly take the Prophet with him.

On the evening of 26 June, Joseph and Hyrum Smith were accompanied in jail by John Taylor, Willard Richards, John Fullmer, Stephan Markham, and Dan Jones. Part of the evening was spent listening to Hyrum read Book of Mormon accounts of God's servants being delivered from prison.[30] By afternoon the following day, Fullmer, Markham, and Jones all left the jail to run errands for the prisoners, but were denied reentry. When Markham went to purchase something for Willard Richards (who was feeling ill), he was driven from the city by Carthage Greys, a company of local soldiers. By late afternoon there were only four left in the jail. About their situation Taylor explained, "We all of us felt unusually dull and languid, with a remarkable depression of spirits. In consonance with those feelings I sang a song, that had lately been introduced into Nauvoo, entitled, 'A poor wayfaring man of grief,'" a song which Taylor described as "pathetic, and the tune quite plaintive, and was very much in accordance with our feelings at the

DAN JONES

time." After a short time lapsed, Hyrum requested that he sing the song again. When Taylor replied that he did not feel much like singing, Hyrum remarked, "Oh, never mind; commence singing, and you will get the spirit of it."[31]

After singing a second time, Taylor looked out the window and saw a number of men approaching the jail, their faces painted black. He described the subsequent events as follows:

> The other brethren had seen the same, for, as I went to the door, I found Brother Hyrum Smith and Dr. Richards already leaning against it. They both pressed against the door with their shoulders to prevent its being opened, as the lock and latch were comparatively useless. While in this position, the mob, who had come up stairs, and tried to open the door, probably thought it was locked, and fired a ball through the keyhole; at this Dr. Richards and Brother Hyrum leaped back from the door, with their faces towards it; almost instantly another ball passed through the panel of the door, and struck Brother Hyrum on the left side of the nose, entering his face and head. At the same instant, another ball from the outside entered his back, passing through his body and striking his watch. The ball came from the back, through the jail window, opposite the door, and must, from its range, have been fired from the Carthage Grays, who were placed there ostensibly for our protection, as the balls from the fire-arms, shot close by the jail, would have entered the ceiling, we being in the second story, and there never was a time after that when Hyrum could have received the latter wound. Immediately, when the balls struck him, he fell flat on his back, crying as he fell, "I am a dead man!" He never moved afterwards.
>
> I shall never forget the deep feeling of sympathy and regard manifested in the countenance of Brother Joseph as he drew nigh to Hyrum, and, leaning over him, exclaimed, "Oh! my poor, dear brother Hyrum!" He, however, instantly arose, and with a firm, quick step, and a determined expression of countenance, approached the door, and pulling the six-shooter left by Brother Wheelock from his pocket, opened the door slightly; and snapped the pistol six succes-

sive times; only three of the barrels, however, were discharged. I afterwards understood that two or three were wounded by these discharges, two of whom, I am informed, died. I had in my hands a large, strong hickory stick, brought there by Brother Markham, and left by him, which I had seized as soon as I saw the mob approach; and while Brother Joseph was firing the pistol, I stood close behind him. As soon as he had

THE CARTHAGE JAIL

discharged it he stepped back, and I immediately took his place next to the door, while he occupied the one I had done while he was shooting. Brother Richards, at this time, had a knotty walking-stick in his hands belonging to me, and stood next to Brother Joseph, a little farther from the door, in an oblique direction, apparently to avoid the rake of the fire from the door. The firing of Brother Joseph made our assailants pause for a moment; very soon after, however, they pushed the door some distance open, and protruded and discharged their guns into the room, when I parried them off with my stick, giving another direction to the balls.

It certainly was a terrible scene: streams of fire as thick as my arm passed by me as these men fired, and, unarmed as we were, it looked like certain death. I remember feeling as though my time had come, but I do not know when, in any critical position, I was more calm, unruffled, energetic, and acted with more promptness and decision. It certainly was far from pleasant to be so near the muzzles of those fire-arms as they belched forth their liquid flames and deadly balls. While I was engaged in parrying the guns, Brother Joseph said, "That's right, Brother Taylor, parry

them off as well as you can." These were the last words I
ever heard him speak on earth.

Every moment the crowd at the door became more
dense, as they were unquestionably pressed on by those in the
rear ascending the stairs, until the whole entrance at the door
was literally crowded with muskets and rifles, which, with the
swearing, shouting, and demoniacal expressions of those
outside the door and on the stairs, and the firing of the guns,
mingled with their horrid oaths and excrations, made it look
like Pandemonium let loose, and was, indeed, a fit representation of the horrid deed in which they were engaged.

After parrying the guns for some time, which now
protruded thicker and farther into the room, and seeing no
hope of escape or protection there, as we were now unarmed,
it occurred to me that we might have some friends outside,
and that there might be some chance of escape in that direction, but here there seemed to be none. As I expected them
every moment to rush into the room—nothing but extreme
cowardice having thus far kept them out—as the tumult and
pressure increased, without any other hope, I made a spring
for the window which was right in front of the jail door,
where the mob was standing, and also exposed to the fire of
the Carthage Grays, who were stationed some ten or twelve
rods off. The weather was hot, we all of us had our coats off,
and the window was raised to admit air. As I reached the
window, and was on the point of leaping out, I was struck by
a ball from the door about midway of my thigh, which struck
the bone, and flattened out almost to the size of a quarter of a
dollar, and then passed on through the fleshy part to within
about half an inch of the outside. I think some prominent
nerve must have been severed or injured, for, as soon as the
ball struck me, I fell like a bird when shot, or an ox when
struck by a butcher, and lost entirely and instantaneously all
power of action or locomotion. I fell upon the window-sill,
and cried out, "I am shot!" Not possessing any power to
move, I felt myself falling outside of the window, but immediately I fell inside, from some, at that time, unknown cause.
When I struck the floor my animation seemed restored, as I
have seen it sometimes in squirrels and birds after being shot.

As soon as I felt the power of motion I crawled under the bed, which was in a corner of the room, not far from the window where I received my wound. While on my way and under the bed I was wounded in three other places; one ball entered a little below the left knee, and never was extracted; another entered the forepart of my left arm, a little above the wrist, and, passing down by the joint, lodged in the fleshy part of my hand, about midway, a little above the upper joint of my little finger; another struck me on the fleshy part of my left hip, and tore away the flesh as large as my hand, dashing the mangled fragments of flesh and blood against the wall.

My wounds were painful, and the sensation produced was as though a ball had passed through and down the whole length of my leg. I very well remember my reflections at the time. I had a very painful idea of becoming lame and decrepit, and being an object of pity, and I felt as though I would rather die than be placed in such circumstances.

It would seem that immediately after my attempt to leap out of the window, Joseph also did the same thing, of which circumstance I have no knowledge only from information. The first thing that I noticed was a cry that he had leaped out of the window. A cessation of firing followed, the mob rushed down stairs, and Dr. Richards went to the window. Immediately afterwards I saw the doctor going towards the jail door, and as there was an iron door at the head of the stairs adjoining our door which led into the cells for criminals, it struck me that the doctor was going in there, and I said to him, "Stop, doctor, and take me along." He proceeded to the door and opened it, and then returned and dragged me along to a small cell prepared for criminals. Brother Richards was very much troubled, and exclaimed, "Oh! Brother Taylor, is it possible that they have killed both Brother Hyrum and Joseph? it cannot surely be, and yet I saw them shoot them;" and, elevating his hands two or three times, he exclaimed, "Oh Lord, my God, spare Thy servants!" He then said, "Brother Taylor, this is a terrible event;" and he dragged me farther into the cell, saying, "I am sorry I can not do better for you;" and, taking an old, filthy mattress, he covered me with it, and said, "That may hide you, and you may yet live to tell the tale, but I expect they will kill me in a few moments." While lying in this position I suffered the most excruciating pain.[32]

Willard Richards, who escaped without injury, soon returned to inform Taylor that the mob had fled and that Joseph Smith was indeed dead. Moved from the jail cell to the head of the stairs, Taylor now "had a full view of our beloved and now murdered brother Hyrum."[33] Of the several people who soon thereafter gathered around Taylor, one was a physician. Using a penknife he made an incision to remove the bullet from Taylor's hand. After sawing with the dull penknife for some time and then using a pair of carpenter's compasses, he finally extracted the ball. About his treatment Taylor reported, "Some time afterwards [the physician] remarked to a friend of mine that I had 'nerves like the devil,' to stand what I did in its extraction. I really thought I had need of nerves to stand such surgical butchery, and that, whatever my nerves may be, his practice was devilish."[34]

Eventually, Taylor was taken to Hamilton's Tavern, the place where he and Dr. Bernhisel had stayed only a few nights previous. The owner, however, was reluctant to take him in, as he feared Mormon reprisals. Mr. Hamilton was not the only one worried about an attack from Nauvoo; so many in Carthage fled that it was difficult to find enough people to carry Taylor to the hotel. Concerned that the citizens of Nauvoo might do something rash, Willard Richards sent off a note reporting what had happened and telling the people he promised there would be no attack.

> Carthage jail, 8 o'clock 5 min. p. m., June 27th, 1844.

> Joseph and Hyrum are dead. Taylor wounded, not very badly. I am well. Our guard was forced, as we believe, by a band of Missourians from 100 to 200. The job was done in an instant, and the party fled towards Nauvoo instantly. This is as I believe it. The citizens here are afraid of the 'Mormons' attacking them; I promise them no. W. Richards.

N. B.—The citizens promise us protection; alarm guns have been fired.—John Taylor[35]

Taylor wrote this last note quickly so that his family might not detect his trembling and become fearful.

Despite being shot at five o'clock on 27 June, Taylor did not have his wounds dressed until nearly two o'clock the next morning. Leonora, learning of her husband's injury, immediately sought to go to Carthage. She had some difficulty, though, finding an escort and a doctor to accompany her, but eventually she started out for Carthage to care for her husband. She arrived in time to witness another physician's efforts to remove a bullet from her husband's swollen left thigh. When the doctor asked if he would like to be tied during the operation, Taylor declined. He later commented on the procedure, saying, "So great was the pain I endured that the cutting was rather a relief than otherwise."[36] While the operation was taking place, Leonora retreated to a separate room so that she might pray for her husband. "While on her knees at prayer, a Mrs. Bedell, an old lady of the Methodist association, entered, and, patting Mrs. Taylor on her back with her hand, said, 'There's a good lady, pray for God to forgive your sins; pray that you may be converted, and the Lord may have mercy on your soul.'"[37]

Other family and friends were subsequently able to visit Taylor while he remained at the hotel. After several days, a few men arrived from Nauvoo seeking to return him to his home. A debate ensued. Friends wished to have Taylor make the trip home, while the citizens of Carthage were anxious to have him stay. Taylor had become an unofficial hostage of the city. As long as he remained in Carthage, the citizens felt there was less likelihood of an attack by the Mormons. Though so weak from the loss of blood that he could barely speak, he finally agreed to make the trip home. As he was carried downstairs to a carriage waiting outside, he realized that some of those aiding him had been in the mob at the jail. Once outside he felt strengthened, and he was loaded onto a wagon and escorted out of town. Of his painful trip home, Taylor wrote:

When I got within five or six miles of Nauvoo the brethren commenced to meet me from the city, and they increased in number as we drew nearer, until there was a very large company of people of all ages and both sexes, principally, however, men.

For some time there had been almost incessant rain, so that in many low places on the prairie it was from one to three feet deep in water, and at such places the brethren whom we met took hold of the sleigh, lifted it, and carried it over the water; and when we arrived in the neighborhood of the city, where the roads were excessively muddy and bad, the brethren tore down the fences, and we passed through the fields.

Never shall I forget the difference of feeling that I experienced between the place that I had left and the one that I had now arrived at. I had left a lot of reckless, bloodthirsty murderers, and had come to the City of the Saints, the people of the living God; friends of truth and righteousness, thousands of whom stood there with warm, true hearts to offer their friendship and services, and to welcome my return. It is true it was a painful scene, and brought sorrowful rememberance to mind, but to me it caused a thrill of joy to find myself once more in the bosom of my friends, and to meet with the cordial welcome of true, honest hearts. What was very remarkable, I found myself very much better after my arrival at Nauvoo than I was when I started on my journey, although I had traveled eighteen miles.[38]

The day after his return, Taylor asked his wife to retrieve his purse and watch from Willard Richards. It was only when he saw those two items that he realized the reason for his falling back inside the jail rather than out amidst the mob. A ball had struck the watch, marking the time of events and unquestionably saving his life. Regarding his discovery Taylor explained:

My family, however, were not a little startled to find that my watch had been struck with a ball. I sent for my vest, and, upon examination, it was found that there was a cut as if with a knife, in the vest pocket which had contained my watch. In the pocket the fragments of the glass were found literally ground to powder. It then occurred to me that a ball had stuck me at the time I felt myself falling out of the window, and that it was this force that threw me inside. I had often remarked to

JOHN TAYLOR'S WATCH

Mrs. Taylor the singular fact of finding myself inside the room, when I felt a moment before after being shot, that I was falling out, and I never could account for it until then; but here the thing was fully elucidated, and was rendered plain to my mind. I was indeed falling out, when some villain aimed at my heart. The ball struck my watch, and forced me back; if I had fallen out I should assuredly have been killed, if not by the fall, by those around, and this ball, intended to dispatch me, was turned by an overruling Providence into a messenger of mercy, and saved my life.

Recognizing the divine intervention on his behalf, he went on to express his gratitude.

I shall never forget the feelings of gratitude that I then experienced towards my heavenly Father; the whole scene was vividly portrayed before me, and my heart melted before the Lord. I felt that the Lord had preserved me by a special act of mercy; that my time had not yet come, and that I had still a work to perform upon the earth.[39]

NOTES TO CHAPTER FOUR
1. *CHC* 2:156.

2. *JD* 5:216.
3. "Opinion," *T&S* (16 January 1843):71.
4. *HC* 5:442.
5. "Missouri vs. Joseph Smith," *T&S* (1 July 1843):241.
6. Ibid., 243.
7. *T&S* (1 October 1843):343–44.
8. *HC* 6:65.
9. Garr, "Joseph Smith: Candidate for President of the United States," *Regional Studies in Latter-day Saint History: Illinois,* 152.
10. *HC* 6:187.
11. Ibid., 6:188.
12. "Who Shall be Our Next President?" *T&S* (15 February 1844):439–40.
13. Ibid., 441.
14. *T&S* (1 March 1844):455.
15. "Religion and Politics," *T&S* (15 March 1844):470.
16. Ibid., 471.
17. *HC* 6:325.
18. Ibid., 5:367.
19. Tyler, *A Concise History of the Mormon Battalion in the Mexican War,* 15; hereafter cited as *Mormon Battalion.*
20. Ibid., 16.
21. "The 'Mormon' Question," *MS* (22 March 1870):180.
22. *HC* 6:467.
23. Ibid., 6:496.
24. *Mormon Battalion,* 24.
25. Ibid., 26–27.
26. Ibid., 27.
27. Ibid., 30.
28. Ibid., 31.
29. Ibid., 35–36.
30. *CHC* 2:264.
31. *Mormon Battalion,* 48.
32. Ibid., 48–51.
33. Ibid., 52.
34. Ibid., 53.
35. Ibid., 55.
36. Ibid., 57.
37. Ibid., 57.
38. Ibid., 62–63.
39. Ibid., 63–64.

~ FIVE ~

A CHURCH to LEAD, A PEOPLE to PREPARE

Upon returning to Nauvoo during the early evening of 6 August 1844, Wilford Woodruff observed, "There was a deep gloom [that] seemed to rest over the city of Nauvoo which we never experienced before." The following morning Woodruff set about, seeing friends and meeting with the Twelve at John Taylor's home. "We were received with gladness by the Saints throughout the city," Woodruff wrote. "They felt like sheep without a shepherd, as being without a father, as their head had been taken away."[1] With the death of Joseph and Hyrum Smith, the Church faced a critical period of uncertainty. Just days before his death, the Prophet wrote the Twelve and requested that they return to Nauvoo from their electioneering missions. As none had yet returned when Joseph was killed, Nauvoo was largely devoid of the usual Church leadership. By the beginning of July, Willard Richards and the wounded John Taylor, as the only Apostles in the city, had begun to allay concerns and reassure members about the Church's future.

Although he did not return to Nauvoo until 2 July, John Taylor's name was attached to an editorial published in the 1 July 1844 issue of the *Times and Seasons*. Also signed by Willard Richards and W. W. Phelps, it read:

> Deeply impressed for the welfare of all, while mourning the great loss of President Joseph Smith, our "prophet and seer," and President Hyrum Smith, our "patriarch," we have considered the occasion demanded of us a word of consolation. As has been the case in all ages, these saints

have fallen martyrs for the truth's sake, and their escape from the persecution of a wicked world, in blood to bliss, only strengthens our faith, and confirms our religion, as pure and holy. We, therefore, as servants of the Most High God, having the Bible, Book of Mormon and the book of Doctrine and Covenants; together with thousands of witnesses, for Jesus Christ; would beseech the Latter Day Saints in Nauvoo, and elsewhere, to hold fast to the faith that has been delivered to them in the last days, abiding in the perfect law of the gospel. Be peaceable, quiet citizens, doing the works of righteousness, and as soon as the, "Twelve" and other authorities can assemble, or a majority of them, the onward course to the great gathering of Israel, and the final consummation of the dispensation of the fullness of times, will be pointed out; so that the murder of Abel; the assassination of hundreds; the righteous blood of all the holy prophets, from Abel to Joseph, sprinkled with the best blood of the Son of God, as the crimson sign of remission, only carries conviction to the business and bosoms of all flesh, that the cause is just and will continue; and blessed are they that hold out faithful to the end while apostates, consenting to the shedding of innocent blood, have no forgiveness in this world nor in the world to come. Union is peace, brethren, and eternal life is the greatest gift of God. Rejoice then, that you are found worthy to live and die for God: men may kill the body, but they cannot hurt the soul, and wisdom shall be justified of her children: Amen.[2]

With this editorial the two Apostles made clear the appropriate course of action: the Saints were to remain unified in the faith and wait until at least a majority of the Twelve returned so that they might guide the Church onward.

Richards and Taylor continued their efforts at shepherding the Saints by means of their writings. On 9 July the two Apostles wrote a letter of "instruction and information" to the president of the British mission. In their correspondence they provided Ruben Hedlock with details concerning Joseph's and Hyrum's deaths, outlining the events that took place in Carthage. Following this account, they reassured Hedlock that "God has not left his church without witnesses; as in former days so shall it be in the latter days, when one falls another will arise to occupy a similar station. Our heavenly Father always has had a leader to his people, always will have, and the gates of hell can never prevail against the chosen of heaven." They went on to explain that the Prophet's absence would not bring an end to the Lord's work: "It will not stop the Temple; it will not stop the gathering; it will not stop the honest-in-heart from believing the truth and obeying it; but it is a proof of the revelations we have received from heaven through him. He has sealed his testimony with his blood. He was willing to die, and desired only to live for the sake of the brethren."[3] They assured Hedlock the work of the Church must go on as though nothing had happened. The missionaries were to continue to preach the gospel, and Church members were to seek guidance from the Spirit. In a postscript, they added to their account of the martyrdom: "We would have said that while Joseph was on his way to Carthage, and on the prairie, he said to his friends around him, 'I am going like a lamb to the slaughter, but my mind is calm as the summer's morning, I have a conscience void of offense towards God and towards all men.' Joseph also said to his friends, 'I am going voluntarily to give myself up, and it shall be said of me that I *was murdered in cold blood.*'"[4]

As Taylor and Richards wrote this letter to Hedlock, Parley P. Pratt was on the last leg of his journey back to Nauvoo. Informed of the Prophet's death by passengers on a steamboat headed for Chicago, Pratt was taunted as to what would become of the Mormons now that their leader was dead. Disembarking in Chicago, he walked to Peoria, Illinois, and as he traveled he "felt so weighed down with sorrow and the powers of darkness that it was painful for me to converse or speak to any one, or even to try to eat or sleep."[5] As Pratt approached Nauvoo, he grew increasingly concerned about how he would greet the community, what he should say to the Smiths, and what counsel he should give. He wondered if the Saints ought to be dispersed, or if they should build up the temple. Ruminating about these concerns, he walked on, "weighed down as it were unto death." He finally prayed aloud, and "on a sudden the Spirit of God came upon me, and filled my heart with joy and gladness indescribable; and . . . the spirit of revelation glowed in my bosom with as visible a warmth and gladness as if it were fire." The Spirit told him,

> Lift up your head and rejoice; for behold! it is well with my servants Joseph and Hyrum. My servant Joseph still holds the keys of my kingdom in this dispensation, and he shall stand in due time on the earth, in the flesh, and fulfill that to which he is appointed. Go and say unto my people in Nauvoo that they shall continue to pursue their daily duties and take care of themselves and make no movement in Church government to reorganize or alter anything until the return of the remainder of the Quorum of the Twelve. But exhort them that they continue to build the House of the Lord which I have commanded them to build in Nauvoo.[6]

This answer immediately dispelled his despair; he "was comforted above measure" and was filled with "joy and gladness."[7] So sudden had his demeanor changed that he sought a confirmation from the Lord that this inspiration was, in fact, His will. After arriving in Nauvoo on 10 July, Pratt shared his vision for the Saints with individuals he met and before the congregations he preached to. He felt his inspiration affirmed as he "found [the Saints] already renewing their labors on the Temple, under the direction of John Taylor and Willard Richards."[8]

The three Apostles began to meet daily at John Taylor's home, as Taylor was yet convalescing, to discuss Church affairs. Soon after Pratt's arrival, they prepared another letter for the following *Times and Seasons* issue published on 15 July 1844. Signed by the three Apostles and W. W. Phelps, it offered "a word of advice and comfort," reiterating themes of their earlier writings and reaffirming Pratt's revelation. They counseled the Saints to "be still and know that the Lord is God; and that he will fulfill all things in his own due time; and not one jot or tittle of all his purposes and promises shall fail." Rather than despair, they reminded them that "the priesthood, and the keys of power are held in eternity as well as in time; and, therefore, the servants of God who pass the veil of death are prepared to enter upon a greater and more effectual work in the speedy accomplishment of the restoration of all things spoken of by his holy prophets." The cause for lamentation, they explained, was not for what would become of the Church but for what had happened to the

NAUVOO TEMPLE ON THE HILL

ideals and institutions of their country. They then made clear what they all ought to be doing. "Let no vain and foolish plans, or imaginations scatter us abroad, and divide us assunder as a people, to seek to save our lives at the expense of truth and principle, but rather let us live or die together and in the enjoyment of society and union. Therefore, we say, let us haste to fulfill the commandments which God has already given us. Yea, let us haste to *build the Temple of our God*, and to GATHER together thereunto, our silver and our gold with us, unto the name of the Lord; and then we may expect that he will teach us of his ways and we will walk in his paths."[9] Though the Prophet was gone, the Saints' work had not altered; they were instructed to adhere to the revelations that had previously guided them.

However, one claiming to have new revelations soon appeared. Having left Nauvoo just prior to Joseph Smith's death, Sidney Rigdon returned from Pittsburgh at the beginning of August. On the day of his arrival, Pratt invited him to meet at John Taylor's to sit in council with himself, Taylor, and Willard Richards. The Apostles waited the following morning, but Rigdon never appeared. He chose, rather, to attend a scheduled Church meeting where he preached before a large congregation, telling them of a revelation he had received which directed that he be appointed guardian over the Church. The Apostles quickly found out, to their surprise, that Rigdon scheduled a meeting for the coming Thursday so the Saints could select a new leader. Seeking to assume control of the Church while a majority of the Twelve were still absent from Nauvoo, Rigdon was foiled when members of the Twelve arrived on Tuesday evening. They met together at John Taylor's home the following morning and then called a meeting for the afternoon, involving the Nauvoo high council and Sidney Rigdon. At that meeting, Rigdon explained that according to his revelation, no one could "be the successor of Joseph," and as such he had "been ordained a spokesman to Joseph." In this position he was to be "guardian" of the Church. In response Brigham Young declared, "I do not care who leads the church, even though it were Ann Lee [founder of the Shakers]; but one thing I must know, and that is what God says about it. I have the keys and the means of obtaining the mind of God on the subject."[10] At the appointed hour on Thursday, Sidney Rigdon made his case before the gathered Saints, and Brigham Young proposed the Church be led by the Twelve. As the president of the Twelve spoke, many in the audience claimed to have heard Joseph Smith's voice or to have seen the Prophet's face represented in Brigham Young's. At the meeting's conclusion, the vote was in favor of the Twelve leading the Church.

Though unable to attend the meeting due to his wounds, Taylor followed up the Saints' choice with an editorial published in the *Times and Seasons*. It opened with the statement, "Great excitement prevails throughout the world to know 'who shall be the successor of Joseph Smith?'" The one-paragraph article acknowledged that the decision rendered three weeks previous was of a temporary nature. While the Twelve were to preside over the entire Church, Taylor explained that "when any alteration in the presidency should be required, seasonable notice will be given." The editorial advised Saints to demonstrate their wisdom by remaining silent on matters about which they were ignorant. Instead, they were told to "be patient, be patient a little, till the proper time comes, and we will tell you all." As added explanation, and as a foreshadow of the care with which the Twelve would make their decisions, the article explained, "Great wheels move slow."[11] In the same *Times and Seasons* issue, Taylor included a report on the "Special Meeting" held 8 August. As an addendum to this account, Brigham Young, on behalf of the Twelve, advised readers: "Beware of the speculations about the prophet! Believe no tales on the subject: Time will tell who are friends of Joseph Smith, who laid down his life for his brethren."[12] Taylor and his fellow Apostles were to guide the Church through this transitional period.

There was one still in Nauvoo who could not be patient, one who began to spread his own tales: Sidney Rigdon. Not content with the decision rendered in August, Rigdon sought out followers. He continued in his claims of having received revelations to direct Church affairs, and he began to ordain men "to be prophets, priests and kings." When confronted by Brigham Young and Orson Hyde, he reluctantly admitted what he had done. Given his actions, which the Twelve deemed increasingly detrimental to the Church's welfare, a meeting was convened to determine Rigdon's fate on Sunday, 8 September. Held at the meeting grounds in Nauvoo, eight of the Twelve were in attendance, including John Taylor, along with the high council in Nauvoo. Brigham Young led the meeting, telling those in attendance,

> The business of the day will result in this thing: all those who are for Joseph and Hyrum, the Book of Mormon, book of Doctrine and Covenants, the Temple and Joseph's measures, and for the Twelve; they being one party; will be called upon to manifest their principles openly and boldly. Then we wish all who are of the opposite parties to enjoy the same liberty, and to be as decided and bold, and to show their principles as boldly, and be as decided as they are in their secret meetings and private councils. If they are for Sidney Rigdon; and believe he is the man to be the first

president and the leader of this people, we wish them to manifest it as freely as they do in other places; because this will form another party.[13]

Following testimony from many of the Twelve, including Orson Hyde, Parley P. Pratt, and Amasa Lyman, a motion was made by W. W. Phelps that Sidney Rigdon be "cut off from the church, and delivered over to the buffetings of Satan until he repents."[14] Bishop Newel K. Whitney presented the motion to the high council, and their vote was unanimous. Brother Phelps then presented the motion to the body of the Church, and when this second vote was taken, approximately ten refrained from supporting the motion. Those in support of Rigdon then had their membership "suspended" until they could be brought before the high council. For those unable to attend the meeting, Taylor published an account of the trial in the following two issues of the *Times and Seasons* so that all in the Church might know that the man who had accompanied Joseph Smith in visions and in trials, who had been the Prophet's counselor, was now expelled from the Church.

As he recuperated from his injuries, Elder Taylor increasingly resumed his position in Church and city affairs. Whereas he had been unable to attend the meetings in August, he felt well enough to address the Saints at the first conference since Joseph Smith's death. His talk deviated little from themes put forth in his letters and editorials as he explained to those gathered, "If our prophets have been taken, they are gone to plead our cause before the Father. And if we are deprived of their persons, presence and council, that is no reason why we should be deprived of the council of God to direct us in all our movements whilst pressing our journey here below. We are in possession of the same principles, the same priesthood, the same medium of communication and intelligence, and of those things which will not only secure our happiness here, but hereafter." In so many ways, he said, the Church could proceed as if nothing had happened. Built on a true foundation, they were engaged in God's eternal work. As he told them, "We assembled here to bring about great events, to fulfill the things spoken of by the prophets and secure to ourselves an inheritance in the everlasting kingdom of God. Shall we then be led about by the foolish notions of any man? No! We will not, but we will accomplish those things which are commanded us. We will not be diverted from our course, though earth and hell oppose. Shall we fear the puny arm of man, or the prating of a wretched mobocrat? No! What have we to fear? We have nothing but God to fear."[15]

Critical to securing their inheritance in God's everlasting kingdom was building the temple. Taylor addressed this subject at length.

> Why are we taking so much pains to build that Temple? That we may fulfill certain ordinances and receive certain endowments and secure to ourselves an inheritance in the eternal world. Every man, woman and child within the sound of my voice are interested in the building of that Temple. We know very little as a people yet, we don't know so much as the former day saints. The Savior said to his disciples, "whither I go ye know, and the way ye know;" but how many of you know the locality of the Savior and the way to go to him? . . . The first thing we have got to do is to build the Temple, where we can receive those blessings which we so much desire.[16]

In the months immediately following the Prophet's death, Taylor emphasized time and again that the process of revelation the Lord had reinstituted with Joseph Smith did not end with his death.

CONTINUING LIFE IN NAUVOO

Just as the death of Joseph Smith and his brother Hyrum did not mean the end of Mormonism, the martyrdom did not bring about the immediate demise of Nauvoo. Rather, the city and its occupants continued, in many ways, to flourish. Writing about the city after the Saints' exodus, John Taylor explained, "When we went there, the country was wild and uninhabited, with the exception of a few farms scattered here and there, but we turned the desert into a city, and the wilderness into a fruitful field, or fields of gardens. When we first settled in Nauvoo, lands in the city were worth from three dollars to twenty dollars an acre; when we left they were worth five to fifty dollars an acre, . . . and we had made very extensive improvements."[17] For John Taylor, the year and a half before the Saints were forced from the city proved to be a prosperous time.

In his journal, kept from December 1844 to September 1845, John Taylor detailed his business affairs, described social events, and outlined his involvement in Church matters. In entries for the first days of 1845, Taylor gave an account of what his life was like in Nauvoo six months after he had been wounded at Carthage.

> WEDNESDAY, JANUARY 1ST, 1845. In the forenoon attended Seventies' Hall dedication. In afternoon had a party of the Printing Office hands and their wives, in number about twenty, we had a quite a jovial time. I spoke to them on the necessity of union. Judge Phelps also gave them some good advice on this subject; after which we parted.

> THURSDAY, JANUARY 2ND, 1845. I attended to Printing office business. [In the evening John Taylor was among thirty-five English Saints who attended a party at Willard Richards' home.]

> FRIDAY, JANUARY 3RD, 1845. Chiefly at home.

> SATURDAY, JANUARY 4TH, 1845. Went out to my farm, in company with Bro. Bean. [Taylor owned a sixty-acre farm four miles east of Nauvoo]

> SUNDAY, JANUARY 5TH, 1845. In the forenoon at home. In afternoon, engaged in writing letters to Elder Woodruff, England, and Elder Parley P. Pratt, New York. In evening attended a meeting in Bro. Joseph's Store. [Woodruff had been sent to preside over the Church in Europe, and Pratt was overseeing the Church in the East and was publishing a newspaper called the *Prophet*.]

> MONDAY, JANUARY 6TH, 1845. Engaged Elias Smith in examining books belonging to Printing Office. [Elias was Joseph Smith's cousin who worked as a business manager for the *Times and Seasons* and *Nauvoo Neighbor*.]

> TUESDAY, JANUARY 7TH, 1845. Attended to various business in forenoon. In evening attended the Mechanic's

Association meeting. ["The Nauvoo Agriculture and Mechanical Association" was a joint-stock corporation established to promote agriculture, husbandry, and manufacture goods necessary for daily living. Taylor was extensively involved with the association.]

WEDNESDAY, JANUARY 8TH, 1845. Attended a large family meeting of Elder Young's. A great number of his relations were present, the band and choir were also in company. Much useful instruction was given; It was there Elder Kimball first preached his Bee Sermon. The meeting was held in the Seventies' Hall. [Involving the Youngs, Kimballs, and Richardses, the meeting was conducted to instruct the family members and determine the Church standing of those in attendance.]

THURSDAY, JANUARY 9TH, 1845. I attended a dinner party accompanied by Mrs. Taylor; given by the Old Police at Bros. Tuft and Dunn's; the Twelve with their wives were most of them present on the occasion.

FRIDAY, JANUARY 10TH, 1845. I attended a meeting of the Twelve, Trustees-in-Trust, and a committee of the Manufacturing Association.

SATURDAY, JANUARY 11TH, 1845. Attended City Council at 10 o'clock A.M., and continued in Council till 3 o'clock P.M. In the evening at my own house in company with Pres. B. Young, Willard Richards, and Amasa Lyman; assisted to write an epistle of the Twelve to the churches throughout the world, the following of which is a copy.[18]

Though the epistle was signed only by Brigham Young and Willard Richards, Taylor's journal described the others' involvement in its writing. The epistle, which Taylor copied into his journal, opened by explaining their reasons in writing to the Saints: "As the purposes of God roll forth and the work of the Lord hastens to its accomplishment, it is necessary that we, as watchmen upon the towers of Zion, communicate with you from time to time, and put you in possession of such information as may be deemed necessary for your welfare, for the furtherance of the cause of God, and for the fulfilling of those great purposes which our heavenly father has designed in the rolling forth of the dispensation of the fullness of times, 'spoken of by all the prophets since the world was.'"[19] Describing the progress made in building the temple, the Twelve expressed their desire that "all the young, middle aged, and able bodied men who have it in their hearts to stretch forth this work with power, to come to Nauvoo, prepared to stay during the summer; and to bring with them means to sustain themselves with, and to enable us to forward this work."[20] The letter also reminded Saints of their duty to pay tithing, and it warned of "designing men" who sought to lead Church members astray.

For a time following Joseph Smith's death, opposition to the Church subsided somewhat. However, this lull in anti-Mormon activity was short-lived. On 15 May 1845 Taylor reported, "I with some others of my brethren had to secrete ourselves, to escape the hands of mobbers, who would have murdered us, if they had us in their power; they with the design of entrapping us, had made out writs against us to appear at this session of the Court to answer to charges preferred against us. We went to Brother Hunter's, and afterward to Bro. Pierce's to hide; and were employed in correcting and preparing Church history for the press."[21] Concerning these persecutions Taylor reported, "Several of the Twelve, as well as myself, had to have a guard of two men in our houses every night, to preserve us from assassination for the space of two years before we left [Nauvoo] finally."[22]

In addition to escaping would-be assassins, John Taylor also had to watch out for the law. As the prosecution readied for the trial of those arrested in connection with the murder of Joseph and Hyrum Smith, Taylor, along with other Mormons, was sought by prosecutors as a witness. However, he remained adamant about not returning to Carthage for trial. He felt, as did other Church leaders, that his testimony would accomplish little and would only serve to jeopardize the lives of those who went. So strong were Taylor's feelings on the subject that he told a congregation gathered on Sunday, 13 April 1844, that "if they made an attempt to serve writs on him it would cost them their lives, and . . . if they wished to magnify the law and make it honorable they should bring to justice the murderers of Joseph and Hyrum, two of our best men, who were treacherously butchered while in the custody of officers pledged for their safety." He went on to declare "he would not submit any more to such outrages on our lives and liberties, for under present circumstances the law is only powerful to hold men still while the lawless massacre them."[23] He continued his remonstration against the law in an editorial published in the *Nauvoo Neighbor* shortly thereafter. Here he advocated that "until the blood of Joseph and Hyrum Smith have been atoned for by hanging, shooting, or slaying in some manner, every person engaged in that cowardly assassination, no Latter-day Saint should give himself up to the law."[24] Although Taylor's advocacy was subsequently repudiated in Willard Richards's letter written on behalf of the General Council of the authorities of the Church,[25] it nonetheless reflected his sentiments concerning the injustice that had been committed against him, his close friends, and fellow Church members.

In April 1845 Taylor was presented with the opportunity to purchase property from James Ivins, who had become "disaffected" with the Church, having had the inclination first to follow William Law and then Sidney Rigdon. By 1845, Ivins sought to leave Nauvoo. His holdings included a two-story red brick home, a brick store, and a large pine-board barn, which were located on half an acre of land on the corner of Main and Kimball Streets. The cost was $3,000, and Taylor consulted some of the brethren, who advised him to go ahead with the purchase. About these events, Taylor wrote in his journal: "I took measures forthwith to procure it, not that I wanted to build myself up; but my idea in getting it was to keep it out of the hands of our enemies, as it was offered so cheap; and I thought the store would suit us for a Printing office." He went on to add, "My feelings after I had traded for this were the same as ever, I felt like sacrificing all things when called upon; my heart is not set upon property, but the things of God: I care not so much about the good things of this life, as I do about the fellowship of my brethren, and to fulfilling the work the Lord has called me to do; and the favor of the Lord, and securing to myself, my family, and friends an inheritance in the Kingdom of God."[26] The Taylor family moved into the brick home, which still stands, on 10 May 1845.

Despite the numerous accusations against the Saints, the attacks by "mobbers," and the legal bullying, the Saints continued building a house unto the Lord. In the early morning hours of 24 May 1845, the

THE NAUVOO TEMPLE

Twelve "repaired to the Temple with great secrecy for the purpose of laying the cornerstone." Many Saints gathered when they heard a band playing on the temple grounds. About this meeting Taylor wrote, "About six o'clock A.M., the brethren being assembled, we proceeded to lay the stone; at quarter past six the stone was laid; after which Bro. Young prayed, his voice being heard distinctly, by the congregation below; and the congregation shouted Hosanna, Hosanna, Hosanna to God and the Lamb, Amen, Amen, and Amen. Bro. Kay sung a song composed for the occasion by W. W. Phelps, called the capstone. Although there were several officers watching for us to take us; yet we escaped without their knowledge; when the singing commenced we left unnoticed, and they had not an opportunity of seeing us." A hole was made in the cornerstone as a type of a time capsule. Taylor sent to be placed in the hole volumes one through five of the *Times and Seasons*, copies of the *Nauvoo Neighbor*, his history of the Missouri persecutions, and three pamphlets he printed while on the Isle of Man.[27]

During the latter half of 1845, Church leaders recognized that their stay in Nauvoo would be of a short duration. In the August and September entries in his journal, Taylor documented some of the preparations for moving west and his nearly daily participation in Church affairs.

WEDNESDAY, AUGUST 27TH, 1845. In council with the Twelve. Bro. Parley P. Pratt was present, he had just returned from the East. I [was] much gratified to meet with him again, he being my father in the gospel.

THURSDAY, AUGUST 28TH, 1845. In council with the Twelve, wherein we made arrangements, and voted for an expedition of a number of people to go to California in the ensuing spring. After which we had our Quorum meeting.

FRIDAY, AUGUST 29TH, 1845. Chiefly about home.

SATURDAY, AUGUST 30TH, 1845. At Temple and other places.

SUNDAY, AUGUST 31ST, 1845. At meeting in morning. In afternoon at Quorum meeting.

MONDAY, SEPT. 1ST, 1845. Chiefly at home, attending to office matters.

TUESDAY, SEPTEMBER 2ND, 1845. General business, laying hands on the sick &c.

WEDNESDAY, SEPTEMBER 3RD, 1845. About general business. This evening we had a very severe hail storm, hail stones fell nearly as large as hen's eggs, breaking the windows in the North and East, of all the houses in the City.

THURSDAY, SEPTEMBER 4TH, 1845. I was at Council with the Twelve at Dr. Richards'; after which had Quorum meeting.

FRIDAY, SEPTEMBER 5TH, 1845. At a meeting at the Big Field. The Twelve, Bishop Miller, and a few others from Nauvoo, were among the number that partook of the rich bounties of the season, provided by the inhabitants of the 11th ward, under Bishop Evans, and the proprietors of the "Big Field." [The "Big Field" was an agricultural association located southeast of Nauvoo.]

SATURDAY, SEPTEMBER 6TH, 1845. Principally about home.

Sunday, September 7th, 1845. In morning at meeting. Bro's. Kimball and Smith preached. In afternoon in council with Twelve; after which at Quorum meeting.

Monday, September 8th, 1845. At Bro. Benbow's on prairie.

Tuesday, September 9th, 1845. At a meeting of the council of Fifty, where there was some conversation held concerning California.

Wednesday, September 10th, 1845. About various business.

Thursday, September 11th, 1845. This morning we received information from Lima, [Adams County, Illinois] that the mobs were burning houses there; the first report was that there was one burnt; next report that came was, there was four burnt; and finally we heard that there were three burnt. We (the Twelve) held a council and thought it advisable as we were going West in the Spring to keep all things as quiet as possible and not resent anything. [At this meeting Brigham Young selected those of the fifty designated to go west in the spring.]

After the trouble we had to finish the Temple to get our endowments, we thought it of more importance than to squabble with the mob about property, seeing that the houses were not of much importance, and no lives were taken. Thinking by these pacific measures that they would be likely not to molest us; and to show the surrounding country that we were orderly disposed people, and desirous of keeping peace. It was also counseled that the brethren from the surrounding settlements should come into Nauvoo with their grain.

Friday, September 12th, 1845. Reports came in about their further mobbing. We sent a number of teams off for grain to the settlements.[28]

PREPARING TO LEAVE NAUVOO

When Joseph Smith first arrived at Commerce, Illinois, he commented, "It is a beautiful site but not long a resting place for the Saints."[29] Even before the Prophet's death, preparations for leaving Nauvoo and moving west were underway. On 21 February 1844, Joseph Smith had held a meeting in the mayor's office, where seven members of the Twelve, including John Taylor, were present, along with a few other men. They had met for the purpose of choosing men to explore Oregon and California with the design of finding a place where the Saints might raise up a new city. Several men had volunteered to go west, and others had been requested by their Church leaders to go with them.[30] By September 1845, the Twelve were making specific plans to leave Nauvoo. They proposed sending agents to metropolitan cities with the aim of selling their property to wealthy investors. Such a course of action, they hoped, might preserve the temple better than if only apostates and opponents to the Church remained in the area. About this meeting Taylor wrote:

> I stated to the brethren that I had some thoughts of disposing of my house, stores, barn &., providing I could get a purchaser, which I expected I could; and after using part of the means that I should need to liquidate some debts that I was owing, turn in the remainder towards assisting in this expedition under the direction of counsel. After some deliberation it was thought best to do so if practicable and as I supposed that probably five or six thousand dollars could be obtained for it might be of essential service in that way. I feel that I am the Lord's and that I and everything I have [is] at his disposal at all times.[31]

Only months after Taylor purchased his new home and office, efforts to sell the property in preparation for leaving began.

At the October conference a few weeks later, the Saints' exodus from Nauvoo was openly discussed by many speakers. Heber C. Kimball told those gathered, "I am glad the time of our exodus is come; I have looked for it for years. It is necessary for us to be faithful and humble, and if we listen to counsel we shall prosper. And although we leave all our fine houses and farms here, how long do you think it will be before we shall be better off than we are now?"[32]

Later in the conference, John Taylor spoke on a matter of business. As he explained,

> There is one piece of business which devolves upon me to bring before this conference; and that is the printing. As we have done preaching, so we have done printing to the people; and now let them alone and mind our own business, and let them print what they have a mind to. It has been thought best to publish the conference minutes, and let that finish the subject; but I have thought it would perhaps be better to continue the Times and Seasons until the volume be completed. And if we do not circulate them abroad, we can at home, in the neighborhood. There are reasons for it. First, many are anxious about items of doctrine which the saints want; and many want to have the volume completed. As to the Nauvoo Neighbor, it is more connected with temporal matters, news, etc., and we don't care so much about that. The world doesn't wish any news from us, and we don't wish to urge it upon them. I have read papers until I have become tired; for they are all villainy, corruption, deceit and abomination; and I shall be glad when we get to a place where we can be at peace. In regard to discontinuing the papers, I will do as I am counseled. Some may consider that they will be injured by stopping the paper; but I will give four or five dollars worth of obligations for everyone they can present against me. No man can say that I have asked pay for a paper, though hundreds here are owing me for it. I will abide counsel, but am willing to publish the Times and Seasons until the end of the volume.[33]

A motion to do as Taylor had proposed was posed by Elder Kimball, and the motion was approved. Despite all that had to be done in order to leave, Taylor published the *Times and Seasons* right up until the exodus began; the last issue was dated 15 February 1846, the day before the Taylor family left their home and crossed the Mississippi River into Iowa.

Despite their pending departure from Nauvoo, the Saints continued to work on the temple. On 10 December 1845, Brigham

Young reported that the east room in the temple was arranged in preparation for giving endowments. At 3:45 that afternoon, approximately 40 people gathered to receive the ordinances that the Apostles had been teaching about for several months. Among the group were John and Leonora Taylor. The ceremony, officiated by Brigham Young and Heber C. Kimball, began approximately 45 minutes later. Brigham Young reported that "we continued officiating in the Temple during the night until three-thirty a.m. of the 11th." Thirty persons received the endowment ordinance that evening.[34]

As Saints flocked to the temple so they might participate in the holy ceremonies, they also busily prepared for their forthcoming journey. In describing the city during this time, Taylor explained, "Nauvoo was converted into one great wagon shop; in fact, nothing else seemed to be spoken or thought of but making wagons, purchasing teams, and preparing for a removal."[35] On 1 February 1846, Taylor commented in the *Times and Seasons* about the upcoming departure:

> All things are in preparation for a commencement of the great move of the Saints out of the United States; (we had like to have said, beyond the power of Christianity,) but we will soften the expression, by merely saying, and lack to their "primitive possessions," as in the enjoyment of Israel. It is reduced to a solemn reality, that the rights and property, as well as the lives and common religious belief of the church of Jesus Christ of Latter-day Saints, cannot be protected in the realms of the United States, and, of course, from one to two hundred thousand souls, must quit their freedom among freemen, and go where the land, the elements, and the worship of God are free.

> About two thousand are ready and crossing the Mississippi to pioneer the way, and make arrangements for summer crops at some point between this and the "Pacific," where the biggest crowd of good people, will be the old settlers.

> To see such a large body of men, women and children, compelled by the inefficiency of the law, and potency of mobocracy, to leave a great city in the month of February,

for the sake of the enjoyment of pure religion, fills the soul with astonishment, and gives the world a sample of fidelity and faith, brilliant as the sun, and forcible as a tempest, and as enduring as eternity.

May God continue the spirit of fleeing from false freedom, and false dignity, till every Saint is removed to where he "can sit under his own vine and fig tree" without having any to molest or make afraid. Let us go—let us go.[36]

And go they did. Leonora Taylor reported that the family left "Nauvoo to go on our journey to California" on 15 February 1846. Given the windy conditions, they returned to Brother Hirum Kimball's home, where they spent the evening. On 16 February they crossed the river and camped at Sugar Creek, where Leonora was "very sick" and where they endured the severe weather. Leaving from Sugar Creek two weeks later, the Taylors began their journey west. About her experience Leonora wrote,

[W]e are now in the Wilderness our Property which was worth ten thousand Dollars is gone, all except the Necessaries we have with us, we have been obliged to sacrifice it to the Mob if the Lord will supply us with food & raiment I care nothing about what we have left.[37]

NOTES TO CHAPTER FIVE

1. Woodruff, *Wilford Woodruff's Journal,* 2:434.
2. "To the Church of Jesus Christ of Latter Day Saints," *T&S* (1 July 1844):568.
3. *HC* 7:174.
4. Ibid., 7:175; emphasis in original.
5. *Autobiography of Parley P. Pratt,* 332.
6. Ibid., 333.
7. Ibid., 333–34.
8. Ibid., 334.
9. "To the Saints Abroad," *T&S* (15 July 1844):586; emphasis in original.
10. *HC* 7:229–30.
11. *T&S* (2 September 1844):632.

12. "Special Meeting," *T&S* (2 September 1844):638.

13. "Trial of Sidney Rigdon," *T&S* (15 September 1844):647.

14. "Conclusion of Elder Rigdon's Trial," *T&S* (15 October 1844):686.

15. "October Conference Minutes," *T&S* (15 October 1844):684.

16. Ibid., 685.

17. "Address to the Saints in Great Britain," *MS* (15 November 1846):115.

18. Jesse, ed., *John Taylor Nauvoo Journal,* 13–16; hereafter cited as *Nauvoo Journal.* Information from some of Jesse's footnotes for this section has been included here to provide further explanation of Taylor's writings.

19. Ibid., 16.

20. Ibid., 17.

21. Ibid., 56.

22. "Letters to the Editor," *MS* (15 June 1850):188.

23. *HC* 7:396.

24. Oaks and Hill, *Carthage Conspiracy,* 71.

25. *HC* 7:406.

26. *Nauvoo Journal,* 55.

27. Ibid., 56–57.

28. Ibid., 101–104.

29. Cowley, comp., *Wilford Woodruff: History of His Life and Labors,* 213.

30. *CHC* 2:120.

31. *Nauvoo Journal,* 108–109.

32. *HC* 7:466.

33. Ibid., 7:473.

34. Ibid., 7:543.

35. "Address to the Saints in Great Britain," *MS* (15 November 1846):113.

36. "February," *T&S* (1 February 1846): 1114; emphasis in original.

37. Madsen, *Journey to Zion,* 208.

~ SIX ~

A TRAVELING MINISTER

An account of the Saints' departure from Nauvoo, written by John Taylor, was published on the opening page of the *Millennial Star*, 1 November 1846. As many British Church members had friends "in the West, and contemplate joining the Saints . . . in a distant land," John Taylor thought it advisable to inform them of the events that had taken place in Nauvoo and on the trail through Iowa. His description emphasized that what had happened to the Saints in Illinois was not merely a chance occurrence that in some way frustrated the designs of God. The "mobbers," as Taylor called them, did not cause the Saints' departure from Nauvoo. As he explained, "the cruel and perfidious persecution that we endured tended to hasten our departure, but did not dictate it."[1] Rather, their exodus from the city had been clearly anticipated by Joseph Smith. As Taylor explained:

> Many a time have I listened to the voice of our beloved Prophet, while in council, dwell on this subject [the Saints' exodus to the Rocky Mountains] with delight; his eyes sparkling with animation, and his soul fired with the inspiration of the Spirit of the living God. It was a theme that caused the bosoms of all who were privileged to listen, to thrill with delight; intimately connected with this were themes upon which prophets, patriarchs, priests and kings dwelt with pleasure and delight: of them they prophesied, sung, wrote, spoke and desired to see, but died without the sight.[2]

The Saints' travails, rather than evidence of defeat, constituted the fulfillment of ancient prophecy: the days which prophets of old had awaited with great anticipation were unfolding. As such, their enemies in Illinois, according to Taylor, were actually "ignorant instruments of rolling forth the purpose of God," who had "opened [the Saints'] eyes to their true situation, raised them from their lethargy, and gave them another opportunity of improving their talent, and of making their calling and election sure."[3] The temporal calamities that had befallen the Saints were actually cause for praise, as these challenges reflected the spiritual destiny of God's people.

According to Taylor's description, the Twelve, the Nauvoo high council, and 400 other families departed Nauvoo in February 1846. They "left at that time for the purposes of assuaging the anger of the infuriated mob, and to preserve the peace, lives and property of our brethren whom we left behind; and as most of their indignation was kindled against the leaders of the church, this step had a tendency to cool their wrath, and give the brethren whom we left behind, a better opportunity to dispose of their property." Those who left, he explained, were very much exposed to the inclement weather as they lived in tents and wagons. They "had frequently to endure the fury of the pitiless storm—the drifting snow—the pelting hail and rain—and the icy chills of storms and tempests." Having "outlived the trying scene," Taylor wrote, "we felt contented and—the songs of Zion resounded from wagon to wagon—from tent to tent."[4]

Spring, he told his readers, brought about "more favorable circumstances." There was grass sufficient enough for their animals, and gone were the "chilling storms." Four boats continually ferried Saints across the Mississippi River so they could join those who had departed before them. By August, Taylor estimated there were 15,000 Saints, 3,000 wagons, and 30,000 head of cattle either at Council Bluffs, Iowa, or somewhere along the Iowa trail. About their trip west, Taylor explained to those in Britain that "in almost every other country it would have been impossible to remove so large a body of people with so little trouble and outlay—provender for cattle would have cost so much. We could not have removed in the eastern or southern states in America, because the land is generally cultivated, and that which is not, is either worthless or covered with timber; not so, however, with the country through which we have traveled and shall travel." He went on to observe, "The land is rich and fertile. There are large prairies or open land, skirted here and there with timber on the banks of the smaller streams and larger rivers."[5] His account also detailed how the "camp of Israel" was organized into companies, how much provisions cost, and how the main body of Saints had set up camp for the winter. Echoing the belief Heber C. Kimball shared in the conference preceding the exodus, Taylor expressed his opinion that, despite the sacrifice the Saints had to make in leaving behind their farms, homes, and property, they were "relatively speaking . . . better off at the present time, and our circumstances much more favorable than if we had continued in Nauvoo."[6]

Prior to Taylor's November 1846 account, the British Saints learned about the exodus when the *Millennial Star* published an excerpt from a letter Taylor wrote to his brother-in-law Joseph Cain on 1 August 1846. From the brief passages, the Saints received a partial glimpse of the challenges faced by those leaving Nauvoo. In his letter, Taylor explained that after leaving Sugar Creek on 2 March, the Saints took almost eight weeks to travel to the West Fork of the Grand River, only 160 miles from Nauvoo. The poor weather and road conditions made traveling tediously slow. Taylor also gave a brief account of his trip back to Nauvoo after having been out on the trail for two months. Of their former home he wrote, "the place has altered very much, *civilization is making rapid strides, and the people are very much improved since we left;* they have built a ten-pin alley opposite the temple, in Mullholland-street; groggeries are plentiful, at night you can hear drunkards yelling and whooping through the streets, a thing formerly unknown." In contrast to the non-Mormon "improvements," he described the temple as follows: "The basement story of the temple is finished, together with the ground floor, and looks elegant. My feelings were very peculiar while standing in the font, which is of stone, and passing through the rooms, when I have thought how the Saints had labored and strove to complete this building, and then be forced to leave, together with their comfortable homes, in the hands of the enemies."[7] Through Taylor's writings, the British Church members gained a sense of what their fellow Saints experienced as they were forced from their homes and made their way across the state of Iowa on their way to Winter Quarters.

If John Taylor's account in the November 1846 *Millennial Star* painted a somewhat optimistic picture of the Saints' journey, with the songs of Zion reverberating across the plains, Leonora Taylor's diary documented the hardships and dangers the family faced as they left Nauvoo and traveled west. At length she detailed the dreadful weather conditions. Just after crossing the Mississippi River, she wrote that they "had very severe Wether. Snow Storm & wind[,] we made a Family Bed all over the tent floor."[8] Only a few days after leaving their camp at Sugar Creek, they arrived at a place called Gospel Valley, where, once they had situated their camp, the rain came on "and spoild our floors." They then had to spend the night "with the wind blowing into our wagon so hard."[9] While spring may have been as beautiful as John Taylor described to the British Saints, along with the improved weather came an enveloping mud, which severely hampered their travels. In mid-April, at a place called Locust Creek, a Brother Benson asked the Taylors if he might borrow a couple of oxen. He requested that Joseph Taylor, John and Leonora's seven-year-old son, go with him. Placing Joseph on his lead horse, the two rode two miles to the camp. When Brother Benson was done using the oxen, he sent them home with Joseph, who had to travel "through mud that would take a man to his knees." When on the way back the oxen ran off into the woods, Joseph followed them and he "cried all the way home." Of his return Leonora wrote, "The dear Child was coverd with mud from head to foot, he several times lost sight of the road but would not leave his Oxen."[10]

In addition to the inconvenience posed by the mud, there were other dangers associated with traveling by wagon across the prairie. One afternoon at the beginning of May, "a hurricane came on," as Leonora described it, blowing down tents and trees. During the storm, Joseph ran away from the tents in fear of falling trees. With the help of a Brother Jones—John Taylor had a few days previous returned to Nauvoo—the family got the tent set up again, but "very soon after the roof pole came down and the tent was soon prostrate." They then retreated to the wagon. Just as Leonora and the children climbed in, the children yelled that a tree was coming down. Some men, Leonora wrote, "ran and by there united efforts gave it a diferund direction, or it must have crushed the cariage and large

Waggon both."[11] Along with the hazards posed by such storms, Leonora documented the many illnesses her family faced. She also detailed the difficulties they had with their animals and the injuries they sustained; on one occasion she badly sprained her knee such that she needed help getting in their tent. About their circumstances Leonora wrote, "Our situation does require all the grace we can muster. I pray the Lord give us all that is needfull that I may never bring a reproach on his cause or people."[12]

On 2 July Leonora described her husband's role in recruiting volunteers for the Mormon Battalion, which was to march to California as part of the United States' efforts in the war against Mexico. About this day she wrote, "Father went on held a meeting along with O. Prat[t], spoke about Voll[u]nteering to the People 500 of our Brethern."[13] On this occasion John Taylor told the men:

> Many have felt something like rebellion against the United States. I have myself felt swearing mad at the government for the treatment we have received at the hands of those in authority, although I don't know that I have sworn much. We have had cause to feel as we have, and any man having a spark of liberty in him would have felt likewise. We are now something like Abraham was, wandering not knowing whither we wander; fleeing from a land of tyranny and oppression we are calculating to settle in some part of California.[14]

Despite the justified distrust of the government, he explained the benefits that would come to the Saints if they enlisted. As he subsequently told the Saints in England, the march of the battalion "amount[ed] to the same as paying them for going to the place where they were destined to go without."[15] Acknowledging that "it is a great journey for a man to leave his family and go on," he explained their loved ones would be cared for, and he concluded by making "a motion that we raise a body of 500 men and make Captain Allen lieutenant-colonel."[16] On 16 July 1846, the volunteers were enlisted in the army. A dance was held on the afternoon of 19 July, and the next day the men began their march to San Diego, California.

17,000 MILES IN 8½ MONTHS

Less than a month after addressing the volunteers, John Taylor was called on to make his own "great journey," leaving his family behind as he traveled to England once again. While in Winter Quarters, the Twelve were apprised of irregularities in the way the mission presidency in England was conducting Church affairs. Earlier in the year Wilford Woodruff had been released from his position as head of the British mission, and his counselor Reuben Hedlock was appointed the new

THE MILLENNIAL STAR

president. Shortly after Woodruff's departure both Hedlock and Thomas Ward, Woodruff's other counselor, established the British and American Joint Stock Company to aid emigrating Saints. The company was also to be involved in trade, and was represented as being associated with the Church, as it was promoted in the *Millennial Star* and in Church conferences. Other than selling stock to British Saints, the company did little more than pay the salaries and traveling expenses of its officers. So great was the presidency's enthusiasm for the company that they encouraged arriving missionaries "to preach Joint Stockism," as was the case with an Elder Sirrine, who paid "deference to them as his presidents" but would not follow their instructions as they contradicted directions he received from the Twelve.[17]

To correct the situation, Elders Orson Hyde, Parley P. Pratt, and John Taylor were called at the end of July 1846 to leave for England. The three Apostles left on 31 July. Pratt described their departure: "[W]e took passage down the river in an open scow, or flat boat, in company with a family of Presbyterian missionaries who had been residing on the Loupe fork of the Platte River, among the Pawnee Indians, and who were now bound for St. Joseph, Missouri. We floated or pulled the oars for some days, tying up and sleeping on shore at night."[18] At St. Joseph, the Apostles purchased the boat from the disembarking missionaries, and they continued down the river. At

Fort Leavenworth, Kansas, they encountered members of the Mormon Battalion who were receiving money for clothing and supplies. The volunteers gave them several hundred dollars for their trip east, and $5,000 to $6,000 was collected for the men's families. It was determined that Pratt would take the money back to the Saints at Council Bluffs. On horseback he made the 170-mile trip in three days. In the meantime, Orson Hyde and John Taylor proceeded to New York. After delivering the money, Pratt took a horse and carriage 450 miles to Chicago. From there he traveled first by steamboat and then by train, arriving in Boston, Massachusetts. By this time, however, Pratt's would-be traveling companions had already arrived in New York, and rather than wait a few more days for him, Elders Hyde and Taylor booked passage on a ship and immediately sailed for England, arriving in Liverpool at the beginning of October. In reporting on his travels Taylor wrote, "We found, upon our arrival, that we had not come away too soon. The teachers of the people were under transgression; they were corrupt; they were acting dishonorably and dishonestly, under false pretenses; stripping the poor of their last pittance," all while the Church leaders "professed that they were doing the will of God." He went on to explain that "under a cloak of religion, [they] were reveling in debauchery, drunkenness, and fraud."[19] Immediately, Elders Hyde and Taylor issued a circular to the Saints, which declared that the company promoted by Hedlock and Ward was "an institution wholly independent of the church," and they advised them "to patronize the Joint Stock Company *no more for the present*."[20] A conference in Manchester was scheduled for two weeks later to further discuss the matter.

ORSON HYDE

When the conference convened on Saturday, 17 October 1846, only two of the three Apostles, Orson Hyde and Parley P. Pratt, were in attendance. Orson Hyde presided over the meeting, and in speaking first to the assembly, he outlined how the meetings were to proceed. The morning was to be dedicated to "speaking and general instructions." In the afternoon they would inquire about the condition of the various English branches of the Church. Then, in the evening, the hall in which they were meeting was to be given up to the British and American Joint Stock Company, even though the business of the company was outside the purview of the conference. Regarding this business Hyde explained:

> This company, though not directly connected with our church, yet as most of the shareholders are members thereof, it stands indirectly connected with our body; and it is just about as much of an auxiliary to aid our onward march to perfection in happiness, as a weight of fifty-six pounds would be to aid a man in running a race, if tied to his heel. Cut the cord asunder by annihilating the company, and let the church go free from this body of sin and death.[21]

Before the meeting was over, Elder Taylor arrived from Liverpool, having been detained due to illness. He gave a short speech that was described as "pointed, instructive, and comforting." On Sunday evening, Taylor again addressed the gathered Saints. Though a summary of his sermon was not published in the conference minutes, the record did observe: "An excellent sermon by Elder John Taylor. It was like the man himself; sympathetic, bold, powerful, and eloquent."[22]

Following the conference, the three Apostles issued a formal statement in the *Millennial Star*. They outlined their views on the Joint Stock Company, explaining that although the company was started without the knowledge of Church leaders in America, it gained their approval when they were informed that it would establish "manufacturies" in Nauvoo and elsewhere that would hire the poor. Rather than pursue this objective, however, the company was ill advised in attempting to trade by sea, paying officer salaries without accumulating any profits, and loaning large amounts of money without collateral. As a result, the elders "*most emphatically* advised a dissolution of the company." They also recommended that shareholders "contribute to the aid of others who have suffered in this enterprise."[23] Accompanying the Apostles' proclamation was the notice that Reuben Hedlock and Thomas Ward had been disfellowshipped the previous

July until they could account for their actions. By the time the Apostles arrived in England, Hedlock had abandoned his calling as president. According to Pratt, he "fled at our approach, leaving many debts unpaid, and finally lived incog[nito] in London with a vile woman—he being severed from the Church."[24]

During the October 1846 conference, it was determined that Orson Hyde would edit the *Millennial Star* and assume control of the publishing office in Liverpool, while Parley P. Pratt and John Taylor would visit the branches of the Church throughout the British Isles. The two published a schedule of their intended visits, and then began their winter travels. Concerning their work Taylor wrote:

> As Elder P. P. Pratt and myself journeyed among the churches, we found them generally doing well, rejoiced to see us, and expressed a willingness to follow our advice in all things. We visited most of the conferences in England and Scotland. In some of the leading conferences, such as Manchester, Liverpool, Birmingham, Sheffield, and Glasgow in Scotland, we found them exceedingly prosperous; nor were they less zealous, loving and affectionate in some of the smaller conferences. I visited the Isle of Man alone, and was glad to meet there some of my old friends. . . . I also visited Wales, and was very much pleased and gratified with the situation of things there. I found the Welsh church in a very flourishing condition. Elder [Dan] Jones is publishing a paper in the Welsh language, which circulates very extensively, he has also published many thousands of tracts, and circulated them throughout the length and breadth of his native land. . . . In speaking of him and the good done by American Elders, I would not forget the English and Scotch; I do not implicate them with their leaders; I found them generally to be good, humble, virtuous, zealous, and honorable men, who are using all their exertions to propagate the cause of truth and build up Zion.[25]

Parley P. Pratt similarly described their travels to the many branches of the Church.

> [W]e traveled from conference to conference by railway, coaches, steamers, etc., visiting nearly all the principal towns in England and Scotland. We were everywhere received and treated with the utmost hospitality, and with demonstrations of joy and gladness not soon to be forgotten. The Saints and others convened from far and near at the sessions of our several conferences, and vast crowds of strangers, as well as Saints, listened to us. Public feasts, tea parties, public dinners and all kinds of demonstrations of joy and welcome greeted us as we visited from place to place. So that our sojourn was more like a triumphal procession than like a dreary pilgrimage. We preached the gospel, set in order the churches, directed the labors of the Elders, comforted the Saints, and reproved and corrected the abuses introduced by President Hedlock and others in relation to the joint stock companies, etc.[26]

In summing up his time in England, Taylor explained, "I have seldom enjoyed myself better than I did on my late visit to the British churches." Had time permitted, he would "gladly have spent two, three, or six months more."[27] Time, however, did not permit a longer stay as the Apostles needed to get back to Winter Quarters before the Saints headed west. While Orson Hyde stayed behind until Orson Spencer arrived from America to assume responsibility for the British mission, Parley P. Pratt and John Taylor went to Liverpool where they secured passage on a new ship, *America*, that would take them home. Pratt and Taylor set sail on 19 January 1847, but a storm that lasted nine days prevented them from leaving the English channel between England and Ireland. Eventually the ship had to return to port. The Apostles left for a second time on 7 February 1847, just four months after arriving in England.

A 36-day journey across the Atlantic took them to New Orleans, where they proceeded up the Mississippi River by steamboat. In St. Louis the two Apostles separated. By traveling apart, at least one of them would arrive at Winter Quarters before the pioneer company left. Pratt rode north on horseback, coming across the Iowa trail near the settlement of Garden Grove. He arrived in Council Bluffs, Iowa, on 8 April 1847, the day after Orson Pratt, Wilford Woodruff, and Brigham Young had departed westward with the pioneer company, the first group of pioneers, led by Brigham Young, to arrive in the Salt Lake Valley. When these Apostles heard of Parley's arrival, they returned to Winter Quarters to counsel with him. On 13 April, Taylor arrived in their midst, having traveled up the Missouri River by steamer. He brought with him 469 gold sovereigns collected as tithing from the British Saints, hundreds of letters, and scientific equipment to be used by those in the first group traveling west.

Both Taylor and Pratt declined to go with the pioneer company, which was in the process of leaving. Rather, they sought to be with their families and decided they would come with the second group of Saints leaving later that spring. The Apostles soon discovered that not all had gone well that winter in their absence. Pratt wrote:

> I found my family all alive, and dwelling in a log cabin. They had, however, suffered much from cold, hunger and sickness. They had oftentimes lived for several days on a little corn meal, ground on a hand-mill, with no other food. One of the family was then lying very sick with the scurvy—a disease which had been very prevalent in camp during the winter, and of which many had died. I found, on inquiry, that the winter had been very severe, the snow deep, and, consequently, that all my horses (four in number) were lost, and I afterwards ascertained that out of twelve cows I had but seven left, and out of some twelve or fourteen oxen only four or five were spared.[28]

During the remainder of the spring, Parley P. Pratt and John Taylor prepared themselves to lead the emigration camp, the second and much larger group of pioneers to leave for the Salt Lake Valley. There was much to do in resolving issues with the local Indians, deciding on the proper organization of the companies, and ensuring that the Saints were properly outfitted for the forthcoming trip.[29] When the group was finally assembled and ready to leave on 15 June 1847 from the gathering spot on the Elkhorn River, there were "1,448 men, women and children and almost 600 wagons—a would-be caravan of some 10 miles long."[30] Originally Brigham Young had instructed that the company be limited to 100 wagons with John Smith (the Prophet's uncle) and Isaac Morley in charge of the camp.

In addition, the pioneers were to be supplied with breadstuffs to last a year and a half, and as many wives of battalion members as possible were to be brought along. In their preparations to take all those who wished to travel west, Pratt and Taylor, as the presiding Church leaders, made numerous changes to Young's directives, which had been given by way of revelation. Two months following their departure, John Taylor wrote Brigham Young a letter, explaining:

> Our numbers far exceed what we anticipated, for instead of numbering 100 wagons we have near 600; the cattle were generally weak in coming off the rushes; we had to recruit our cattle and send to Missouri for breadstuffs. You know, brethren, that it takes a little time and labor to start a large wheel; it has, however, commenced rolling and will, we trust, not stop until it reaches the valley of the Salt Lake.[31]

Brigham Young, however, was not pleased to find out that his instructions had been altered. When Young and those accompanying him back to Winter Quarters encountered the emigration camp, a council meeting was called for, which Wilford Woodruff subsequently described as "one of the most interesting councils we ever held together on the earth." In meetings held on the evenings of 3 and 4 September 1846, involving the returning members of the Twelve and Parley P. Pratt, "there was less excitement [about the pioneer company's success] and more blunt criticism of Pratt and Taylor's handling of the camps."[32] About this meeting Pratt wrote:

> A council was called, in which I was highly censured and chastened by President Young and others. This arose in part from some defect in the organization under my superintendence at the Elk Horn, and in part from other misunderstandings on the road. I was charged with neglecting to observe the order of organization entered into under the superintendence of the President before he left the camps at Winter Quarters; and of variously interfering with previous arrangements. In short, I was severely reproved and chastened.

Though he defended his actions, as he had done nothing out of rebellion, Pratt eventually admitted his mistakes. He explained, "I no doubt deserved this chastisement; and I humbled myself, acknowledged my faults and errors, and asked forgiveness."[33]

After these council meetings, the two groups headed in opposite directions. Eventually, advanced parties from the emigration camp entered the Salt Lake Valley on 28 September 1847, with John Taylor's group arriving on 5 October. Following their arrival Pratt wrote, "After we had arrived on the ground of Great Salt Lake City we pitched our tents by the side of a spring of water; and, after resting a little, I devoted my time chiefly to building temporary houses, putting in crops, and obtaining fuel from the mountains."[34] Describing their building efforts Taylor explained, "Our houses were built on the outside line [of the fort] in shanty form, with the highest wall outside, the roof sloping towards the interior. The windows and doors were placed on the side facing the enclosure, the outside being left solid, excepting loop holes— for protection. Our corrals, hay-stacks and stables were some distance behind and outside the fort." Taylor continued to work throughout the fall, and by Christmas he "had put up, enclosed and covered about ninety feet of building made of split logs, out of which was taken a four-inch plank. The plank was used for partitions, etc. . . . In addition to this, I had built corrals and stables behind, and enclosed a garden spot in front, with a board-rail fence. I assisted in all this labor of sawing, building, hauling, etc.,—enough for one fall."[35]

Along with their many efforts in preparing homes for the coming fall, the Saints participated in a spiritual renewal. Pratt explained, "Having repented of our sins and renewed our covenants, President John Taylor and myself administered the ordinances of baptism, etc., to each other and to our families, according to the example set by the President and pioneers who had done the same on entering the valley."[36] In doing so, they consecrated their work to the building up of the kingdom of God.

NOTES TO CHAPTER SIX

1. "Address to the Saints in Great Britain," *MS* (15 November 1846):97.
2. Ibid., 97–98.
3. Ibid., 98.

4. "Address to the Saints in Great Britain," *MS* (15 November 1846):113.

5. Ibid., 114.

6. Ibid., 115.

7. "Extract," *MS* (1 August 1846):3; emphasis in original.

8. Madsen, *Journey to Zion,* 197.

9. Ibid., 198.

10. Ibid., 199.

11. Ibid., 200–201.

12. Ibid., 205.

13. Ibid., 208. An excerpt from John Taylor's journal quoted in B. H. Roberts's *A Comprehensive History of the Church* indicates that it was Parley P. Pratt who spoke to the volunteers along with John Taylor.

14. *CHC* 3:88.

15. "Address to the Saints in Great Britain," *MS* (15 November 1846):117.

16. *CHC* 3:88.

17. "On Priesthood," *MS* (1 November 1847):326.

18. *Autobiography of Parley P. Pratt,* 345.

19. "Elder Taylor's Letter to the Editor of the Star," *MS* (1 June 1847):162.

20. "Circular," *MS* (15 October 1846):92; emphasis in the original.

21. "General Conference at Manchester," *MS* (15 November 1846):119.

22. Ibid., 121.

23. "The Joint Stock Company," *MS* (1 November 1846):103; emphasis in original.

24. *Autobiography of Parley P. Pratt,* 347.

25. "Elder Taylor's Letter to the Editor of the Star," *MS* (1 June 1847):162.

26. *Autobiography of Parley P. Pratt,* 346–47.

27. "Elder Taylor's Letter to the Editor of the Star," *MS* (1 June 1847):161.

28. *Autobiography of Parley P. Pratt,* 357.

29. For a discussion of the events that took place between Pratt's and Taylor's return from England and their departure for the Salt Lake Valley, see Stephen F. Pratt, "Parley P. Pratt in Winter Quarters and the Trail West," *BYU Studies* (Summer 1984):373–88.

30. Bennett, *We'll Find This Place,* 255. For a detailed account of the emigration camp's trip west, see chapter nine of this book.

31. Ibid., 251.

32. Ibid., 268.

33. *Autobiography of Parley P. Pratt,* 359–60.

34. Ibid., 360.

35. *Life of John Taylor,* 193.

36. *Autobiography of Parley P. Pratt,* 360.

~ SEVEN ~

A PREACHER *and* PUBLISHER *in* EUROPE

> Arrivals—Elder John Taylor, one of the Quorum of the Twelve Apostles, with Elders John Pack, Senior President of the Eighth Quorum of the Seventies, and Curtis E. Bolton, High Priest, arrived in Liverpool, on the 27th of May, in good health, per ship Jacob A. Westervelt, of New York. These brethren are on a mission to France, to preach the gospel. May the Lord abundantly bless them in their labors for the spread of truth, and may the inhabitants of that great nation soon feel the awakening powers and sanctifying influences of the gospel of peace.[1]

John Taylor's initial stay in the Salt Lake Valley only lasted two years. In the October conference of 1849, he was called on a mission to France. Weeks after his call, he took leave of his family yet again to travel across the Atlantic to preach the gospel. Along with Lorenzo Snow, who was going to Italy, Erastus Snow to Denmark, and Franklin D. Richards to England, John Taylor left on 19 October, heading east across the mountains and prairies.

While in St. Louis in February 1850, Elder Taylor wrote his family a letter reporting on his travels. Given the time of year he left Salt Lake, traversing the mountains and then crossing the plains had been a "cold and dreary" journey. Despite the unpleasant weather, Taylor and his traveling companions felt the Lord's protection. "The snows," he explained, "fell on our right and left, before and behind, but we never encountered a snow storm until the last day."[2] As his group traveled at a leisurely pace, he studied French so that he might be better prepared once he arrived at his final destination. As he told his family, "I have made some progress in the language and hope to be able to speak it on my arrival there."[3]

Crossing the plains, the group followed the pioneer's path, which took them to Kanesville, Iowa, on the east side of the Missouri River just across from Winter Quarters. Despite the many pioneer companies that had left from the area on their way to Salt Lake, there were many Saints still living in the area. When the elders arrived in Iowa, they "were saluted with the firing of guns." Parties were held, musical performances were conducted, and other celebrations took place during the three weeks Elder Taylor stayed with the Saints in Kanesville. Leaving this settlement, Taylor and his companions journeyed across Iowa and then down the Mississippi River to St. Louis. Approximately 3,000 Church members lived in this city downriver from Nauvoo. Elder Taylor recorded in the letter to his family that they had "a magnificent hall and a splendid band" and they did "things up in good style." As they had done in Kanesville, the Saints in St. Louis, Taylor reported, "flocked around me like bees," at times preventing him from "being able to fulfill the many engagements that have pressed themselves upon me."[4] At the time of writing to his family in mid-February, he had been in St. Louis about three weeks.

Further in the letter he explained his purpose in writing: to express his feelings toward his family upon their separation. To this end he wrote:

> "But," say you, "do you not think of us and home? and do you never think of me, and of me?" This is what I have been wanting to get at for some time, and this long, tedious preface has become wearisome to me—let me tell my feelings if I can. Home! Home! Home! What shall I say? can I tell it? No, a thousand times no! Your forms, your countenances, your bodies and your spirits are all portrayed before me as in living characters. You are with me in my imaginations, thoughts, dreams, feelings; true our bodies are separated, but there you live—you dwell in my bosom, in my heart and affections, and will remain there forever. Our covenants, our hopes, our joys are all eternal and will live when our bodies moulder in the dust.

Oceans, seas, mountains, deserts and plains may separate us—but in my heart you dwell.

Do I see an amiable, lovely woman—my feelings are not there, they fly to my home. Do I see a beautiful infant—hear the prattle of lovely innocents, or the symmetry and intelligence of those more advanced in years? My mind flies to my home—there I gaze upon my wives, there I fondle and kiss my children and revel for a time in this mental delight; but I awake from my reverie and find that it is but a dream, and that mountains, deserts and plains separate us! Do I murmur? No! Do you? I hope not—shall I not say for you, No?

He went on to describe how he felt about the work in which he was involved, reminding his loved ones that their separation was but for a short time and greater rewards awaited them.

I am engaged in my Master's business; I am a minister of Jehovah to proclaim His will to the nations. I go to unlock the door of life to a mighty nation, to publish to millions the principles of life, light and truth, intelligence and salvation, to burst their fetters, liberate the oppressed, reclaim the wandering, correct their views, improve their morals, save them from degradation, ruin and misery, and lead them to light, life, truth and celestial glory. Do not your spirits co-operate with mine? I know they do. Do you not say, "Go, my husband, go, my father; fulfill your mission, and let God and angels protect you and restore you safe to our bosoms?" I know you do. Well, our feelings are reciprocal, I love my family and they love me; but shall that love be so contracted, so narrow, so earthly and sensual as to prevent my doing the will of my Father in heaven? No, say I, and you echo, No. No! our thoughts and feelings soar in another atmosphere. We live for time, and we live for eternity; we love here and we will love forever. . . .

Our separations here tend to make us more appreciative of each other's society. A few more separations and trials, a few more tears, a few more afflictions, and the victory will be ours! We'll gain the kingdom, possess the crown, inherit eternal glory, associate with the Gods, soar amidst the intelligences of heaven; and with the noble, the great, the intellectual, the virtuous, the amiable, the holy, possess the reward held in reserve for the righteous, and live and love forever. . . . May the spirit of peace be and abide with you forever; and when you bow before the Throne of Grace remember your affectionate husband, father and friend.[5]

Following his stay in St. Louis, Elder Taylor, Brother Curtis Bolton, and Brother John Pack journeyed on to New York, where they boarded the *Jacob A. Westervelt* for a 22-day trip across the Atlantic. They enjoyed a pleasant journey, at least, according to Elder Taylor "as pleasant as a temporary imprisonment (such as is a voyage across the Atlantic) will at any time admit of."[6] When their ship arrived in Liverpool, England, it was the third and final time Elder Taylor disembarked in this city, which nearly 40 years earlier had been the place of residence for the Taylor household.

Two days after landing in England, Taylor addressed a letter to the editor of the *Millennial Star*, dated 29 May 1850, in which he reflected on his previous trips to the British Isles. "I am necessarily led to a variety of reflections on landing in this town. Some nine or ten years ago I arrived here on a mission, with the rest of the Twelve to preach the gospel to England. It fell to my lot to come to Liverpool[, where a]t that time there was not one Saint here." Despite the challenges they faced, "the truth . . . triumphed" as 5,000 people were baptized into the Church. His second visit, he reminded readers of the *Millennial Star*, was precipitated by the presidency of Elder Reuben Hedlock "seeking to aggrandize themselves instead of advancing the pure principles of eternal truth."[7] His stay in England, he explained, would necessarily be short, as he was now "on my way to France, in company with my brethren and others of the Twelve on the way to various missions in Italy, Denmark, and Sweden."[8] In the following issue of the *Star*, Franklin D. Richards, president of the British Mission, informed readers that on 8 June, "Elders Taylor, Lorenzo Snow, and Erastus Snow left London for their several places of appointment on missions assigned them. . . . Truly it was an occasion of great joy to these servants of God to meet with others of their brethern from Zion, and attend the London Conference."[9]

Ten days after leaving London, Curtis Bolton, William Howell (from Wales), and John Taylor landed in Boulogne-sur-Mer, a town on the north coast of France. After securing lodgings in a room where they were "comparatively comfortably situated," they sought the town's mayor to find out if they could preach publicly. In meeting with Monsieur le Marie, Taylor explained that as "our principles taught us to uphold all laws, government, and authority wherever our lots might be cast . . . we wished to be acquainted with the laws and usages of this country, in order that we might not infringe upon them." The mayor first asked for their credentials and then informed them there would be no problems if they preached in dedicated churches. Were they to meet in a public hall, however, they had to notify the mayor of the time and place of the meeting, identifying their intentions and what doctrines they would preach. In respect to these policies, Taylor indicated that "it [was] necessary for the Mayor to confer with the Prefect of the Police about any public meeting of this kind, that if a person was to hold a public meeting, or even advertise for one without this [permission], they would be in danger of being taken up, and imprisoned, or expelled [from] the country."[10] The conversation with the mayor proceeded somewhat humorously as Brother Bolton interpreted for Elder Taylor. However, the mayor requested that Taylor speak to him in English, which the mayor spoke "imperfectly." Noticing how the mayor spoke, Taylor explained, "before I was aware, [I] was answering in French, 'oui Monsieur' &c. Thus he was trying to accommodate me in English, and I him in French."[11]

John Pack arrived in France on 18 June 1850. The missionaries soon arranged to use a hall in the town center for their preaching. They put up placards announcing a series of lectures on the principles of the everlasting gospel to be given by Elder Taylor. At this same time, Taylor made acquaintance with the town's newspaper editor, who agreed to publish several articles written by Elder Taylor. The first piece, published in both French and English, described the Church's beginnings, and a second, printed the following week, outlined the first principles of the gospel. In a letter written to the editor of the *Interpreter Anglais et Francais*, Taylor explained the reasons for the missionaries coming to France. He informed the residents, "We have come to Boulogne for the purpose of preaching or lecturing on the religious principles believed by us as a people, and we are desirous of laying those principles as fully before all classes of the citizens of Boulogne as circumstances will admit of." Pointing out that they had no political intentions, he added they were neither Protestant nor Catholic "in common acceptance of the term," but they were like them "in many particulars."[12] Briefly outlining the doctrines which they taught, Taylor concluded: "We have come from the territory of Deseret, near the Great Salt Lake, Upper California, United States, a distance of eight thousand miles, over mountains, deserts, plains, and oceans, in the name of Israel's God as His servants to make known to the inhabitants of this nation, the things in which ourselves rejoice, and to call upon all men in the name of Jesus to repent and be baptized for the remission of sins."[13]

Despite the missionaries' efforts, Elder Taylor's lectures were poorly attended, which led Taylor to suggest that "the people of Boulogne [were] more disposed for pleasure than any thing else."[14] Among the attendees, however, were several ministers who sought to disrupt the proceedings. While Taylor expressed a willingness to meet them at his residence or in their homes to discuss the gospel, he would not debate with them in public. After the first evening's lecture, several ministers followed John Taylor out the door of the hall and into the street, challenging his teachings and claiming they could prove "Joe Smith" an imposter. Taylor responded, "I told them to prove whatever they liked in their own way, I cared nothing for their opinions—that I was personally acquainted with Joseph Smith—that he was a gentleman, and would not treat a stranger as they had treated me—that I wished no further conversation."[15] He then refused to acknowledge the men who continued to follow him. Later he found out the same men had disrupted a meeting held by Brother Howell.

On 4 July 1850, a messenger arrived with a note addressed to Taylor, Bolton, Pack, and Howell. Signed by three ministers, C. W. Cleeve, James Robertson, and Philip Cater, it requested an "open and public debate" concerning the "extraordinary nature of your pretensions and announcements." The missionaries accepted the challenge, appointing Elder Taylor to respond on their behalf. Concerning the challenge, Taylor explained, "I must say that I considered the note [from the ministers] too ungentlemanly, abusive, and insulting to be deserving of notice. I should have considered it and its authors worthy only of contempt, had I been in a place where I was known."[16] Wishing to defend the gospel against the misrepresentations of these men, the missionaries made plans for the debate. Starting on 11 July and continuing for the following two evenings, the debates started at seven o'clock and were intended to last until ten o'clock each evening.

As part of the debate, the ministers challenged the character of Joseph Smith, to which Taylor replied:

> I testify that I was acquainted with Joseph Smith for years. I have traveled with him; I have been with him in private and in public; I have associated with him in councils of all kinds; I have listened hundreds of times to his public teachings, and his advice to his friends and associates of a more private nature. I have been at his house and seen his deportment in his family. I have seen him arraigned before the courts of his country, and seen him honorably acquitted, and delivered from the pernicious breath of slander, and the machinations and falsehoods of wicked and corrupt men. I was with him living, and with him when he died, when he was murdered in Carthage [Jail] by a ruthless mob, headed by a Methodist minister, named Williams, with their faces painted. I was there and was myself wounded: I at that time received four balls in my body. I have seen him, then, under these various circumstances, and I testify before God, angels and men, that he was a good, honorable, virtuous man—that his doctrines were good, scriptural and wholesome—that his precepts were such as became a man of God—that his private and public character was unimpeachable—and that he lived and died as a man of God and a gentleman. This is my testimony.[17]

The debate afforded Taylor the opportunity to discuss how the organization of the primitive Church compared with the doctrines of

Mormonism and how Mormonism compared to what the ministers taught.

> Now let us examine how this doctrine agrees with that of these gentlemen; for be it remembered that St. John says, "He that transgresseth and abideth not in the doctrines of Christ hath not God, but he that abideth in the doctrines of Christ hath both the Father and the Son." (2 John 9.) Now, have they Apostles? No.

> They ridicule the idea of them. Have they Prophets? No. They tell us there is to be no more prophecy. Have they evangelists, pastors and teachers, inspired men? No. They don't believe in inspiration, and tell us the cause of inspiration has ceased. Do they speak in tongues? No. You have heard it turned into ridicule time and again. Do they have prophets among them who prophesy? This they call a delusion. If any are sick, do they do as St. James says, "send for the Elders of the Church that they may pray for them, and anoint them with oil in the name of the Lord?" No. That they call fanaticism. Do they baptize in the name of the Lord for the remission of sins? No. Do they lay on hands for the gift of the Holy Ghost? No. What have they got that in the least resembles the gospel? They have not even a clumsy counterfeit. How will they stand the test? "He that abideth not in the doctrines of Christ hath not God."[18]

When Taylor went on to discuss the tenets of Methodism and the Baptist Association, both Mr. Cleeve and Mr. Cater denied their affiliations with these religions. To these statements Taylor responded:

> I certainly think the gentlemen have taken a strange position, they seem to be afraid of acknowledging what their profession is. However, I will proceed. I have three different ministers to do with of some persuasion, for they all call themselves Reverends. Now, do their doctrines agree with the scriptures? Have they the organization, ordinances, gifts, prophecy, revelations, visions, tongues, apostles, and prophets? No! This they cannot deny, for they

have all of them opposed these things; yet all of these things were associated with primitive christianity. Their offices, their doctrines, their calling, their teaching, their ordinances are all incorrect, they are devoid of the blessings, powers, unity, certainty and revelation, and are left struggling in the mazes of confusion, division, strife, uncertainty and error. They know not God nor the power of God. (Interruption.) There is scarcely a principle that these gentlemen have that is correct, even the doctrine of baptism for the remission of sins they treat lightly; yet Philip baptized the Ethiopian eunuch—when he believed, he immersed him in water; John baptized in Aenon because there was much water there; St. Paul was told to "arise and be baptized, and wash away his sins," and Jesus says that "except a man be born of water and of the spirit, he can in no wise enter the kingdom of God."

Not wanting to pursue the topic further, the ministers were satisfied to have the discussion rest, to which Taylor replied, "If they have no reply to make, of course I must let it rest."[19]

A local newspaper reporter was in attendance to get an account of the deliberations, which was to be printed in an extra section of the paper. However, Taylor later wrote to the *Star* that the reporter "only got one-third of it in, and that so imperfect, that it conveys no correct idea of the debate."[20] (Not satisfied by the reporter's account, Taylor returned to Liverpool later that year and, using Brother Bolton's notes taken each evening, published, in a lengthy pamphlet, his own account of the discussion.)

Regarding their efforts in Boulogne, Taylor wrote, "Several respectable persons have told me that they believe the doctrine; but some want more time to investigate; others seem afraid, or ashamed of their neighbors, for the present."[21] After the debate, John Pack remained in Boulogne, while the other three missionaries left for Paris, arriving in the French capital on 19 July. In Paris, Brother Bolton and Elder Taylor began translating the Book of Mormon. The translation work was aided by several converts who were "men of intelligence and education." Despite repeated delays in finishing the translation, Elder Taylor said of the final copy that it is "as good a one as it is possible for anybody to make. I fear no contradiction to this statement from any man, learned or illiterate. I had it examined and tested by some of the best educated men in France." He did make some changes to the book by numbering paragraphs and dividing paragraphs in places where they were too long. Despite the small alterations, "the original simplicity of the book is retained, and it is as literal as the genius and idiom of the French language would admit of."[22]

RETURN TO ENGLAND

In the fall of 1850, Elder Taylor returned to Manchester, England, for the Church conference held there. Of the Twelve, Orson Pratt, Franklin D. Richards, and John Taylor were present. On Saturday morning, 5 October 1850, Elder Taylor spoke to the British Saints about revelation and Church organization. Reiterating themes that he addressed when he was in England four years previous, he reminded the Saints they did not have to sustain Church leaders in their wrongdoings. "But if an elder should do wrong, are we to vote for him? no, lift up your hands to cut him off, if he repents not. That is the way I want you to do with me, brothers Pratt and Richards, and with all of us, we do not want you to sustain iniquity under false cover." He added, "When men do right, then it is that we have to sustain them."[23]

In a subsequent address, he spoke at length concerning the financial affairs in Deseret, explaining the Saints' need to manufacture their own materials. "It is upon this principle," he explained, "that England has been sustained, namely, her manufactures."[24] In accordance with Brigham Young's epistle on the subject, Elder Taylor's speech advocated the immigration of "mechanics" to the Salt Lake Valley. The Saints in Deseret, he said, "suffer for lack of home manufactures," and yearly they send out hundreds of thousands of dollars for items that might be produced in the valley. Hoping to encourage their participation he suggested, "If I had the money, and wished to speculate, there is nothing I would rather do than enter into this work. If I had the means, I would take out a company of potters; I would go to the presidents of the conferences, and say, I want you to show me some of your best potters.—I want to organize a company of them to go right to the Valley . . . to manufacture the same kind of articles, and as good as they do here in England."[25] His speech also outlined the religious reasoning behind the desire for independence in manufacturing the goods they needed: "We do not want to go among the nations buying from them the things we want to consume, for there will be earthquakes and distress of nations, and an overflowing scourge from the Almighty will perplex them. We do not want to be among these nations when these things take place."[26] To rely on others would be to the Saints' folly. Of his own speculative adventures, Taylor told the Saints that he, along with others, planned to raise beets in Salt Lake to make sugar. For this purpose he organized the Deseret Manufacturing Company. Despite expending extensive capital in purchasing first-rate equipment to refine sugar and importing the machinery from England to Deseret, the operation largely proved to be a failure as it did not produce the desired sugar.

Following the conference in Manchester, John Taylor announced he was having busts made of Joseph and Hyrum Smith. Having brought with him drawings of the men and casts taken immediately following their deaths, he had procured the services of a well-known artist in England. Assisted by two men who knew the Prophet and his brother, Taylor supervised the modeling himself. The busts, Taylor explained, "are neatly executed, and will make a beautiful ornament for the chimney piece or library." Lest those planning to emigrate be deterred from purchasing the busts, he added that they "are of such a size as to be easily conveyed to the Valley." Following Taylor's announcement in the *Star*, the editor indicated that the prices asked were "very reasonable," commenting that "we hope Elder Taylor will realize his expectations in disposing of them to the Saints, seeing he has been at such an amount of trouble and expense for their gratification."[27]

AN EDITOR IN PARIS AND HAMBURG

Following his return to Paris, Taylor wrote back to Elder Richards in England, explaining it would not be necessary to take up collections from the Saints for publication of the Book of Mormon in French. He had procured donations from several wealthy Saints, and he arranged it so that the sales of the first books would fund printing 200,000 additional copies without further expense. Taylor apologized for this announcement. "I may have deprived some of an anticipated blessing. I hope they will excuse me; for perhaps there may be an opportunity afforded them of assisting some of my brethren in another way."[28] His letter also informed Richards that Taylor planned to return to his publishing background and begin a newspaper called *L'Etoile du Deseret* (The Star of Deseret). When the paper came out, it described Joseph Smith's visions, provided an account of Church history, and outlined important doctrines. Regarding the content Taylor explained, "Instead of filling it with the news of the day, we have filled it with all that is good for the people to read, that it may be a standing work for years to come. It contains articles written on baptism, the Gift of the Holy Ghost, the necessity of gathering together, and all the leading points associated with the religion we believe in."[29]

In the first issue, Taylor wrote a lengthy article comparing the philosophical systems of man with the theological designs of God. The subject became one on which Taylor would discourse extensively. In the opening paragraphs he explained his thesis: "The wise, the learned, the pious, the philosopher, the legislator, the divine, and Christian have been in search of something to ameliorate the condition of man." Despite their considerable and well-intended efforts, he explained, "every plan put into operation by man, to regenerate the world, only exhibits more fully his folly and incompetency; and in spite of every effort, religiously, morally, and politically, the world is getting worse and worse."[30] The failure of men to accomplish their aims and the world's "unhappy, debased, corrupt, and unsettled state," he suggested, were due to "the lack of pure principles of true philosophy." Having forsaken God's ways, men were left to their own designs, which "have been weighed in the balance and found wanting."[31] In contrast, he wrote, "Our religion is not a wild phantasy, as some have supposed, based upon some obscure vision, or idle tale. It is a revelation of God to us and the world. It accords with every principle of reason, revelation, intelligence, and philosophy."[32]

The focus on philosophy reflected what Taylor saw as the cultural bias of the French people. Concerning their preaching in France, Elder Taylor explained, "We do not preach religion much to them, for a great many of them are philosophers, and, of course, we must be philosophers too." The challenge the missionaries faced was to "make it appear that our philosophy is better than theirs, and then show them that religion is at the bottom of it." He indicated that to proceed otherwise would be unproductive: "It would be nonsense to talk about justification by faith: they would say it was moonshine, or something else. You have got to talk common sense, you have got to affect their bodies as well as their souls, for they believe they are possessed of both."[33]

Of the French fascination with philosophy, Taylor was quite critical. On one occasion several philosophers came to visit him. "While conversing," he explained, "I had to laugh a little at them, for the word philosophy is about every tenth word they speak. One of them, a Jesuit priest, who had come in the Church, a well educated man, was a little annoyed in his feelings at some of my remarks, on their philosophy. I asked them if any of them had ever asked me one question that I could not answer. They answered in the negative. But, said I, I can ask you fifty that you cannot answer." At another time while walking around the *Jardin des Plantes* he purchased an "exceedingly light cake," which was "so thin that you could blow it away." When someone asked him the name of the cake, he, in the absence of knowing the proper name, suggested it be called "philosophy or fried froth," as it was "so light you can blow it away, eat it all day, and at night be as far from being satisfied as when you began."[34]

In Paris Elder Taylor baptized a Brother Bertrand, who belonged to a group that advocated Fourierism, "a species of French philosophy, established by one Fourier, a Frenchman." At the time of his baptism, Bertrand had been an editor of the group's newspaper, and one of the paper's other editors, a Mr. Krolokoski, approached Elder Taylor to discuss the gospel. During their conversation Mr. Krolokoski asked, "Mr. Taylor, do you propose no other plan to ameliorate the condition of mankind than that of baptism for the remission of sins?" When Taylor acknowledged that mankind was to be redeemed by the first principles of the gospel, Krolokoski wished him well but claimed it could not be done. In response, Taylor challenged him.

> Mr. Krolokoski, you sent, some time ago, Mr. Cabet to Nauvoo. He was considered your leader—the most talented

man you had. He went to Nauvoo when it was deserted—
when houses and lands were at a mere nominal value: he
went there with his community at the time we left. Rich
farms were deserted, and thousands of us had left our
houses and furniture in them, and there was everything that
was calculated to promote the happiness of human beings
there. Never could a person go to a place under more happy
circumstances. Mr. Cabet, to try his experiment, had also
the selection in France of whom he pleased. He and his
company went to Nauvoo, and what is the result? You have
seen the published account in the papers. We were banished
from civilized society into the valleys of the Rocky
Mountains to seek for that protection among savages which
Christian civilization denied us. . . . There our people have
built houses, enclosed lands, cultivated gardens, built
school-houses, opened farms, and have organized a government and are prospering in all the blessings and immunities
of civilized life. Not only this, but they have sent thousands
and thousands of dollars over to Europe to assist the
suffering poor to go to America, where they might find an
asylum. You, on the other hand, that went to our empty
houses and farms—you, I say, went there under most favorable circumstances. Now, what is the result? I read in all of
your reports from there, published in your own paper in
Paris, a continued cry for help. The cry is to you for money,
money: "We want money to help us to carry out our
designs." The society that I represent comes with the fear of
God—the worship of the great Eloheim: they offer the
simple plan ordained of God—viz., repentance, baptism for
the remission of sins, and the laying-on of hands for the gift
of the Holy Ghost. Our people have not been seeking the
influence of the world, nor the power of government, but
they have obtained both; whilst you, with your philosophy
independent of God, have been seeking to build up a
system of communism and a government which is,
according to your own accounts, the way to introduce the
millennial reign. Now, which is the best—our religion, or
your philosophy?[35]

To Elder Taylor's question, Krolokoski had not an answer, commenting only, "Well, I cannot say anything."[36] As Taylor emphasized time and again, he believed it was the philosophy of Jesus Christ, not the world's philosophy, which would meliorate the ills of society.

While yet in Paris, Elder Taylor petitioned the government for the privilege of preaching throughout all of France. When he spoke with cabinet members, they told him his request would be granted. His efforts proved futile, however, as eventually he was denied the permission he sought. Taylor felt this might have been due, at least in part, to reports of a mob in Denmark tearing down a building of the Saints and assaulting them. As a result, the only place where they could preach was in a private room. France was, at the time, amidst a period of revolution, and the law prohibited the missionaries from having any more than 20 people attend a meeting. Those in attendance at larger gatherings, if discovered, could be put in prison. Concerning the political conditions, Taylor reported that "the officers were continually on the alert, and when we would meet, lest there should be more than twenty people, they would be counting how many there were in the room, and thus the Saints were continually under the spirit of fear of the authorities."[37] Even though "'Liberty, Equality, Fraternity, and Brotherhood,' was written almost upon every door," the people, as Taylor observed, "had liberty to speak, but might be put in prison for doing so."[38] Under these circumstances, Elder Taylor and his companions labored to raise up the Church in Paris. Branches were also established in the cities of Le Havre, Calais, and Boulogne.

When the translation of the Book of Mormon was finished, Taylor felt inclined to return home, having been away for nearly two years. However, he received an epistle from the First Presidency indicating the elders ought to stay yet another year and outlining a need for the gospel to be taken to other countries. When Elder Taylor read this, he explained, "it immediately occurred to my mind to go to Germany."[39] Before getting out of bed the next morning, he developed a plan to publish the Book of Mormon in German. Without delay he set about finding someone with the requisite skills in German to accompany him. He wrote to Orson Hyde, asking him to send someone from the Salt Lake Valley to help with the work. He then enlisted the help of a new convert in France, George Viett, who spoke both French and

German. Before making his way to Germany, Taylor returned to England to find a qualified person to help. Though he found many Germans, none of them had the requisite Church experience to be of aid. As he was preparing to depart, Taylor happened to encounter George P. Dykes, who had previously considered going to Germany but had gone to help Elder Snow since Dykes knew Danish. As Dykes was getting ready to go home, Taylor persuaded him to go to Germany for a few months. In Hamburg, Taylor and Dykes set about translating the Book of Mormon, along with Viett and Charles Miller, who had just been baptized in Germany.

As he had done in Paris, Elder Taylor sought to spread the gospel by publishing another newspaper. The paper, called *Zions Panier* (Zion's Banner), was "mostly occupied by an account and testimony of the editor, of the rise and progress of the Church, and its first organization by revelation and ministration of the Holy Angels, to the young man Joseph."[40] Concerned about the quality of the translation, Taylor had the paper read by several professors in Hamburg. One professor indicated that had he not known the paper was first written in English and then translated, he would have thought the paper originally written in German. Regarding the paper, the *Millennial Star's* editor expressed confidence that "with the spreading of *Zion's Banner* upon the breezes of the German shore, opens up a new dispensation to that people . . . ; and we hesitate not to express our firm conviction that many thousands will be gathered out of the German tongue, who will flock to Zion."[41] Since the translation of the Book of Mormon was well underway and in competent hands, Taylor left Germany. In Liverpool, Taylor met the one person whom he wished to have help in the German translation work—Daniel Carn, who had just arrived from Salt Lake.

A FINAL CONFERENCE IN FRANCE

Taylor returned to France and arrived in Paris a few days after the revolution precipitated by Louis Napoleon. Upon his arrival, he "saw the place where the houses had been battered down, and the people killed by wholesale; where [they] were shot down promiscuously, both big and little, old and young, men, women, and children."[42] Despite the prohibition against large meetings, a secret conference was scheduled for the day the French people were to "vote" for the man who had just overthrown the government. About this coincidence, Taylor reported "at the very time they were voting for their president, we were voting for our president, and building up the Kingdom of God."[43] During their meeting, Taylor prophesied that the Saints' cause would yet stand when Napoleon's regime was "crushed to pieces." Given the political situation, some elders were afraid to come to Paris, yet nearly 400 Saints attended the meeting. Many elders, priests, and teachers were ordained, and a presidency was established for the country, with Curtis Bolton chosen as the president.

After the conference, Elder Taylor's mission in France was complete, and he soon departed. When he arrived in England, a letter from Brother Bolton informed him that the day he left, the high police had come to his lodgings to inquire of him. Concerning these events Taylor later reported:

> It was not more than ten minutes after I had taken the cab and started to the railroad station to take my last departure from France, when one of the High Police came to inquire after me. The gentleman with whom I stayed was a very affectionate friend to me, and he kept the police in conversation for two hours, speaking very highly of me; he told them I was a respectable, high-minded man, &c. The police told him of every place I had been at since I came to Paris; when I came to France; what hotel I stayed in; when I went to England, and how long I staid there; when I went to Germany, and how long I staid there; which books I had printed, &c. &c. He gave my friend a most minute account of every step I had taken; and all this is recorded in the books of the police.[44]

The police might have caught up with him, except Elder Taylor did not take a direct route to England. Not knowing the police sought him, he stayed another week in a small town on the coast of France.

Before leaving England, Elder Taylor worked to finish the first of two books he wrote in his lifetime, *The Government of God*. So busy was he in finishing this work that he did not have time to address a final letter to the British Saints. The editor of the *Star*, however, informed readers that the book was ready for press, and he hoped that it would soon be available. He went on to add, "To those who are acquainted with Elder Taylor's writings, a word from us is quite unnecessary; they will know at once what to expect from his vastly extended and comprehensive mind, while surveying the economy of God's Government, and bringing into direful contrast the frail and corrupt policies of mankind at the present age of the world."[45] Concerning Taylor's book, historian Hurbert H. Bancroft wrote, "As a dissertation on a general and abstract subject it probably has not its equal in point of ability within the range of Mormon literature. The style is lofty and clear, and every page betokens the great learning of the author. As a student of ancient and modern history, theologian, and moral philosopher, President Taylor is justly entitled to the front rank."[46] After giving his manuscript to James Linforth to publish, Taylor boarded the steamship *Niagara*, which set sail for Boston on 6 March 1852.

Upon his return to Salt Lake, Elder Taylor talked to the Saints gathered in the Tabernacle about his missionary efforts.

> I have felt to rejoice all the day long, that God has revealed the principle of eternal life, that I am put in possession of that truth, and that I am counted worthy to engage in the work of the Lord, and be a messenger to the nations of the earth. I rejoice in proclaiming this glorious Gospel, because it takes root in the hearts of the children of men, and they rejoice with me to be connected with, and participate in, the blessings of the kingdom of God. I rejoice in afflictions, for they are necessary to humble and prove us, that we may comprehend ourselves, become acquainted with our weakness and infirmities; and I rejoice when I triumph over them, because God answers my prayers, therefore I feel to rejoice all the day long.[47]

NOTES TO CHAPTER SEVEN
1. *MS* (15 June 1850):185.
2. *Life of John Taylor,* 206–207.
3. Ibid., 206.

4. Ibid., 207.
5. Ibid., 207–209.
6. "Letters to the Editor," *MS* (15 June 1850):186.
7. Ibid., 186.
8. Ibid., 187.
9. "President Richards' Letter to the Editor," *MS* (1 July 1850):202.
10. "Letters to the Editor," *MS* (1 September 1850):268.
11. Ibid., 268.
12. "Letter From John Taylor," *MS* (1 August 1850):235.
13. Ibid., 236–37.
14. "Letters to the Editor," *MS* (1 September 1850):269.
15. *Three Nights' Public Discussion,* 1.
16. Ibid., 2.
17. Ibid., 23–24.
18. Ibid., 35.
19. Ibid., 36, emphasis in original.
20. "Letters to the Editor," *MS* (1 September 1850):270.
21. Ibid., 270.
22. *JD* 1:21.
23. "General Conference," *MS* (1 November 1850):323.
24. "General Conference," *MS* (1 December 1850):358.
25. Ibid., 360.
26. Ibid., 361.
27. "To the Saints," *MS* (1 November 1850):330.
28. *MS* (15 April 1851):123.
29. *JD* 1:21.
30. "An Address to the Elders in France, Switzerland and Italy as Published in the First Number of the 'Etoile Du Deseret,' *MS* (15 August 1851):241.
31. Ibid., 243.
32. Ibid., 242.
33. *JD* 1:23.
34. Ibid., 1:27.
35. Ibid., 5:237–38.
36. Ibid., 5:238.
37. Ibid., 1:24.
38. Ibid., 1:22.
39. Ibid., 1:24.
40. *MS* (15 December 1851):375.
41. Ibid., 375.
42. *JD* 1:26.

43. Ibid., 1:26.
44. "Special Conference at Great Salt Lake City," *MS* (Supplement 1853):4.
45. *MS* (1 April 1852):105.
46. Bancroft, *History of Utah,* 433.
47. *JD* 1:17.

~ EIGHT ~

A NEW PHASE *in the* HISTORY *of* MORMONISM

Elder John Taylor is presiding in the United States, and publishing the Mormon, in New York city. That publication commends itself to the favorable consideration and patronage of the Saints, being ably conducted and exercising a very salutary influence in correcting public opinion and defending our people and the principle of our holy religion from the calumny, abuse, and misrepresentation of the world.
—Fourteenth General Epistle of the Presidency of the Church[1]

With regard to brother John Taylor, I will say that he has one of the strongest intellects of any man that can be found; he is a powerful man, he is a mighty man, and we may say that he is a powerful editor, but I will use a term to suit myself, and say that he is one of the strongest editors that ever wrote. Concerning his financial abilities, I have nothing to say; those who are acquainted with the matter, know how "The Mormon" has been sustained. We sent brother Taylor, and other brethren with him, to start that paper without purse or scrip, and if they had not accomplished that object, we should have known that they did not trust in their God, and did not do their duty.—Brigham Young[2]

PROSPECTS FOR A NEW PAPER

After returning from Britain in 1852, John Taylor was called on a mission the following year to preach the gospel to the Saints in the

Rocky Mountains. Rather than traveling abroad as he had done with his other missionary service, Taylor, along with several other Apostles and Presidents of the Seventies, visited nearly all of the Mormon settlements in Utah. Instead of seeking new converts, their missionary efforts were intended to spiritually strengthen the Saints with whom they visited: their meetings aimed to remind Saints of their duties and inspire them to live according to the covenants they had made.

After returning to Salt Lake, Taylor was elected a member of the territorial legislature. He did not, however, have a chance to serve in this office. Before the legislature convened, he received yet another mission call at a conference in June 1854. This call, which took him back to the United States, where eventually he took up residence in New York City, was, in many ways, similar to his previous proselyting efforts. While in New York, Taylor presided over the Church in the eastern states and preached the gospel to those willing to listen. As he had done in both France and Germany, Elder Taylor established and edited a newspaper. He also oversaw the immigration efforts of the Church as Saints from the British Isles arrived in ports along the northeast coast of the United States.

In starting on this mission, John Taylor left Salt Lake in the fall of 1854 accompanied by Jeter Clinton, Nathaniel H. Felt, Alexander Robbins, Angus M. Cannon, and his oldest son, 23-year-old George John Taylor. Making his second trip east across the Rocky Mountains and the following plains, Taylor and his group traveled to St. Louis, where they arrived by November. From that city, Taylor wrote to Franklin D. Richards, who still presided over the British Mission and with whom he would coordinate the immigration activities. He told Richards that "our present mission" represented "a new phase in the history of 'Mormonism.'" In the past, proselyting efforts had been "strictly religious," at least as the world understood the missionaries' labors. This practice had now changed: "Hitherto, with the exception of home officers, we have not meddled in politics." However, with their new calling, "we are now entered fairly into the political arena."[3] In addition to attempting to exert influence on the political decision-making in Washington, their foray into the political arena involved publishing a newspaper aimed at defending the Church from spurious claims about its doctrine and the conduct of its people. The

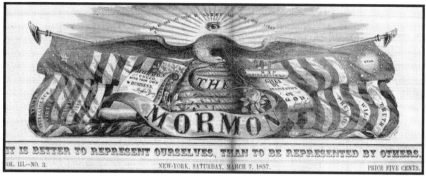

IT IS BETTER TO REPRESENT OURSELVES, THAN TO BE REPRESENTED BY OTHERS.

VOL. III.—NO. 3.   NEW-YORK, SATURDAY, MARCH 7, 1857.   PRICE FIVE CENTS.

THE MORMON

newspaper sought to challenge common misrepresentations of the Church and, in so doing, correct public opinion. In these efforts, Taylor's paper, which he called the *Mormon*, was to be much different than the newspapers he published in France and Germany.

The paper's function as an advocate for the Mormon cause was clearly stated in the prospectus Taylor sent to Richards in England. It explained, "THE MORMON will be devoted to the cause and interests of the 'Church of Jesus Christ of Latter-day Saints,' and will be the advocate of its claims, social, moral, political and religious; and will also treat upon all subjects which the Editor may deem instructive or edifying to his readers, among which will be science, literature and the general news of the day." In fulfilling this objective, Taylor explained that while he "would, by all proper means, court [the] respect and patronage" of honorable men, as editor he had "no promises to make," but would rather leave "himself at liberty to examine any principle, and pursue such a course as to him may seem best." With broad editorial discretion, Taylor intended to draw on his wide range of intellectual abilities in advocacy for the Church. As he told Richards in a postscript to the prospectus, "We are now going to be the representatives of our own opinions" in place of "having others represent them for us."[4] This idea—"It is better to represent ourselves, than to be presented by others"—outlined Taylor's philosophy for their publishing efforts. It also became the paper's motto, appearing in capital letters at the bottom of the paper's masthead.

In December 1854, the party of missionaries arrived in New York City. Despite limited resources, they rented out rooms in a boarding house, which also served as headquarters for the Eastern Mission. As he had done on other missions, Taylor traveled without purse or scrip. Since Church members in Utah were unable to provide them with the means necessary to publish the paper, he sought the aid of scattered Saints in New York. With their limited assistance, Taylor rented out two rooms in a building located at the corners of Nausau and Ann Streets, in the heart of New York's newspaper district. On either side of the building housing the *Mormon* were offices for venerated papers: the *New York Herald* and the *Tribune*, the latter edited by Horace Greely, a man Taylor came to loath. Concerning his efforts to get the paper started, Taylor wrote Brigham Young explaining, "We commenced our publication not because we had means to do it, but because we were determined to fulfill our mission, and either make a spoon or spoil a horn. . . . How long we shall be able to continue, I don't know. We are doing as well as we can, and shall continue to do so; but I find it one thing to preach the gospel without purse or scrip, and another thing to publish a paper on the same terms."[5]

The newspaper's first issue came out on 17 February 1855, and it clearly reflected the bold fervor of Taylor's tenure as editor. Concerning the paper, B. H. Roberts wrote, "As a defender of the faith and character of the Saints that Elder Taylor in *The Mormon* is most conspicuous." With this publication, Taylor "leaped into the public arena, threw down his gage of battle and dared the traducers of the Saints of God to take it up. The very name Mormon—which they had derided and made the synonym for all that was absurd in religion, impure in social life, or disloyal to government, he took up and made the title of his paper."[6] The paper's masthead, which took up nearly a quarter page and was designed by Taylor's son, George, depicted a large eagle atop a beehive at the paper's center. From the eagle's mouth dangled a banner inscribed with the paper's name, and to each side was an American flag. Above the eagle an all-seeing eye was surrounded by a blaze of glory and the words "Let there be light; and there was light." Written on the stripes of the left flag were the words "Truth, Intelligence, Virtue and Faith," and on the stripes of the other flag it read "Truth will prevail." The two scrolls on either side of the eagle included the following statements: "Mormon creed. Mind your own business—Brigham Young" and "Constitution of the

United States, given by inspiration of God—Joseph Smith." With this distinct heading, according to Roberts, Taylor took the mocked name *Mormon* and placed it "in bold letters and surrounded it with the symbols of liberty, intelligence and truth, and defied its slanderers to pluck from it the emblems in which he enshrined it."[7]

On the inside page, at the head of the editorial column, was another large eagle perched atop a beehive, again with American flags on either side. Leaning against the beehive, on one side, were copies of the Doctrine and Covenants, Book of Mormon, and Bible. "Peace and good will to man" was written on a tablet on the opposite side of the beehive. The eagle held in its beak a scroll that read "Holiness to the Lord." Under this heading, in the initial issue, Taylor gave his "Introductory Address," in which he admitted his reluctance at once again becoming an editor.

> We now present ourselves before the public to make our editorial bow; to be frank, however, we do not feel ourselves particularly honored in being re-called to the editorial chair; but as a matter of duty to ourselves, our church, and the world, we undertake it.
>
> We are well aware of its responsibilities and labor; and take hold of it as we would any other piece of drudgery; and we shall feel better pleased when we get through our labors, than at its commencement; and leave any one who covets the honor to gather the laurels. At the same time we do not shirk from the task; but shall try to entertain and instruct our readers, according to our ability.

Despite admitting his open reluctance in undertaking to publish another newspaper, Taylor was not reluctant to share his decisive opinion or explains his beliefs. In the first issue, his column boldly pronounced:

> It is true we are Mormon, inside and outside; at home or abroad, in public and private—everywhere. We are so, however, from principle. We are such, not because we believe it to be the most popular, lucrative, or honorable (as

the world has it); but because we believe it to be true, and more reasonable and scriptural, moral and philosophic; because we conscientiously believe it is more calculated to promote the happiness and well-being of humanity, in time and throughout all eternity, than any other system which we have met with.[8]

The publication of the *Mormon* meant that the Church had an oracle in one of America's leading cities, a means to counter the derisive commentary and descriptions disseminated by writers and editors throughout the country.

"REPRESENTATIVES OF OUR OWN OPINIONS"

In part the need to be representatives of their own opinions was precipitated by a speech given by Orson Pratt, under the direction of Brigham Young, on 29 August 1852. Pratt began by saying, "It is quite unexpected to me, brethren and sisters, to be called upon to address you this forenoon; and still more so, to address you upon the principle which has been named, namely, a plurality of wives." He then added, "It is rather new ground for me; that is, I have not been in the habit of publicly speaking upon this subject; and it is rather new ground to the inhabitants of the United States, and not only to them, but to a portion of the inhabitants of Europe; a portion of them have not been in the habit of preaching a doctrine of this description; consequently, we shall have to break up new ground."[9] The fact was no one had been in the habit of publicly speaking on the topic. His announcement, which explained the doctrine of plural marriage, provided the Church's opponents abundant fodder for renewing the criticisms raised by J. C. Bennett's exposé of the practice nearly a decade earlier.

As polygamy had become a popular subject in the preceding year and a half, Taylor took it upon himself to address the issue in the newspaper's first edition. In a column simply entitled "Polygamy," he explained:

Since this doctrine has been promulgated by us, as a part of our religious creed, every variety of opinion has been expressed, by men in all classes of society. It has been talked about by religious and irreligious, professor and profane. It has been the theme in the Legislative Hall, the Pulpit, the Bar-room, and the Press. Polygamy and the Mormons, the Mormons and Polygamy, has resounded everywhere. A universal hue and cry has gone through the length and breadth of the land; from California to Texas, and from Louisiana to Maine.

Given this situation, he explained, "it may be expected that something should be said by us in relation to this matter." He then told readers that it was for all to know that "we are not ashamed . . . to declare that we are polygamists." He further explained that "we unhesitatingly pronounce our full and implicit faith in this principle, as emanating from God, and that under His direction it [polygamy] would be a blessing to the human family."

The remainder of the article took a deliberate and reasoned approach to the subject, suggesting the topic "demand[ed] the most serious, calm, and dispassionate consideration." He acknowledged why "men of reflection and virtue, having a knowledge of the world" would "feel indignant at Polygamy." From appearances, it could easily be seen "as something pandering to the brutal passions of man; and from the exceeding low standard of virtue, can scare conceive of anything but lasciviousness associated with the sex." Mormons, however, he explained, "have higher aims and more exalted views of marriage." They seek to be married not until a separation at death, but they "expect an eternal union in the eternal worlds." As such, their marriages represented a sacred and lasting act, not an act of debauchery and lewdness. After suggesting possible motives for practicing polygamy (other than the debased ones typically ascribed to Mormons), he concluded by pointing out how the world's moral, social, and political systems had done nothing to solve the evils of prostitution. "We would just remark that philosophy, morality, law, and Christianity, as now taught, have signally failed to stop this monstrous social and moral evil. The present state of the world proves their incompetency. The Lord's way, as practiced by ancient men of God . . . we think will stop it among us."[10]

The paper, however, was not always as calm and dispassionate as it was in its treatment of polygamy. An article, entitled "Horrible State of Affairs in Utah," was a direct critique of editors and writers so willing to condemn the debauchery in Utah.

> We have read so much about the corruption of Utah, that one could hardly think of putting it anywhere else; and as some of our contemporaries have been up in the mountains so long, that they never can find time to look about home, we publish the following for their especial information; for it is but neighborly for us to attend some little to their affairs when they manifest such special interest in the affairs in Utah.
>
> The following took place in the chaste city of Gotham, where so many of our editors are shocked with polygamy.[11]

Following this brief commentary was an account of "Dealers in Human Flesh." The story told of a woman who was sold for two dollars to Christian Herman, the "keeper of [a] house of prostitution." The article clearly reflected Taylor's contempt for the hypocrisy manifested by those who condemned Mormons' marital relations. While so many were outraged at the practice of polygamy, he argued they did little to address the moral shortcomings of the societies in which they lived. As Taylor put it, they spent too much time in the mountains of Utah while ignoring the debauchery that permeated their own communities.

In addition to outlining the Church's religious doctrine, part of representing "our opinions" involved responding to the many distorted portrayals of Mormonism. In these responses, the paper was direct and often biting. In the first issue of February 1855, an article on the second page declared "An Editor in Mistake."

> We have read in the New York Times a long, labored, scurrilous article, well besprinkled with "barefaced falsehood," "filthy imposturez," "knaves of Utah, "huge blasphemy,"

and other mild, courteous and polite epithets flowing from the chaste and virtuous bowels of our immaculate censorian. We wonder that a gentleman of such high toned moral feelings, breathing the pure un-adulterated(?) atmosphere of the chaste city of New York, would have tarnished his vestal purity so far as to descend from his lofty pinnacle of morality and virtue, to mouth such "filthy impostures." . . .

If he thinks such things will pass current among common mortals, we think he has made a great mistake; his unsupported statement . . . we think will not go far against the testimony of hundreds of honest men.

We have been at a loss to know why he should pen such an article. It could not be for the improvement of the morals of the people of Utah; for such an object can never be attained by falsehood.

Having censored the censorian, the paper went on to explain, "We have nothing to hide; we are willing to compare Utah any day with an other part of the world, and have no secrets." Satire dripping from the page, the article ended with a suggestion: "We would recommend him [the writer], before he makes another attempt, to read Howe, John C. Bennett, Turner, and a few other anti-Mormon publications that we could mention, that he may be able to make out a more plausible story; (for being lately re-introduced into the editorial corps, we begin to be ashamed of the cloth) and hope, by a thorough examination of these various 'Mormonism's Expose' that he may be more successful next time."[12]

In an issue a month later, Taylor used his editorial column to respond to an article entitled "The Mormons; shall Utah be admitted to the Union?" While he explained "we have no particular objections to be written about," Taylor objected to Mormonism being "cooked and hashed," much like French cuisine, "so that you cannot discover the original substance." The blatant distortions of Mormonism were in many ways quite laughable, and he wrote, "We are really amused both at the cupidity of readers and the ignorance of writers generally when they enter upon the subject [of Mormonism]." Setting humor aside, he made clear his satirical contempt for writers who were profuse in their allegations yet cared little for supporting their claims. "There is no need of proof, of course, to such small and gentle allegations; that would be superfluous; . . . besides it is so much easier to get up an article without proof." Taylor's criticism was accompanied by a feature common in his writings—a challenge to the presumptuous writer or editor. Addressing the author, Taylor wrote, "What may be in strict accordance with Mr. Putnam and his readers' views may not exactly suit our taste, and as we believe in matter of fact, we ask for proof, and we will agree to bring fifty testimonies in favor, to his one against, the morality of the Mormons." Continuing the challenge, he added, "We dare him to compare the morals, chastity and propriety of the Mormons with those of the chaste city of Gotham, or any city or territory in the United States."[13] Although bold in their initial declarations, these writers most often met Taylor's challenges with curious silence.

Taylor spent so much time responding to other writers that four months after the paper's commencement, he issued an apology: "We have to apologize to our readers for having so much in our paper lately in relation to the falsehood and misrepresentation of many of our contemporaries." With this column he delineated the paper's philosophy and purpose. "We are not, nor do we desire to be captious; our creed is to 'mind our own business;' part of that business, however, is, as will be seen by our prospectus, to defend that character of Mormonism against the slanderous attacks of a corrupt, venal press." While small attacks were not worth his time, he saw it his duty to counter the "huge bare-faced falsehoods, unblushingly set forth, and fabricated and circulated, by a certain clique, for the most infamous purposes."[14]

In addition to attacking the oft-published misrepresentations, Taylor was quick to comment on and, when he felt necessary, condemn propositions for solving the "Mormon problem." Upon hearing that a company of United States troops on their way to California were able to prostitute numerous "squaws" and "white women" during their stay in Utah, the *New York Herald* proposed sending out "to the Great Salt Lake, a fresh detachment of young, goodlooking soldiers, and at the end of two or three months, order them off to California and replace them by a new detachment at Salt Lake City and so on until those Turks of the desert are reduced, by female desertions, to the standard Christian regulation of one wife apiece." This suggestion was followed by the recommendation that "a corps of regular disciplined woman's rights women" accompany the army detachment so they might "lay down the law to their sisters among the Mormons, [and] . . . soon compel the patriarchal authorities of Salt Lake to an exodus to some other region beyond the reach of our gallant army, and our heroic warriors in petticoats, who know their rights, and knowing, dare maintain them."[15]

Taylor's response to the *Herald* lambasted the debased nature of the proposal.

> Such then is the modus operandi proposed! Gentlemenly debauchee officers are to be sent out; good looking ones, that they may be the better able to take away from vice the horrid appearance it would have dressed in another garb; after these shall have performed their work of misery and death, they are to be recruited by others—fine, dashing, "young, good-looking fellows," —who will be quite competent to deceive and destroy; real Christian gentlemen, "with a new, showy uniform," who will be able to corrupt the daughters of Utah, and to introduce Christianity in all its beauty, as practiced in the United States. They are to take with them a number of pals,— "woman's rights women," — who are to assist in their conversion, and "show them their rights," that the inhabitants of Utah may have ocular demonstration of the beautiful workings of monogamous Christianity, and be brought back to "the standard Christian regulation of one wife apiece;" and as many misses or fast young women as suits our convenience; that a deadly blow may be struck at the virtue of Utah; that she may be crowded with voluptuaries, and prostitutes like all other good Christian states and cities; that debauchery and corruption may run riot, that we may have our procuresses, pimps, cyprians, hotel accommodations, and houses of assignation; that virtue, chastity, and purity may be banished from Utah; that our daughters may be prostituted and our wives debauched; . . . that when officers, lawyers, judges, soldiers and Gentiles in general go to Utah, they can find the same conveniences and accommodations that are to be met

with everywhere among the virtuous Gentile monogamous Christians; and all this glory is to be achieved by the gallant officers and soldiers of our army, under the auspices and direction of James Gordon Bennett [editor of the *Herald*].[16]

Taylor often directly addressed articles to his fellow editors. A commentary, with the not-so-subtle heading "Mind Your Own Business," observed how "MORMONISM has been made the common property and stock-in-trade of the whole fraternity of Editors, from Maine to Georgia, and from the Atlantic Ocean to the western bounds of Missouri." Given this editorial free-for-all, the article suggested, "Seriously, gentlemen, it is none of your business; here you comfortably sit behind your desks throwing your squib shells into Utah, as though that were a part of your commission."[17] In other columns, he repeatedly demanded that editors prove their imaginative accusations. When one New York paper suggested sending out the army to solve the "Mormon Question," Taylor commented, "Come gentlemen, bring on your reasons; we call for proof; these frothing, fuming, bleating, empty words are nothing. We know you don't want the will; but give us your reasons; come, you have most of you been dabbling in the monstrosities of Mormonism; if you can't show them, the people will begin to disbelieve you. What a pity you can't make your exhibits!"[18] In addition to demanding proof, he challenged editors to explain the rationale for the abuse heaped upon the Mormons. He wanted to know the ground for the never-ending criticism, suggesting, "Let each [editor] review all that he is cognizant of and weigh the matter in his own mind, and see if he has sufficient evidence of a nature that would convict a prisoner at the bar of a court of justice."[19] While B. H. Roberts suggested that Taylor's tone in the paper's columns was not "a supplicant pleading for toleration" but a demand for justice,[20] at the very least, Taylor's efforts can be seen as a demand for a more ethical and responsible reporting about Mormons and Mormonism—reports supported by proof and justified by something more than mere sensationalism.

PREACHING THE GOSPEL TO THE SAINTS AND UNCONVERTED

In addition to publishing *The Mormon*, Taylor oversaw the Church in the eastern states. In the newspaper's second issue, Taylor used his editorial column to address "the Saints Scattered through out the East." Concerning these Saints, Taylor acknowledged that they had been without proper guidance from Church leadership. "You have been scattered abroad in the world, exposed to the powers of darkness and gainsayings, falsehood and ridicule of a corrupt generation, without teaching, and dependent, in many instances, upon your own resources and your God, with very little opportunity of receiving teaching, either from his servants or by the written word. You have had very little opportunities of becoming acquainted with the progress of Zion . . . or the revelations given for their guidance." Given their situation, these one-time Saints had missed out on the "very nature and genius of the gospel," namely, continued revelation through inspired leaders. While the gospel they had received years previous was "still the same eternal, unchangeable truth," the Church had progressed much and received additional "principles of truths."[21] With this commentary, Taylor sought to persuade these Saints not to reject new truths (i.e., polygamy) simply because they were not part of the teachings with which they had originally been familiar.

After Taylor arrived in New York, he met many of the leaderless Saints described in his column. When he convened a meeting of a group who claimed to be Church members, Taylor discovered that nearly all were Mormons in name only. There were only two whom Taylor acknowledged as true adherents to the Church's doctrines and beliefs. Addressing the remaining would-be Saints, Taylor reported that "I told the rest to go their own way; told them what I acknowledged to be 'Mormonism,' and if they would not walk up to that, they might take their own course."[22] When Taylor met in conference with the New York Saints nearly two years later on 2 November 1856, he continued to address the subject of what it meant to be a Mormon. Focusing on why he was a Mormon, he outlined the purported reasons those in attendance had joined the Church. In so doing, Taylor was able to both remind some of what had been and suggest to others what ought to be. For example, he explained that "notwithstanding the rumours that were brought in opposition, you found [Mormonism] to be Scriptural in all its parts, and necessarily reasoned, that it was impossible for so many separate and distinct truths, to make one grand lie."[23] Later he told those gathered, "You began to realize your position and responsibility, to live for eternity as a mortal and immortal being; to discover, that the great, omnipotent Being whom you so much dreaded, was not so austere, was not so rigid as you had supposed Him to be, not so awful and inaccessible."[24] In this manner, Taylor outlined the beliefs that united Mormons in their faith, highlighting how they had "found out the value of union, and appreciate its worth."[25]

Not all of the branches of the Church were in such disarray. Taylor reported that in Tom's River, New Jersey, "there was as good a Church when I first went there as I found in the East."[26] By early 1856 he reported in the *Mormon*:

> It affords me very much pleasure to have to state that since the arrival of myself and brethren in these eastern states, Mormonism assumes quite another aspect: we have large and flourishing churches in different parts of this state [New York], which are continually increasing, not only by emigration but by baptisms. The Spirit of the Lord rests among the assemblies of the Saints; the inquiries after truth are many; the floods of falsehood with which this country was deluged before our arrival are being dissipated, and the light of eternal truth is bursting forth with resplendence and glory.[27]

There was also another established branch in Philadelphia, which Taylor and his associates visited for several conferences in 1856.

Taylor's efforts at gaining converts met little success. In reporting to the Saints in Salt Lake about his work, Taylor told them, "It is almost impossible to produce any effect on the feelings of the people." He described a series of meetings he held in New Jersey "to see if something could be done." The people came out in great numbers. He explained that "'Mormonism' was popular; as many as 200 carriages were present. We were treated well, and preached faithfully. Somebody came and set up a little groggery, and it was removed forthwith. Was anybody converted? No. They turned their ears like a deaf adder to the cause, and that is the general feeling, so far as I have discovered." It was his assessment that "those who love the truth are scarce." While he found "a great many scattered all over the United States, who believe 'Mormonism' is truth," many people did not have the "moral courage to embrace it."[28]

ADDITIONAL RESPONSIBILITIES

While in New York, Elder Taylor also aided the Church's immigration efforts. In writing Elder Franklin D. Richards, who oversaw the immigration from the British end, Taylor told him, "I know that a heavy responsibility rests upon you in your present position, and I would rather assist to lighten, than add to, your already onerous engagements."[29] Whereas immigrants had previously sailed from England to New Orleans and then traveled up the Mississippi River, by the mid-1850s this practice had been altered. Brigham Young had directed immigrants to now come by way of northern ports in America, including New York and Boston. In doing so they could avoid "the tedious and unhealthy voyage through the Gulf, and by over-crowded steamers along the sultry 'bayous,' and the sickly miasma concentrated in the 'air currents' of the great Mississippi."[30] When Taylor and his party originally left Salt Lake and traveled to New York in 1854, Taylor had several men go from Council Bluffs, Iowa, to the northern cities to find "out the expense, convenience, distance, and prices for emigration."[31] Directed by Elder Taylor, Church representatives helped the arriving Saints make arrangements for the journey to Iowa, where they started their overland trek to the Salt Lake Valley. When those arriving from England lacked the necessary means, Taylor helped them find jobs until they were fiscally ready to complete the trip.

By June 1855, the first year Taylor oversaw the immigration efforts, the *Mormon* reported that 2,300 Saints had arrived in Philadelphia and New York. Their travels had been "altogether satisfactory; not only in relation to life and health, but to the kindness and gentlemanly . . . officers of the several ships to their passengers, during their voyage, and on arrival the prompt and efficient municipal authority and laws in protecting strangers from the heartless sharpers that invariably infest our sea-board towns." There had been but a few infant deaths among the immigrating Saints, and when they arrived, many in the two cities praised the "good order, good feelings, and . . . spirit of union and kindness one to another, as was exhibited by the emigration of the Latter Day Saints." The *Mormon* credited President Franklin Richards for the "good condition" of the Saints. It lauded him and the Saints "for the manner in which they are fitted out, and their general police and organization, for their excellent selection of presiding officers over the companies, and the entire willingness of those over whom they presided to listen to their counsel and wholesome instructions."[32] For the next few years, Taylor helped thousands of immigrants make their way to the Salt Lake Valley.

In March 1856, a convention was held in Salt Lake City, and a constitution was adopted. As part of the convention, John Taylor and George A. Smith were appointed to make the case for statehood on behalf of the territory of Deseret. During the summer of 1856, Taylor took leave of his other responsibilities to join his colleagues in Washington and lobby members of Congress to introduce a bill admitting a new state. The Mormon delegates, however, found themselves working against the political current of the era. By this time, the Republican Party had largely based its party platform on eliminating the "twin relics" of barbarism: polygamy and slavery. The Democrats, not wanting to be perceived as supporting polygamy, were even more pronounced in their denunciation of the Mormons. Concerning their efforts in Washington, Taylor reported:

> Brother George A. Smith, Dr. Bernhisel, and myself were appointed as delegates to go to Washington. . . . I was in Washington several times, and counseled with my brethren on the subject of our admission. We counseled with some of the most prominent men in the United States in relation to this matter; and those that dare say anything at all, dare not, if you can understand that.
>
> I believe that brother George A. Smith and brother Bernhisel labored with indefatigable zeal to the best of their knowledge and intelligence to accomplish the thing they set about; and I did, while I was with them. But it was not necessary for me to remain there; and I told the brethren, if I was wanted, by sending me a telegraphic dispatch, I would be there in a little time. I believe these brethren did all that lay in their power.[33]

Given the political climate and the antagonism against the Mormons due to the practice of polygamy, little was accomplished and the petition for statehood was eventually withdrawn. Despite the lack of apparent success, Brigham Young commended Elder Taylor and his companions for the work they did in Washington, saying "they discharged their duty manfully and satisfactorily to their God and to their brethren."[34]

It was while in the East that John Taylor met with his "father in the gospel," Parley P. Pratt, for the last time. In September 1856, Pratt was called on a mission to the eastern states. Pratt's letter from the First Presidency stated, in part, "Owing to the extra duties of delegate being placed upon Brother John Taylor, it is suggested that you also aid him in writing for *The Mormon*, and such other duties as may devolve upon you by the united counsel of brethren now in charge on that mission."[35] After a two-month journey to St. Louis, Pratt stayed in that city nearly a month while he engaged in "visiting, instructing, writing history, and writing for *The Mormon*."[36] In December he traveled on to Cincinnati, where he continued to write correspondences for Taylor's paper. Finally, on 24 December 1856, Pratt met up with his fellow Apostle in Philadelphia. A week later they took the train to New York, where they celebrated the new year with several hundred Church members.

For the week Pratt was in New York, most of his time was spent meeting with John Taylor and others discussing Church affairs. On 7 January 1857 Pratt recorded in his journal, "I was in council all day at brother Taylor's residence with the brethren of the Twelve. We resolved to concentrate our energies this year in forming settlements on or near the Platte River, on the route of our emigration, according to the instructions of President Young. We voted that the *Mormon* be continued, and that it is not expedient for brother Snow to resuscitate the *Luminary* at present."[37] The following day Pratt left for Trenton, New Jersey, continuing on with his mission. He preached where he could and continued writing articles for the *Mormon*. On 21 January he wrote a lengthy poem, entitled "My Fiftieth Year," commemorating his fiftieth birthday. Taylor published the poem in the newspaper, as well as a poem that he wrote in honor of his dear friend.

On 30 May 1857, the *Mormon* published one last piece about Pratt:

Our readers will doubtless be startled with the above announcement; our heart is deeply pained to say it, but we have no reason for doubting the sad intelligence that has reached us, though, as yet, only by the way of the public press. A few days ago we were advised of his apprehension near Fort Gibson; and, close upon the receipt of that information, we learned, by telegraphic dispatch, that he had been assassinated near Van Buren, Arkansas, May 13. . . . Though we deeply deplore the loss to the Church of such a great and upright man, and the bereavement to his family, yet we mourn not. His life has been one of honor and faithfulness; his days have been well spent in the service of his God; his name is revered by thousands and tens of thousands, and will be honored by millions yet unborn; while that of his cowardly assassins, and those who have cheered them on to this damning deed, and who now rejoice over their crime, will be loathsome, and a stink in the nostrils of God and good men.[38]

EVALUATING THE MORMON

When Taylor returned to Salt Lake in August 1857, he reported on his mission efforts in the East. Regarding his work as an editor, he had relatively little to say.

We have been engaged in publishing a paper, which is generally known, because it has been circulated here. About my proceedings and acts, I have got very little to say, only that I have done as well as I could, the Lord being my helper; and I believe my brethren here have prayed for me, and that I have been sustained by their prayers and faith.

I have not been in that place, because it was my desire to be there; for I have had a hard struggle and a good deal to pass through: but that is common with us all; and if there were no struggle, there would be no honour in a victory.[39]

Brigham Young, however, was more profuse in his accolades for Elder Taylor's work. When Taylor completed his missionary report, President Young immediately followed him in addressing the gathered Saints. Of Taylor's work he commented:

With regard to the labors of brother Taylor in editing the paper called *The Mormon*, published in the city of New York, I have heard many remarks concerning the editorials in that paper, not only from Saints, but from those who do not profess to believe the religion we have embraced; and it is probably one of the strongest edited papers that is now published. I can say, as to its editorials, that it is one of the strongest papers ever published, so far as my information extends; and I have never read one sentence in them but what my heart could bid success to it and beat a happy response to every sentence that I have read or heard read. Brother Taylor, that is for you; and I believe that these are the feelings and the sentiments of all in this community who have perused that paper.[40]

JOHN TAYLOR'S CONTINUING DEFENSES OF THE CHURCH

When John Taylor wrote to Franklin D. Richards in 1854 announcing a "new phase in the history of 'Mormonism,'" explaining they would "meddle in politics" where previously they had abstained, it is unclear whether Taylor completely understood the prophetic nature of this statement. In the ensuing years, the Church's doctrines and practices became more than fodder for editorial critique. The issues of polygamy and the Church's considerable influence in territorial business increasingly became political concerns that Congress felt necessitated government intervention. Given the political pressure from Washington in the form of legislation and federal officers appointed to govern the territory, the Church and its leaders no longer had a choice but to "meddle" in the political sphere as the religious and political became inextricably linked.

While the Republican Party in the 1850s incorporated as part of its platform the abolition of both slavery and polygamy, Congress addressed the issue of polygamy during the Civil War, passing the Anti-Bigamy Act in 1862. In addition to establishing penalties for practicing polygamy, the act sought to disincorporate the Church, limiting its real estate holdings to $50,000. Though deemed unconstitutional by many, this legislation served as the basis for subsequent bills in Congress that aimed to legislate against polygamy and limit the Church's influence within the territory.

In 1869, on a return trip from the Pacific Coast, Vice President Schuyler Colfax stopped in Salt Lake and addressed a gathering there, as he had done four years previous. Colfax began his speech by praising what he had seen at the Territorial Fair and complementing the Saints on the recently constructed Tabernacle. In addressing the political purpose of his speech, the vice president acknowledged the civil and religious liberty of Americans, suggesting that "the faith of every man is a matter between himself and God alone." While the Saints had a right to "worship the Creator through a president and twelve apostles," he claimed that "no assumed revelation justifies anyone in trampling on the law." He went on to argue that the issue of polygamy was not a matter of religion, and, citing the Book of Mormon and Doctrine and Covenants, he pointed out that the practice went against "the original and publicly proclaimed and printed creed on which your church was founded."[41]

Though not in Salt Lake when Colfax spoke, Taylor heard of the vice president's speech several weeks later. Staying in Boston at the time, he immediately took up his pen and wrote a lengthy reply, which was published in the New York *Tribune* and Salt Lake *Deseret News*. In his letter, he challenged Mr. Colfax's assertions: "That our country is governed by law we all admit; but when it is said that 'no assumed revelation justifies any one in trampling on the law' I should respectfully ask, What! not if it interferes with my religious faith, which you state 'is a matter between God and myself alone?' Allow me, sir here to state that the assumed revelation referred to is one of the most vital parts of our religious faith; it emanated from God and cannot be legislated away."[42] Taylor suggested that if the vice president "carefully examined our religious faith he would have arrived at other conclusions." Taylor added, "In the absence of this [careful examination] I might ask, who constituted Mr. Colfax a judge of my religious faith?"[43] The remainder of Taylor's letter picks apart the vice president's examples and critiques his reasoning. He derided Colfax's claims of toleration toward the Mormons, pointing out that "your tender mercies were exhibited by letting loose an army upon us, and you spent about forty millions of dollars to accomplish our ruin."[44] Taylor dismissed claims that there was no interference in the Mormons' religious beliefs, suggesting the 1862 Anti-Bigamy Act was a "direct attack upon our religious faith," explaining "it is the old story of the lamb drinking below the wolf, and being accused by it of fouling the waters above. The big bully of a boy putting a chip on his shoulders, and daring the little urchin to knock it off."[45] Taylor concluded by chiding Christian society for doing nothing about the "great institution of monogamy," prostitution, and "its twin sister," infanticide. Admonishing his critics, he asked why their moral system did not "bring forth better fruits."[46]

When Taylor returned to Salt Lake, he was praised for his articulate defense of the Church's beliefs. The scope of Taylor's reply and the fervor of his criticisms, along with the national attention which it received, led the vice president to issue his own reply—though some have claimed it was authored by someone other than Colfax—in which he critiqued "the favorite themes of the Mormon leaders."[47] In response to the vice president's rejoinder, Taylor wrote another detailed critique of the vice president's additional criticisms of the Church and its people. Concerning this discussion B. H. Roberts wrote:

> Taking it all in all, this is doubtless the most important discussion in the history of the Church. The great reputation of Mr. Colfax as a speaker and writer; the fact that he had for many years been a member of Congress and accustomed to debate, together with the high station he occupied at the time of the discussion, gave to it a national importance. It occurred, too, at a critical time in the history of the Church. The Republican party had pledged itself to the accomplishment of two objects: the suppression of slavery and polygamy. Slavery it had abolished; and it was now expected that polygamy would receive its attention.
>
> There was also, just then, an effort being made by prominent and wealthy members of the Church, to destroy the influence of President Brigham Young, or, if that failed, to weaken it by dividing the Church into parties. Of this movement the Vice-President was aware, as was also the President and the members of his Cabinet; and lent their influence as far as they could, to this scheme of disintegration; hoping, by fostering it, to solve the Mormon

problem. That it failed miserably is notorious; but these considerations make the discussion between Elder Taylor and the Vice-President all the more important.[48]

Along with defending the Church, the debate demonstrated Taylor's considerable intellectual abilities. His writing evidenced the skills developed over his editorial career as he challenged his opponent's arguments and provided articulate expressions of his beliefs. Roberts suggested that in comparing Taylor with Mr. Colfax, "Elder Taylor loses nothing. In fact he gains by it; for, [in spite of] the experience and learning and position of his opponent, he (Taylor) surpassed him not only in the force of argument, but in literary style, in the elegance, ease and beauty of his diction; while for courtesy, fair dealing and frankness, he was not surpassed by the Vice-President, who was noted for possessing these admirable qualities."[49]

Two years later, recently appointed federal judge James B. McKeon convened a non-Mormon grand jury and indicted Brigham Young on charges of "lascivious cohabitation." Brigham Young, George Q. Cannon, and Daniel H. Wells were arrested. When Young appeared in court in October 1871, Judge McKeon stated that "it is therefore proper to say, that while the case at bar is called *The People vs. Brigham Young*, its *other* and *real* title is, FEDERAL AUTHORITY *versus* POLYGAMIC THEOCRACY." Following Young's court appearance, Taylor wrote a lengthy letter published in the *Deseret News*. While cynically commending McKeon for his honesty in acknowledging the true aims of the court, he challenged the judge's assertion and questioned whether "President [Ulysses S.] Grant, with or without the consent of his cabinet, is making war upon the citizens of Utah for their religious belief for private political purposes."[50] At length he condemned the federal government's blatant intrusions into the religious affairs of the Mormons. Taylor again took up his pen in defense of the Saints when Congress debated and then passed the Poland Act in 1874, which transferred criminal, civil, and chancery cases to federal jurisdiction, as well as made the territorial attorney general and marshal federal appointees. He wrote six letters outlining in detail the judicial abuses the Mormons had faced and countering the allegations made against them. As the debate concerning polygamy proliferated, and the federal government sought to increasingly dictate the affairs of the territory, Taylor's political writings abounded. Detailed in his analysis and biting in his criticism, Taylor sought to highlight the injustices imposed upon the Saints and challenge the misdoings of the federal government and its representatives in Utah.

NOTES TO CHAPTER EIGHT

1. "Fourteenth General Epistle of the Presidency of the Church," *MS* (18 April 1857): 246.
2. *JD* 4:34.
3. "Foreign Correspondence," *MS* (23 December 1854):811.
4. "Prospectus," *MS* (23 December 1854):810.
5. *Life of John Taylor,* 245–46.
6. Ibid., 248–49.
7. Ibid., 249.
8. "Introductory Address," *Mormon* (17 February 1855).
9. *JD* 1:53–54
10. "Polygamy," *Mormon* (17 February 1855).
11. "Horrible State of Affairs in Utah," *Mormon* (3 March 1855).
12. "An Editor in Mistake," *Mormon* (17 February 1855); emphasis in original.
13. "The Mormons," *Mormon* (17 March 1855).
14. "The Mormons and their Slanders," *Mormon* (9 June 1855).
15. *Life of John Taylor,* 260.
16. "Soldiers, Attention!" *Mormon* (15 September 1855); emphasis in original.
17. "Mind Your Own Business," *Mormon* (30 June 1855).
18. Ibid.
19. "Why the Hue and Cry Against Mormons?" *Mormon* (29 September 1855).
20. *Life of John Taylor,* 253.
21. "To the Saints Scattered Abroad Throughout the East," *Mormon* (24 February 1855).
22. *JD* 5:121.
23. "Discourse by President John Taylor," *MS* (21 March 1857):180.
24. Ibid., 181.
25. Ibid., 179.
26. *JD* 5:121.

27. *Life of John Taylor,* 266.
28. *JD* 5:121–22.
29. "Foreign Correspondence," *MS* (23 December 1854):812.
30. "Emigration," *Mormon* (9 June 1855).
31. "Foreign Correspondence," *MS* (23 December 1854):812.
32. "Emigration," *Mormon* (9 June 1855).
33. *JD* 5:122.
34. Ibid., 5:123.
35. *Autobiography of Parley P. Pratt,* 433.
36. Ibid., 435.
37. Ibid., 437.
38. Ibid., 451.
39. *JD* 5:113–14.
40. Ibid., 5:123.
41. "The Mormon Question," 4.
42. Ibid., 6.
43. Ibid., 7.
44. Ibid., 8.
45. Ibid., 9.
46. Ibid, 10.
47. Ibid.,11.
48. *Life of John Taylor,* 309–310.
49. Ibid., 310.
50. "The United States vs. The Church of Jesus Christ of Latter-day Saints," *MS* (14 November 1871):722.

~ NINE ~

PROPHET of GOD, EXEMPLAR to a PEOPLE

When the Quorum of the Twelve was first organized, seniority was determined by age rather than length of service as an Apostle. Thus, when Brigham Young was sustained as President of the Quorum during the Twelve's mission to England, Wilford Woodruff (who was older than John Taylor) was placed before Taylor in the order. Subsequently, when it was considered that Taylor was ordained an Apostle before Woodruff and had, in fact, assisted in his ordination, it was determined that Taylor was the senior Apostle of the two. Further reorganization of the Quorum took place in June 1875 during a meeting held in Sanpete County, Utah. It was at this time that Brigham Young turned to John Taylor and declared: "Here is the man whose right it is to preside over the council in my absence, he being the senior Apostle."[1]

Up until that meeting, Orson Hyde and Orson Pratt had come before Taylor in seniority, as both were Apostles when Taylor was ordained in December 1838. Both Hyde and Pratt, however, had been disfellowshipped and dropped from the Quorum: Hyde in 1839 when he sided with Thomas Marsh and issued an affidavit against the Church, and Pratt in 1842–43, when he disagreed with Joseph Smith over polygamy. Both men subsequently repented earnestly and were welcomed back into the Church and the Quorum. When each returned, they assumed the position they once held. For over 25 years, Orson Hyde served as Acting President of the Twelve during the presidency of Brigham Young. John Taylor reported that some years before the change in seniority was made, George A. Smith asked him if he had noted "the impropriety of the arrangement." Elder

Smith believed that questions concerning seniority "might become very serious ones, in case of change of circumstances arising from death or otherwise." While Taylor acknowledged "the correctness of the position assumed by him" and admitted that he had been aware of it for years, he explained that personally he "cared nothing for the matter"[2] and that he held the two Apostles in high esteem. Yet, he did acknowledge the potential complications were the circumstances to alter. These complications were avoided when President Young determined that those Apostles who had remained constant in their faith ought to have precedence over these two brethren, and the change was made. Concerning the matter Taylor explained, "Thus our positions at that time seemed fully defined; and what had been spoken by Elder George A. Smith, without any action of mine, was carried out by President Young; and from that time to the death of Brigham Young, I occupied the senior position in the Quorum."[3]

The import of Brigham Young's decision was felt two years later when the Church's second President and prophet died on 29 August 1877. Following President Young's funeral, ten members of the Twelve (Orson Pratt and Joseph F. Smith were in England), along with Young's two counselors, met together "and waited upon the Lord" as they "sought to learn His mind and will concerning us and His church."[4] Having received that guidance, the men unanimously sustained John Taylor as the President of the Twelve and voted that the Quorum of Twelve be the presiding authority in the Church. President Young's two counselors, John W. Young and Daniel H. Wells, though not Apostles themselves, were sustained as counselors to the Twelve. In this meeting it was also determined that Young, Wells, and John Taylor's nephew, Elder George Q. Cannon, would assist Elder Taylor in handling the business affairs of the Church. Subsequently, an epistle was issued that acknowledged the service rendered by Brigham Young and announced to the Church: "The President of the Church having been taken from us by death, the Church is now placed in the same position it was at the martyrdom of the Prophet Joseph Smith—there is no quorum of First Presidency."[5] The Quorum's actions were ratified at the following October 1877 conference, when the Church officially sustained John Taylor as President of the Quorum of the Twelve Apostles.

THE FIRST PRESIDENCY

As they had done following Joseph Smith's death, the Twelve Apostles took the responsibility of directing the Church after Young's death. It was still in his capacity as President of the Twelve (the First Presidency had yet to be reorganized) that John Taylor presided at the April 1880 conference. Addressing the Saints the morning of 7 April 1880, Elder Taylor announced, "As it is a jubilee year to you— although I suppose the forty-ninth year would be the proper jubilee—it is the fiftieth anniversary of The Church of Jesus Christ of Latter-day Saints. It occurred to me that we ought to do something, as they did in former times, to relieve those that are oppressed with debt, to assist those that are needy, to break the yoke off those that may feel themselves crowded upon, and to make it a time of general rejoicing."[6] As $704,000 in principal and $900,000 in accumulated interest were owed to the Perpetual Emigration Fund, Elder Taylor proposed that half of the amount be stricken from the books. Those who would be forgiven of their debt in its entirety were the poor, those "struggling with the difficulties of life." Additionally, in the preceding years, many Saints had put on record, when they were unable to pay, the tithing they owed. The total owed by the Saints in 1880 had come to $151,789. Again Taylor proposed that half that amount be forgiven. Expunging these debts was not the only charitable action undertaken. Taylor suggested that the Saints donate 700 cows and 3,000 sheep, which would be added to those provided to the Church, so that 1,000 cows and 5,000 sheep could be passed on to the needy. In addition, 34,000 bushels of wheat (which had been collected and stored by the Relief Society) were to be loaned, without interest, to those who needed it for seed. Just as the Church had forgiven the debt of many, individuals should do likewise, Taylor recommended. "If you find people owing you who are distressed, if you will go to work and try to relieve them as much as you can, under the circumstances, God will relieve you when you get into difficulties."[7] The Jubilee Conference, as this came to be known, provided spiritual instruction and temporal reprieve from the financial troubles that besought many Saints.

Speaking on Sunday afternoon in the October 1880 conference, John Taylor discussed how the Twelve had assumed the position of the First Presidency and officiated in that role for the previous three years. Concerning Orson Pratt's morning announcement that the First Presidency had been reorganized with John Taylor as the new President of the Church, Taylor told the gathered Saints:

> Had it not been our duty to have the Church organized fully and completely in all its departments, I should have much preferred to have continued with the brethren of the Twelve, speaking of it merely as a matter of personal feeling. But there are questions arising in regard to these matters that are not for us to say how they shall be, or what course shall be pursued. When God has given us an order and has appointed an organization in his Church, with the various quorums of Priesthood as presented to us by revelation through the Prophet Joseph Smith, I do not think that either the First Presidency, the Twelve, the High Priests, the Seventies, the Bishops, or anybody else, have a right to change or alter that plan which the Lord has introduced

and established. And as you heard Brother Pratt state this morning, one duty devolving upon the Twelve is to see that the churches are organized correctly. And I think they are now thus organized throughout the land of Zion.[8]

Setting his personal feelings aside, John Taylor was sustained as the third President of the Church, choosing as his counselors George Q. Cannon and Joseph F. Smith. With these three Apostles now making up the First Presidency, three vacancies in the Quorum of Twelve emerged. In the 1880 conference, Francis Marion Lyman and John Henry Smith filled two of the openings. In 1882 Taylor called George Teasdale and Heber J. Grant to be Apostles, filling the one remaining vacancy from two years before and the one created by Orson Pratt's death.

While John Taylor was President of the Church, the political intrusions that had hounded the Church for many years intensified. In 1882, Congress passed the Edmunds Act, named for Senator George F. Edmunds of Vermont, which shored up the Anti-Bigamy Act passed 20 years earlier. The act sought to eliminate The Church of Jesus Christ of Latter-day Saints as a political power in Utah. The act specifically addressed the practice of polygamy, making cohabitation with a polygamous wife a misdemeanor punishable by a fine not to exceed $300 and a prison term not to exceed six months. The act also disfranchised anyone practicing polygamy and created a five-man commission to supervise elections in the territory.

Because of questions about the constitutionality of the Edmunds Act, government officials proceeded carefully in its enforcement. In October 1884, a test case was brought before the state court as Rudger Clausen, a leader from Brigham City, was arraigned on charges of polygamy and unlawful cohabitation. President Taylor was called on to testify in the case. In response to what he witnessed at the court, Taylor explained:

> I could not help thinking as I looked upon the scene, that there was no necessity for all this; these parties need not have placed themselves in this peculiar dilemma. Here was a young man blessed with more than ordinary intelligence,

bearing amongst all who know him a most enviable reputa-
tion for virtue, honesty, sobriety, and all other desirable characteristics that we are in the habit of supposing go to make a
man respected and beloved, the civilized world over.

Taylor pointed out that had Clausen lived with his second wife
outside the bonds of marriage, the law would have had no effect on
them. Instead, he explained, "this heroic young man is the one now
arraigned before the courts of his country, for an alleged offence
against the morality of the age."[9] Clausen's conviction, which was
upheld by the Supreme Court, emboldened government officials, and
they began to seek out information on practicing polygamists.
Spotters and spies were paid to monitor the activities of suspected
polygamists. Children were questioned about their parents, and wives
were subpoenaed and interrogated about their private relations with
their husbands.

As further arrests were made, those officials charged with
enforcing the law sought ways to increase the penalties involved, and
so they determined that each act of unlawful cohabitation was subject
to the maximum fine and imprisonment allowed by the law. As such,
those arrested could rack up thousands of dollars in fines and incur
multiple six-month sentences. The Utah commission in charge of the
elections also stepped up enforcement of the law, denying the vote
not only to those who practiced polygamy but to any who believed in
it. Those who cohabitated with more than one woman, yet were only
married to one, were neither prosecuted nor prevented from voting.

As enforcement of the law was stepped up, President Taylor left
Salt Lake on 3 January 1885. Traveling via train, he went through
Colorado and New Mexico on his way to Arizona. He held regional
meetings with the Saints and counseled them as he had done in Utah.
President Taylor discovered that the persecution of polygamists in
Arizona was just as intense as it was in Utah. In fact, some men found
guilty of polygamy were sent off to jail not in the territory peniten-
tiary but were shipped to Detroit. While in Arizona President Taylor
encouraged the Saints to pursue possibilities of setting up colonies in
Mexico, outside the reach of the American government. Taylor's
return trip took him to Los Angeles and then to San Francisco, from

whence he made the last leg of his journey to Salt Lake, arriving on 27 January 1885.

A few days later, on Sunday, 1 February 1885, President Taylor addressed a group of Saints gathered in the Tabernacle. In what would be his last public appearance before his death in 1887, Taylor sought to counsel them about the political difficulties they faced. Reiterating previous advice given at the pulpit, he told them:

> Are we suffering any wrongs? Yes. Well, what would you do? I would do as I said some time ago. If you were out in a storm, pull up the collar of your coat and button yourself up, and keep the cold out until the storm blows past. This storm will blow past as others have done; and you will see that many of the miserable sneaks who are active in those measures, and who are crawling about your doors, and trying to spy into your houses, etc., will be glad to crawl into their holes by-and-by. Well, what will you do? Get angry? No, not at all. Let these men have their day and pursue their own course; we will protect ourselves from them as well as we can.[10]

Clearly foreshadowing what his future course of action would entail, he told the Saints to "avoid them as much as you possibly can—just as you would wolves, or hyenas, or crocodiles, or snakes, or any of these beasts or reptiles; avoid them as much as you can, and take care they do not bite you. And get out of the way as much as you can."[11] That evening, President Taylor went into hiding in an attempt to ride out the storm. He was accompanied by his counselor George Q. Cannon, L. John Nuttal (Taylor's secretary), and Charles H. Wilcken, who served as a bodyguard.

JOHN TAYLOR AS A MESSENGER OF SALVATION

His last public speech was, in many ways, representative of John Taylor's many years as a messenger of salvation. Just as he had repeatedly demonstrated throughout his life, John Taylor's actions both prior to and following the February 1885 speech evidenced his willingness to put the kingdom of God first. Before returning to Salt Lake from Arizona, there were rumors that federal authorities were waiting in Utah to arrest him. Several Church leaders and associates suggested that it might be best if he did not travel back to Salt Lake. Despite these cautions, he risked the return and resumed his normal Church business. However, after addressing the Saints on 1 February, he chose to withdraw from public view. Rather than abandoning the Saints in their time of need (as some claimed) or hiding out of fear, Taylor sought to do what was best for the Church. About this decision his counselors subsequently wrote:

> In taking this step he did so more to preserve peace and to remove all possible cause of excitement, than from any desire of personal safety. He perceived that there was a determination on the part of men holding official position here to raise an issue, and, if possible, involve the Latter-day Saints in serious trouble. He had not broken any law. He knew he was innocent and that if he were arrested and could have a fair trial, nothing could be brought against him. He had taken every precaution that a man could take under his circumstances to make himself invulnerable to attack. He was determined that, so far as he was concerned, he would furnish no pretext for trouble, but would do everything in his power to prevent the people over whom he presided from being involved in difficulty.[12]

This choice to go "underground," however, had significant personal ramifications. During Taylor's absence, his wife Sophia became seriously ill. Because the law was constantly on the lookout for the President of the Church, he was unable to visit her before her death, nor was he able to attend her funeral. The continual travel from one hiding place to the next and the seclusion forced upon him ultimately affected his health. In writing about Taylor's death, Joseph F. Smith and George Q. Cannon suggested that the government's actions had brought about his demise.

> There is no room to doubt that if he had been permitted to enjoy the comforts of home, the ministrations of his family, the exercise to which he had been accustomed, but of which he was deprived, he might have lived for many

years yet. His blood stains the clothes of the men, who
with insensate hate have offered rewards for his arrest and
have hounded him to the grave. History will yet call their
deeds by their right names; but One greater than the
combined voices of all historians will yet pronounce their
dreadful sentence.[13]

For being wounded in Carthage, he was considered by his counselors
a "living martyr for truth," and now he became, in their eyes, a
"double martyr."

As had become commonplace over the last 30 years of his life,
John Taylor's religious position within the community necessitated
that he speak politically. In addressing an audience in Ogden three
months before he went into hiding, his message was a mixture of religious instruction and political commentary. Concerning his initial
responses to the Edmunds Act, Taylor told the Saints:

> [A]fter looking carefully over the Edmunds law I thought to
> myself, why Congress is growing very wild; this
> Government is getting very, very foolish; they are trampling
> upon Constitutional rights. No matter, I said, I will obey
> this law. I had comfortable places for my family elsewhere,
> and I requested my wives to go to their own homes, and
> live there, and they did so in order that I at least might
> fulfill that part of the law; for foolish or not foolish, my idea
> was to fulfill as far as practicable the requirements of the
> law, and not place myself and my family or my friends in
> jeopardy, through any foolishness of mine. It was expected
> by many of those corrupt men—I do not say in speaking of
> these that all are corrupt—that when these laws were passed
> we should turn our wives out and deal with them as they do
> with their women under such circumstances—make strum-
> pets of them. There is no such feeling as that in my bosom,
> nor in the bosoms of this people.[14]

During the speech he also informed the Saints of a visit he had
with the attorney general under President Ulysses S. Grant. During
their conversation, President Taylor explained, "Now, Mr. Pierpont,

you are well acquainted with all these legal affairs. Although I have yielded in this matter in order that I might not be an obstructionist, and do not wish to act as a Fenian, or a Nihilist, or a Communist, or a Kuklux, . . . yet, sir, we shall stand up for our rights and protect ourselves in every proper way, legally and constitutionally, and dispute inch by inch every step that is taken to deprive us of our rights and liberties."[15] In reporting these events, President Taylor made clear to the Saints his intended course of action during this political crisis: he aimed not to provoke the ire of the government officials, but he would not simply surrender to the injustices inflicted by these men.

In the difficult times, he set himself up as an exemplar to his people. He made clear his political opinions and staunchly set forth his convictions. Above all, as he explained to the Saints, nothing would come between him and his sacred beliefs.

> I would like to obey and place myself in subjection to every law of man. What then? Am I to disobey the law of God? Has any man a right to control my conscience, or your conscience, or to tell me I shall believe this or believe the other, or reject this or reject the other? No man has a right to do it. These principles are sacred, and the forefathers of this nation felt so and so proclaimed it in the Constitution of the United States, and said "Congress shall make no law respecting an establishment of religion, or prohibiting the free exercise thereof." Now, I believe they have violated that, and have violated their oaths, those that have engaged in these things and passed that law, and those that are seeking to carry it out. Congress and the President of the United States and the Judiciary, and all administrators of the law are as much bound by that instrument as I am and as you are, and have sworn to maintain it inviolate. It is for them to settle these matters between themselves and their God. That is my faith in relation to this matter. Yet by their action they are interfering with my rights, my liberty and my religion, and with those sacred principles that bind me to my God, to my family, to my wives and my children; and shall I be recreant to all these noble principles that ought to guide and govern men? No, Never! No, NEVER!

NO, NEVER! I can endure more than I have done, and all that God will enable me to endure, I can die for the truth.[16]

Though willing to die for the truth, he was not willing to give up his convictions. "I cannot as an honorable man disobey my God at their behest, forsake my wives and my children, and trample these holy and eternal obligations under foot, that God has given me to keep, and which reach into the eternities that are to come. I won't do it, so help me, God."[17] Emphatic in his convictions concerning the gospel and absolute in his faith concerning God's dealings, Taylor repeatedly exhibited, both in his speeches and his actions, his passion for the cause of Zion and ardor with which he defended the Church.

In addition to boldly stating his conviction, as he had done throughout his life, President Taylor provided the Saints with a unique historical perspective on the persecutions they faced. An Apostle for over 46 years, Taylor had been a personal witness to all the major challenges that had besought the Church: the expulsion from Missouri, the martyrdom of Joseph Smith, the exodus from Illinois and the trip across Iowa, the journey to Salt Lake, the Utah War, and the political harassment of the federal government. During all these troubling events, Elder Taylor had provided fellow Church members with the counsel and leadership they needed. He encouraged the Saints to see their persecutions not as evidence of their defeat but as an opportunity to become something greater, to do more than they had already accomplished. Concerning the hardships the Saints faced, Taylor, in his 1 February 1885 speech, commented:

> There is nothing new in these affairs, nothing strange in this at all. Many of you have had much to do with these matters. Some of these grey-headed men that I see before me know a little more about those matters than some of the younger portion do. Many of you have been driven from your homes, robbed of your property, dispossessed of your possessions and had to flee from your homes to these mountain valleys, and seek an asylum among the red savages which was denied you by your so-called Christian brethren. Before you came here you were banished from the State of Missouri into the State of Illinois. What for?

Because you had the audacity to worship God according to the dictates of your own consciences. I have had to flee from blood-thirsty bandits time and time again. Brother Snow had to do it, and many of you grey-headed men and women have had to do it. What for? Because of polygamy? No, there was no such thing then alleged. What for? Because you had the hardihood, in this land of freedom, to worship God according to the dictates of your own consciences. For this crime you had to leave your homes, and you were despoiled and robbed and plundered, and had to flee as exiles into another land. I had to do it, you have had to do it. You fled from Missouri to Illinois, and then from Illinois to this land, and why? Why did you leave Illinois and come here? Did you injure anybody? No. They killed your Prophets, and I saw them martyred, and was shot most unmercifully myself, under the pledge of protection from the Governor, and they thought they had killed me; but I am alive yet by the grace of God. . . .

The history of these things is quite familiar to you as Latter-day Saints, and you do not think it anything strange. Some of our young people think that the present proceedings are very remarkable. But many of us, grey-headed folks, have seen plenty of such proceedings, and have had many experiences of this kind; they are nothing new to us at all.[18]

Noting Taylor's wealth of Church experience, his counselors in the First Presidency wrote, "His judgment was remarkably sound and clear, and through life he has been noted for the wisdom of his counsels and teachings. His great experience made his suggestions exceedingly valuable; for there has scarcely been a public movement of any kind commenced, carried on, or completed, since he joined the Church in which he has not taken part."[19]

DEATH OF A PROPHET
During the last two and a half years of his life, Taylor was on the run, moving from house to house, staying just beyond the reach of the law. During these years, he and George Q. Cannon conducted

Church business by way of correspondence. As he could not attend general conference, his speeches were read for him. Ultimately, this lifestyle of constantly moving from one place to another, of never being free to move about as he wished, took its toll on his health. Thirteen days before Taylor's death, Joseph F. Smith returned from his "exile" to the Hawaiian Islands and joined Elder Cannon at President Taylor's bedside. Smith's return to Utah marked the first time the First Presidency had been together since December 1884. Taylor's strength continued to dwindle, and he died on 25 July 1887 at the home of Thomas F. Rouche in Kaysville, Utah.

A letter from his two counselors, published in the *Deseret News*, announced his death. Aptly summarizing the service John Taylor provided the Church, they wrote:

> Once more the Latter-day Saints are called upon to mourn the death of their leader—the man who has held the keys of the kingdom of God upon earth. President John Taylor departed this life at five minutes to eight o'clock on the evening of Monday, July 25th, 1887, aged 78 years, 8 months and 25 days.

> In communicating this sad intelligence to the Church, over which he has so worthily presided for nearly ten years past, we are filled with emotion too deep for utterance. A faithful, devoted and fearless servant of God, the Church in his death has lost its most conspicuous and experienced leader. Steadfast to and immovable in the truth, few men have ever lived who have manifested such integrity and such unflinching moral and physical courage as our beloved President who has just gone from us. He never knew the feeling of fear connected with the work of God. But in the face of angry mobs, and at other times when in imminent danger of personal violence from those who threatened his life, and upon occasions when the people were menaced with public peril, he never blenched—his knees never trembled, his hand never shook. Every Latter-day Saint always knew beforehand, on occasions when firmness and courage were needed, where President John Taylor would be found and what his tone would be. He

JOHN TAYLOR

met every issue squarely, boldly and in a way to call forth the admiration of all who saw and heard him. Undaunted courage, unyielding firmness were among his most prominent characteristics, giving him distinction among men who were distinguished for the same qualities. With these were combined an intense love of freedom and hatred of oppression. He was a man whom all could trust, and throughout his life he enjoyed, to an extent surpassed by none, the implicit confidence of the Prophets Joseph, Hyrum and Brigham and all the leading men and members of the Church. The title of "Champion of Liberty," which he received at Nauvoo, was always felt to be most appropriate for him to bear.[20]

In concluding their letter, George Q. Cannon and Joseph F. Smith wrote of John Taylor's continuing influence on the Church.

And though we have lost his presence here, his influence will still be felt. Such men may pass from this life to another, but the love which beats in their hearts for righteousness and for truth cannot die. They go to an enlarged sphere of usefulness. Their influence is extended and more widely felt, and Zion will feel the benefit of his labors, as it has the labors of others who have gone before him. The work of God will roll forth. One after another of the mighty men—the men who have spent their lives in the cause of God—may pass away, but this will not affect the purposes of our Great Creator concerning His latter-day work. He will raise up others, and the work will go on increasing in power, in influence, and in all true greatness, until it will accomplish all that God has predicted concerning it.

We feel to say to the Latter-day Saints: Be comforted! The same God who took care of the work when Joseph was martyred, who has watched over and guarded and upheld it through the long years that have since elapsed, and who has guided its destinies since the departure of Brigham, still watches over it and makes it the object of His care. John has gone; but God lives. He has founded Zion. He has given His people a testimony of this. Cherish it in your heart of hearts, and live so each day that when the end of your mortal lives shall come, you may be counted worthy to go where Joseph, Brigham and John have gone, and mingle with that glorious throng whose robes have been washed white in the blood of the Lamb.[21]

NOTES TO CHAPTER NINE

1. *JD* 23:365.
2. Taylor, *Succession in the Priesthood,* 16–17.
3. Ibid., 17.
4. Clark, comp., *Messages of the First Presidency,* 2:300.
5. Ibid., 2:299.
6. Pease, comp., *The Mind and Will of the Lord,* 39.
7. Ibid., 41.
8. *JD* 22:39.
9. Ibid., 25:356.
10. Ibid., 26:155.
11. Ibid., 26:155–56.
12. *Life of John Taylor,* 412.
13. Ibid., 414.
14. *JD* 25:349.

15. Ibid., 25:349.
16. Ibid., 26:152.
17. Ibid., 26:152–53.
18. Ibid., 26:150–51.
19. *Life of John Taylor,* 411.
20. Ibid., 410–11.
21. Ibid., 415–16.

~BIBLIOGRAPHY~

Allen, James B., Ronald K. Esplin, and David J. Whittaker. *Men With a Mission, 1837–1847: The Quorum of the Twelve Apostles in the British Isles*. Salt Lake City: Deseret Book, 1992.

Anderson, Karl Ricks. *Joseph Smith's Kirtland: Eyewitness Accounts*. Salt Lake City: Deseret Book, 1989.

Arrington, Leonard J. *Brigham Young: American Moses*. Urbana: University of Illinois Press, 1986.

Bancroft, Hubert Howe. *History of Utah, 1540–1886*. Las Vegas: Nevada Publications, 1992.

Bennett, Richard E. *We'll Find this Place: The Mormon Exodus of 1846–1848*. Salt Lake City: Deseret Book, 1997.

Clark, James R., comp. *Messages of the First Presidency of The Church of Jesus Christ of Latter-day Saints*. 6 vols. Salt Lake City: Bookcraft, 1965–75.

Cowley, Matthias F., comp. *Wilford Woodruff: History of His Life and Labors*. Salt Lake City: Bookcraft, 1964.

Esplin, Ronald K. "Joseph, Brigham, and the Twelve: A Succession of Continuity." *BYU Studies* 21 (Summer 1981):301–41.

____. "Sickness and Faith, Nauvoo Letters." *BYU Studies* 15 (Summer 1975): 425–34.

Garr, Arnold K. "Joseph Smith: Candidate for President of the United States." In *Regional Studies in Latter-day Saint History: Illinois*. Ed. H. Dean Garrett. Provo, Utah: Brigham Young University, 1995.

Jesse, Dean, ed. *John Taylor Nauvoo Journal*. Provo, Utah: Grandin Book, 1996.

Johnson, Clark V., ed. *The Mormon Redress Petitions: Documents of the 1833–1838 Missouri Conflict*. Provo, Utah: Religious Studies Center, Brigham Young University, 1992.

Johnson, Clark V. "Government Responses to Mormon Appeals, 1840–1846." In *Regional Studies in Latter -day Saint History: Illinois*. Ed. H. Dean Garrett. Provo, Utah: Brigham Young University, 1995.

Jolley, Jerry C. "The Sting of the Wasp: Early Nauvoo Newspapers, April 1842 to April 1843." *BYU Studies* 22 (Fall 1982):487–96.

Latter-day Saints' Millennial Star. Liverpool, England. 1840–1970.

Madsen, Carol Cornwall. *Journey to Zion: Voices from the Mormon Trail*. Salt Lake City: Deseret Book, 1997.

Miller, David E., and Della S. Miller. *Nauvoo: The City of Joseph*. Salt Lake City: Peregrine Smith, 1974.

"Missionary Sketches." *Juvenile Instructor* 5 (15 October 1870):166–67.

Nibley, Preston. *Brigham Young: The Man and His Work*. 4th ed. Salt Lake City: Deseret Book, 1960.

Oaks, Dallin H., and Marvin S. Hill. *Carthage Conspiracy: The Trial of the Accused Assassins of Joseph Smith*. Urbana: University of Illinois Press, 1975.

Pratt, Stephen F. "Parley P. Pratt in Winter Quarters and the Trail West." *BYU Studies* 24 (Summer 1984): 373–88.

Pease, Harold W., comp. *The Mind and Will of the Lord: Indexed Discourses of John Taylor Speaking in General Conferences*. Springville, Utah: Bonneville Books, 1999.

Parley P. Pratt, *Autobiography of Parley P. Pratt*. Ed. Parley P. Pratt, Jr. 5th ed. Salt Lake City: Deseret Book, 1961.

Roberts, B. H. *A Comprehensive History of the Church*. 6 vols. Provo, Utah: Brigham Young University Press, 1965.

_____. *Life of John Taylor*. Salt Lake City: Bookcraft, 1963.

_____. *The Rise and Fall of Nauvoo*. Salt Lake City: Deseret News, 1900.

Smith, Eliza R. Snow. *Biography and Family Record of Lorenzo Snow*. Salt Lake City: Deseret News Printers, Inc., 1884.

Smith, Joseph. *History of the Church*. rev. ed. 7 vols. Salt Lake City: The Church of Jesus Christ of Latter-day Saints, 1932–51.

Smith, Paul Thomas. "Young John Taylor." *Ensign* 23 (June 1993):7–9.

Taylor, John. *Succession in the Priesthood*. Salt Lake City: Deseret News, 1882.

_____. "Reminiscences." *Juvenile Instructor* 10 (30 October 1875):256.

_____. "Reminiscences." *Juvenile Instructor* 10 (13 November 1875):267–68.

"The Echo Canyon War." *Contributor* 3 (March 1882):177–79.

The Mormon. New York City, New York. 1855–57.

"The Mormon Question. Being a Speech of Vice-President Schuyler Colfax, at Salt Lake City. A reply thereto by Elder John Taylor . . ." Salt Lake: Deseret News Office, 1870.

Three Nights' Public Discussion Between Reverends C. W. Cleeve, James Robertson and Philip Cater, and John Taylor of The Church of Jesus Christ of Latter-day Saints, at Boulogne-Sur-Mer, France. Liverpool: published by John Taylor, 1850.

Times and Seasons. Commerce and Nauvoo, Illinois, 1839–46.

Tyler, Daniel. *A Concise History of the Mormon Battalion in the Mexican War*. Glorietta, New Mexico: The Rio Grande Press, 1969.

Watt, George D., comp. *Journal of Discourses*, London: F. D. and S. W. Richards and Sons, 1854–86.

Woodruff, Wilford. *Wilford Woodruff's Journals*. Ed. Scott G. Kenny. 9 vols. Midvale, Utah: Signature Books, 1983.

PHOTO CREDITS

p. 12   Brigham Young, courtesy of LDS Family and Church History Department Archives. Albumen print, Marsena Cannon, ca. 1851. Photograph of print possibly by Charles R. Savage.

p. 13   John Taylor, courtesy of LDS Family and Church History Department Archives. Engraved by Frederick Piercy.

p. 28   The Kirtland Temple, courtesy of LDS Family and Church History Department Archives. Photograph by George Edward Anderson.

p. 33   Parley P. Pratt, daguerrotype by Marsena Cannon, ca. 1853, courtesy of LDS Family and Church History Department Archives.

p. 50   Wilford Woodruff, courtesy of LDS Family and Church History Department Archives.

p. 54   Joseph Fielding, courtesy of LDS Family and Church History Department Archives. Photographer: Crawshaw.

p. 66   Heber C. Kimball, courtesy of LDS Family and Church History Department Archives.

p. 72   *Times and Seasons,* Vol. IV, No. 1, Nov. 15, 1842.

p. 77   *Times and Seasons,* Vol. IV, No. 9, March 15, 1843.

p. 79   *Times and Seasons,* Vol. IV, No. 9, March 15, 1843.

p. 86   Lilburn W. Boggs, courtesy of LDS Family and Church History Department Archives.